Silvia Schultermandl
and
Şebnem Toplu (Eds.)

A Fluid Sense of Self

Contributions to Transnational Feminism

edited by

Erin Kenny
(Drury University, MO)
and
Silvia Schultermandl
(University of Graz, Austria)

Volume 2

LIT

A FLUID SENSE OF SELF

The Politics of Transnational Identity

edited by

Silvia Schultermandl and Şebnem Toplu

LIT

Cover Art: Enes Zuljevic

Gedruckt mit Unterstützung des Bundesministeriums
für Wissenschaft und Forschung in Wien
Gedruckt mit Unterstützung der Universität Graz

Bibliographic information published by the Deutsche Nationalbibliothek
The Deutsche Nationalbibliothek lists this publication in the Deutsche
Nationalbibliografie; detailed bibliographic data are available in the Internet at
http://dnb.d-nb.de.

ISBN 978-3-643-50227-8

A catalogue record for this book is available from the British Library

©**LIT** VERLAG GmbH & Co. KG Wien 2010
Krotenthallergasse 10/8
A-1080 Wien
Tel. +43 (0) 1-409 56 61
Fax +43 (0) 1-409 56 97
e-Mail: wien@lit-verlag.at
http://www.lit-verlag.at

LIT VERLAG Dr. W. Hopf
Berlin 2010
Fresnostr. 2
D-48159 Münster
Tel. +49 (0) 2 51-620 320
Fax +49 (0) 2 51-922 60 99
e-Mail: lit@lit-verlag.de
http://www.lit-verlag.de

Distribution:

In Germany: **LIT** Verlag Fresnostr. 2, D-48159 Münster
Tel. +49 (0) 2 51-620 32 22, Fax +49 (0) 2 51-922 60 99, e-mail: vertrieb@lit-verlag.de

In Austria: Medienlogistik Pichler-ÖBZ, e-mail: mlo@medien-logistik.at

In Switzerland: B + M Buch- und Medienvertrieb, e-mail: order@buch-medien.ch

In the UK: Global Book Marketing, e-mail: mo@centralbooks.com

In North America by:

Transaction Publishers
New Brunswick (U.S.A.) and London (U.K.)

Transaction Publishers
Rutgers University
35 Berrue Circle
Piscataway, NJ 08854

Phone: +1 (732) 445 - 2280
Fax: + 1 (732) 445 - 3138
for orders (U. S. only):
toll free (888) 999 - 6778
e-mail: orders@transactionpub.com

To our daughters, Aviva Müller and Selen Toplu,
and the transnational worlds they live in

TABLE OF CONTENTS

ACKNOWLEDGMENTS

INTRODUCTION   11
A Fluid Sense of Self: The Politics of Transnational Identity in Anglophone Literatures
    Silvia Schultermandl and Şebnem Toplu

PART ONE: POLITICS OF MOTION

CHAPTER ONE   27
Theorizing Experience, Locating Identity, Writing Selfhood: Lisa Suhair Majaj's and Shirley Geok-lin Lim's Transnational Life-Writing
    Silvia Schultermandl

CHAPTER TWO   45
Identity Trajectories in V.S. Naipaul's Work
    Anna Izabela Cichoń

CHAPTER THREE   61
"Pleased to meet you!": The Paradox of Identity in Zadie Smith's *The Autograph Man*
    Jonathan P. A. Sell

CHAPTER FOUR   81
Transnational Identity and Saumya Balsari's *The Cambridge Curry Club*
    Joel Kuortti

CHAPTER FIVE   95
Transnational Axes of Identity Articulation in Bernardine Evaristo's *Lara*
    E. M. Ester Gendusa

CHAPTER SIX 113
"All the difficult names of who we are": Transnational Identity Politics
in Chang-Rae Lee's and Karen Tei Yamashita's Fiction
    Kathy-Ann Tan

PART TWO: POLITICS OF LONGING

CHAPTER SEVEN 139
Diasporic Hereafters in Jhumpa Lahiri's "Once in a Lifetime"
    Delphine Munos

CHAPTER EIGHT 159
Gendered Transnational Spaces: Arab "Safari" Situated in
Hanan Al-Shaykh's *Only in London*
    Şebnem Toplu

CHAPTER NINE 175
"Merely a Trick of Moonlight": The Accidental Triangulation
of Love, Power, and Narrative in Zadie Smith's *White Teeth*
    Jessica Weintraub

CHAPTER TEN 197
Borderland Strangers in Caryl Phillips's *A Distant Shore*
    Josiane Ranguin

CHAPTER ELEVEN 215
Globalizing Africa, Universalizing the Child: Towards Transnational
Identity in Ishmael Beah's *A Long Way Gone: Memoirs of a Boy Soldier*
    Jopi Nyman

CHAPTER TWELVE 231
Fronteras Americanas and the Latino Canadian Diaspora:
Guillermo Verdecchia's Border Texts
    Astrid M. Fellner

ABOUT THE CONTRIBUTORS 247

INDEX 251

ACKNOWLEDGMENTS

The idea for this collection first emgered during the 2008 conference of The European Society for the Study of English (ESSE) in Århus, Denmark, where we hosted a panel on transnational Brisith literature. Our biggest thank you goes therefore to the conference organizers who allowed us to put together a double-panel on transnationalism. We equally thank all the contributors to this collection for their dedicated and meticulous revisions of their manuscripts. Their enthusiasm made this collection happen.

This collection of essays is the second volume in the series Contributions to Transnational Feminism. Our thanks go to LIT Verlag for providing this publication venue, to Richard Kisling in their Vienna office for his indispensible help with all matters that pertain to the production of this book, and to their Münster office for their excellent layout work.

A special word of gratititude goes to Martina Koegeler for her assistance with the formatting and the preparation of the index.

As with all work we do, we thank our families for their continuous inspiration. It is their patience, their love and their support that sustains us through long hours of revision and night shifts of compositon.

INTRODUCTION

A Fluid Sense of Self: The Politics of Transnational Identity in Anglophone Literatures

Silvia Schultermandl and Şebnem Toplu

In this era of increasing global mobility, the nation-state can no longer serve as primary means of identification of selfhood. Identities are too complex to be captured by concepts that rely on national borders for reference. Instead, they spill out over the boundaries and rims of nation-states, thus exposing the very limits that these borders conjure. Such identities are not unified or stable, but are fluid entities which constantly push at the boundaries of the nation-state, thereby re-defining themselves and the nation-state simultaneously.

In the United States, Canada, and Great Britain, countries in which many of the authors discussed in this collection have lived for long periods of their lives, this emergence of complex identities has long contested the very definitions of what constitutes "American," "Canadian," and "British" respectively. This includes questions emerging from the interdependence of cultural geographies in the formation of Western modernity, as Lisa Lowe has argued in her analysis of the "Intimacies of Four Continents" in the late 18th century, as well as from ongoing bi-lateral cultural exchanges facilitated through global consumer culture, as Inderpal Grewal has demonstrated in her discussion of Mattel's launching of an Indian Barbie doll.

While scholarship in the closing decades of the 20th century set out to formulate re-definitions of Great Britain, Canada, and the United States as multicultural and heterogeneous nations, more recent approaches argue in favor of a consideration of British, Canadian, and American cultures that are not solely defined by the respective national concepts. Such approaches do not seek to uncover the diverse cultural heritage within Great Britain and North America but look beyond the boundaries of these nations in order to trace the myriad global connections that impact British, Canadian, and American identities. These transnational approaches examine the cultural exchanges facilitated through the trans-Atlantic slave trade and the colonial and postcolonial routes of travel and commerce as integral parts of these three cultural formations, including in the context of global power relations between Britain, Canada, the United States and the so-called Third World. This shift towards the transnational highlights the movements of knowledge and circulation of theories and animates discussions about literary canon formation at large.

This collection offers a discussion of literary texts discussed that challenge these power relations. The individual chapters follow Inderpal Grewal and Caren Kaplan's assertion that "advanced capitalist societies are in a period of transition" through an increasing "transnationalization of accumulation, [through] shifts that challenge the older, conventional boundaries of national economies, identities, and cultures" (9). These occurring shifts no doubt also call for new definitions of identity as well as for new approaches to the politics of identity. Cultural identity has become a highly contested concept in this interaction between global power relations that impact a person's social and material realities on the one hand and the choice of how a person "imagines" him or herself. If we assume that identity is purely based on choice, it is difficult to account for the social and material realities that result from existing power relations and their impositions on the individual. If we assume identity to be solely inscribed by society onto the individual, we overlook the self-determination and agency of every individual. This dialectics between chosen and ascribed identities is at the center of this collection. Based on Benedict Anderson's concept of nations as "imagined communities" and Salman Rushdie's concept of nations as "imaginary homelands," this collection examines the political moves protagonists make when they attempt definitions of their complex identities.

The individual chapters in this collection are arranged in two sections, one entitled "Politics of Motion" and the other one "Politics of Longing." These two modes of belonging mutually inform each other and thus offer a sense of the complexity of the politics of identity in a global era. While motion and belonging at first glance may refer to two different degrees of mobility – one more dynamic, the other one more static – this collection illustrates that they equally evoke the ongoing identity negotiations depicted throughout contemporary Anglophone literatures. The tension between the concepts of motion and belonging seeks to capture the ambiguity and contradictions that can be detected in many works, where they serve as strategic interventions that counter binary oppositions and essentialist identity politics. These politics of motion and politics of longing epitomize the patterns of "globalization from below," that is, the effects of transnationalism on a person's everyday life (Fox 171).

Such moves away from cultural essentialism are at the core of many contemporary texts in Anglophone literatures. Many writers, including Shirley Geok-lin Lim, Lisa Suhair Majaj, V.S. Naipaul, Saumya Balsari, Hanan Al-Shaykh and

Ishmael Beah, have themselves lived in more than one home, located in more than one country. Others, including Zadie Smith, Jhumpa Lahiri, Chang-Rae Lee, Karen Tei Yamashita, Caryl Phillips, Bernadine Evaristo and Guillermo Verdecchia look back on a complex family genealogy that spans not only several countries, but several continents. Such experiences of transnational identity also characterize their protagonists, whose quests take them on journeys across the globe: physical journeys from place to place as well as reflections on the routes that their cultural heritage has taken. These protagonists learn, often at crucial moments in their character development, that only by embracing a fluid sense of self can they reach a sense of belonging amidst this hyper-mobility. This fluid sense of self repudiates all notions of a unified identity. What it proposes instead is a way of reading identity as a political performance in everyday social interactions. These social interactions include cultural encounters that cannot be defined by the nation-state but are testimony to the velocity with which culture travels. The essays featured in this collection discuss internal and external notions of belonging on the one hand and definitions of selfhood on the other.

The Politics of Transnational Identity

The fluid sense of self with which many contemporary Anglophone authors attempt locations within a transnational world goes beyond the identity politics of multiculturalism. Identity politics, an intervention of the field of multiculturalism which takes to task the creation of more political visibility of so-called minority groups, has become a contested idea due to its inherent practices of assigning specific labels to identities, such as *one* artificially directed race, class, or gender. The politics of identity that we see evidenced in critical investigations within this collection do not seek to label along these or similar terms. On the contrary, the fact that identities cannot be labeled is the key assumption with which this collection conducts inquiries into the modes of belonging depicted in Anglophone literatures. From a transnational perspective, a perspective that defines borders as permeable and flexible, the significance of cultural identity as a political practice raises a number of relevant questions about viable modes of self-representation.

When Sandra Kumamoto Stanley describes identity as "a border in a borderless world" (7), she pinpoints a variety of issues in contemporary discussions of the politics of identity. Stanley argues that identity is based on difference, and difference often entails a reification of borders to draw a distinction between the self and others. This distinction between self and other, which lies at the heart of Western modernity, has been challenged by postmodern, feminist, and transnational scholarship. In particular, feminist philosophy exposes the dialectical function of identity which epitomizes the ontologically ambiguous relationship between "that which is" and "that which can be represented." Gillian Howie, for instance, points out this conundrum when observing that "it is possible to identify objects and subject while, at the same time, arguing that identification is in itself philosophically problematic" (163).

The fact that identity operates with borders raises the question whether contemporary scholarship can do, or would do much better, without considering the parameter of identity as a core within the representational logic of communities. The post-ethnicity or post-identity discourse as maintained by Stuart Hall and David Hollinger, for instance, regards the concept of identity as counterproductive to definitions of the self. In its place, Hall proposes the concept of "identification," a concept that refutes static notions of identity as something inherited or assigned (222). Similarly, Hollinger appropriates the concept of "affiliation" in order to underline the fluidity of identity. In his *Postethnic America: Beyond Multiculturalism* (1995), Hollinger argues in favor of a "postethnic perspective on communities of descent within the United States [which] entails the principle of affiliation by revocable consent" (13). Applying Werner Sollors's distinction between consent and descent, Hollinger's definition of identity as an act of affiliation highlights personal "choice over prescription" (ibid.) and thus accredits a highly agentic potential to the politics of identity. In other words, a person's cultural identity is the result of his or her deliberate embracing of certain cultural features. Identity politics is thus a person's conscious decision to perform an identity sustained by these personal choices. In the context of racism, xenophobia, and colonial domination, for instance, such performance of a self-chosen identity deconstructs prevalent notions of "otherness."

A much more critical stance can be observed in the scholarship of Todd Gitlin, who considers identity politics to be a "stylized marginality" that only minorities pursue in their continuous struggles for recognition within the national landscape of a country (173). Gayatri Chakravorty Spivak's notion of essentialism as a "strategic" means with which to achieve postcolonial agency also falls within this category (205). In her more recent book, *Other Asias* (2008), Spivak, however, points out that she has since "thoroughly repudiate[d] the idea of 'strategic essentialism'" (260). That essentialist self-representation can backfire is also Diana Fuss's contention in *Essentially Speaking: Feminism, Nature and Difference* (1989), where she argues that the politics of essentialism are often misunderstood and discredited by white academics, a fact that fuels racial stereotypes.

Such discourses on identity politics portray a general dissatisfaction in cultural studies with approaches that generate assumptions about social 3communities solely based on identity. In part, as Carmen Tirado Bramen observes astutely, identity politics is primarily an academic intervention coming out of the West with a moderate "trickle-down effect in improving the lives of all minority groups" (2). As such, so Bramen elaborates further, the problem with many identity discourses seems to be rooted in the fact that identity politics is often seen as synonymous with multiculturalism (1). And multiculturalism, because it is a phenomenon that investigates the constituency of the nation-state at the expense of examining the broader global interconnectedness, cannot adequately account for the social shifts generated by transnational movements.

Throughout the field of multi-ethnic studies, there has been a similar paradigmatic shift from a multicultural to a transnational focus of study. This shift can also be detected in discussions of hybridity in British and North American contexts. As the essays in this collection underscore, hybrid identities are more complex than can be described through the concept of cultural hyphenation. Cultural identity in these British and North American literary productions ceases to be indicative of national diversity. In this sense, this collection follows Arjun Appadurai's assertion that the appropriation of the hyphen as discursive practice of classifying multiplicitous American cultural identities fails to acknowledge the complexity of transnational identities:

> The formula of hyphenation (as in Italian-Americans, Asian-Americans, and African-Americans) is reaching the point of saturation, and the right-hand side of the hyphen can barely contain the unruliness of the left-hand side. [...] The politics of ethnic identity in the US is inseparably linked to the global spread of originally local national identities. For every nation-state that has exported significant numbers of its population to the United States as refugees, tourists, or students, there is now a decolonized transnation, which retains a special ideological link to a putative place or origin but is otherwise a thoroughly diasporic collectivity. No existing conception of Americanness can contain this large variety of transnations. (424)

Appadurai's contention that hybridity cannot be aptly defined if we only look at ethnic diversity within the nation-state is based on his observation that all communities that are labeled ethnically diverse "are far from being culturally pure or homogenous entities nor do they exist in isolation" (ibid.). In other words, cultural identities draw on and come into existence through the interaction with other cultural entities. Identity is therefore not only a process of identification, it is a continuous cultural dialogue between self and other.

This cultural dialogue between self and other is inevitably a complex one; but due to the increasing global mobility of the self, more and different "others" qualify as conversational partners. Many protagonists in contemporary Anglophone literatures even experience that these potential others are not so different from themselves. This does not mean, however, that the politics of transnational identity animates premature postulations of a global kinship, assuming that everybody is on the same plane and that the world is one happy place. On the contrary, the politics of transnational identity takes a critical stance towards the effects of postmodern phenomena such as neoliberal opportunism and global sisterhood. In particular, the politics of transnational identity that emerge from these cultural dialogues between self and other often mirror global power dynamics. In the introduction to their collection of essays, *Minor Transnationalism* (2005), Francoise Lionnet and Shu-mei Shih consider these underlying power dynamics by emphasizing the difference between the terms "global" and "transnational":

> Whereas the global is, in our understanding, defined vis-à-vis a homogenous and dominant set of criteria, the transnational designates spaces and practices acted upon by border-crossing agents, be they dominant or marginal. The logic of globalization is centripetal and centrifugal at the same time and assumes a universal core or norm, which spreads out across the world while pulling into its vortex other forms of culture to be tested by its norm. It produces a hierarchy of subjects between the so-called universal and particular, with all the attendant problems of Eurocentric universalism. The transnational, on the contrary, can be conceived as a space of exchange and participation wherever processes of hybridization occur and where it is still possible for cultures to be produced and performed without necessary mediation by the center. (5)

Within the field of feminist studies, this distinction between global and transnational marks a particularly consequential move toward a conscious acceptance of the global power divisions and their inevitable influence on the formulation and dissemination of theoretical approaches that it generated. Shirley Geok-lin Lim, for instance, observes that global feminism often tends to be confused with "an international feminism coming out of the West" (8). Transnational feminism, on the other hand, recognizes that the attempt to analyze the specific locations that are detrimental factors in people's experience of culture is concerned with the global inequalities emergent from a world order that is based on binary oppositions. Unlike global feminism, which is characterized by a "tendency to essentialize, homogenize, and centralize Western social and cultural concepts of women" (Lim 8), transnational feminism offers a more dynamic set of parameters, language, and frameworks for a discussion of experiences of migration across times and places.

The dynamic parameters that many writers, including the ones discussed in this collection, depict in their works, suggest new insights into the ways in which identity operates in a world in which borders (physical borders, at least) are becoming more and more permeable. This collection also invites new questions about the reasons why these borders are less permeable for some people and pinpoints the parameters that have made these seemingly penetrable borders solid and reactionary. This includes the borders we all carry within ourselves when we examine the lives of others.

Transnational Shifts in Anglophone Literatures

Recent scholarship in British literature echoes this move toward a transnational understanding on various levels. In a special issue of *Contemporary Literature* entitled *Immigrant Fictions*, Rebecca L. Walkowitz examines the dynamic site of production and reception of literary works. In answer to Gauri Viswanathan's question "Precisely where is English literature produced?," Walkowitz offers that "the location of literature depends not only on the places where books are written but also in the places where they are classified and given social purpose" (527). Walkowitz identifies two parameters of immigrant literatures: "the transnational book" and "the migrant writer" but does so without adopting essentialist definitions of the two parameters of categorization. With the term transnational book, Walkowitz refers to the multiple languages, locations, and trajectories that the global dissemination of books entails. This multiplicity is reflected both on the level of the actual literary production, such as in the fact that many authors of British literature do not live in Britain, and on the level of the books' circulation, such as through the choice of publishing houses, the act of translation, and the books' international reception. At the same time, Walkowitz distinguishes between migrant literature and migrant writers, contending that one does not necessarily presuppose the other. Walkowitz deconstructs the image of the migrant writer as the primary agent of immigrant literature by suggesting that "[n]ot every book that travels is produced by a writer who travels" (532). Instead, Walkowitz argues that "the political and social processes of immigration shape the whole literary system, the relationships among all of the works in a literary culture, and not simply the part of that system that involves books generated by immigrant populations"

(533). In her assertion that migrant literature needs to be considered in terms of the migratory processes at play in its production and circulation and not only in terms of its physical trajectories of migration, including those determining the national and geographical location of the author, Walkowitz joins Susan Stanford Friedman's call for literary categorizations that privilege "transnational models emphasizing the global space of ongoing travel and transcontinental connection" (906) over models that operate with the nation-state as their primary representational logic.

Walkowitz and Friedman share a deep conviction that literature needs to be reconceptualized and re-canonized in ways that reflect the dynamics of global movements which engender the modern world system. Stephen Greenblatt addresses these issues in his recent comment on the additions and excisions that shaped the seventh edition of the *Norton Anthology of English Literature*. Such altercations of already existing canons and anthologies are always difficult endeavors, endeavors whose poignancy Greenblatt implies by calling this practice "textual triage" (436). This "textual triage" often entails taking out less frequently taught texts for the sake of making room for texts that largely draw students' attention. Such texts include those written by Salman Rushdie, Anita Desai, and V.S. Naipaul, precisely authors that represent the multiplicity of literary projects that shape contemporary British literature. And authors such as Rushdie, Desai and Naipaul, among many others, also demand new ways that reconcile their diverse national backgrounds and their multiple locations as writers with labels as British authors.

In North America as well, such acts of textual triage epitomize the ongoing demographic changes in the literary landscape. Similar to the latest edition of the *Norton Anthology of English Literature*, so, too, has the fifth edition of the *Heath Anthology of American Literature* added a great variety of texts which establish multi-ethnic literature as an intricate part throughout American literary history and not just as a phenomenon that started in the late 19th century. And while many American authors in the 20th century depict ethnic identities as a minority trait that positions their protagonists at the margins of American society, the 21st century has brought forth new works in which a multi-ethnic world seems to be the norm rather than the exception. In texts like Alex Espinoza's *Still Water Saints* (2007) or Toni Morrison's *A Mercy* (2008), the proverbial "white guy" no longer embodies American culture but constitutes himself a minority. This conceptualization of ethnic identity as the new norm highlights the power dynamics among various ethnic communities and allows authors to unearth what may be called minorities within minorities, such as the Chino-Cuban protagonists in Cristina Garcia's novel *Monkey Hunting* (2003).

This shift in prevalent conceptualizations of what constitutes minority makes Paul Gilroy's distinction between "where you're from" and "where you're at" (3) even more acute. In the field of multi-ethnic American literature, the discrepancy between the "where you're from" and "where you're at" of individual authors that is, their national origin and their present cultural location, has recently informed practices of conceiving of ethnic writers in explicitly transnational terms. Eleanor Ty, for instance, observes that due to the multiple positionings that writers address, North Asian American and European ethnic texts are no longer "primarily concerned with the challenges of assimilation, racial prejudice, or with cultural hybridity" (239). Ty's assertion that many North Asian American and European ethnic writers write about subjects other than themselves or from within their own cultural groups. Instead, Ty offers the term "Asian global narratives," meaning the "narratives by Asians in the diaspora whose works fall outside of this hyphenated paradigm of Asian plus adopted country" (242). Ty arranges these Asian global narratives into three different categories: first, works that stress globalization as major point of interest; second, works written by writers of Asian origin which do not offer depictions of the authors' adopted countries; and third, works that do not have anything "Asian" as their subject matter (240). Going beyond the teleological narrative, these works, continues Ty, "highlight movement, instability, and importance of standpoint or location" (241).

Interventions such as Ty's concept of "Asian global narratives" and Gilroy's distinction between "where you're from" and "where you're at" offer an important impetus to consider the literary productions of a specific nation in their fullest transnational realm. As is the case with British and North American cultural productions by non-white authors, the fact that not all writers are occupied with recovering their claims to citizenship and identity in their works repositions the very concept of what constitutes British or American identity.

Politics of Motion and Politics of Longing

The individual novels discussed in this collection exemplify a variety of strategies that facilitate this move towards a politics of transnational identity. Many of the authors discussed in this collection have already acquired one or more of the following labels: minority, multiculturalist, postcolonial, migrant, immigrant, and diasporic. By including them into this discussion of the politics of transnational identity, we do not seek to attach yet another label to their works. On the contrary, this collection examines critically the political acts that the characters in these novels undertake in order to make sense of who they are without subscribing to prevalent labels of identification. Such political acts are not the ones they perform at the voting booth or through the espousal of partisan politics; it is the acts of every-day existence through which they express their political awareness of global power relations and their effects on interpersonal relationships. In this vein, their everyday conversations with other protagonists, their personal reflections and inner monologues, their participation in community acts, and their everyday rites and rituals convey how they position themselves in a dialogue with their national and transnational communities.

Among these various means through which the protagonists maintain their politics of transnational identity, there are two prevalent modes of identification: the first one highlights the multiple routes of migration that the protagonists have undertaken before they reached their respective "homes;" the second examines the interpersonal connections through which the protagonists maintain relationships with their transnational communities. We call the first mode "politics of motion" and the second one "politics of longing." Through such politics, these narratives question the binary between homeland and hostland (basically "Motherland" for Britain) which has informed previous scholarship of British and American ethnic literature. The collection follows this distinction and thus offers essays in these two categories.

The essays in the section "politics of motion" share a sincere interest in refuting essentialist notions of place as location of identity politics. Instead, the papers in this section covey that national borders are permeable and cannot sufficiently encompass the multiple parameters that inform the politics of transnational identity. These essays also emphasize migration and mobility as main vectors of identification, thus liberating identity politics from a rigid anchoring in the nation-state.

The section opens with Silvia Schultermandl's discussion of Shirley Geoklin Lim's and Lisa Suhair Majaj's negotiations of national belonging on the one hand and personal longing to make sense in a particular national context on the other. Majaj's work raises important questions about the classification and dissemination of Arab American literature, and Lim's work raises similar issues about Asian American literature. How and what they write places them at the center of ongoing conversations about the ways in which space figures in transnational life-writing. Anna Izabela Cichon, considering that V. S. Naipaul's fiction responds to the problems that contemporary political geographies and the positioning of subjects generate, focuses on various identity models as a contestation of Naipaul's ever evolving concepts of identity from particularism to universalism, thus liberating identity politics from the claiming of place to the negotiation of those very claims. Cichon concludes that the evolution of Naipaul's attitude to self-identification is based on Western paradigms. Similarly, Jonathan P.A. Sell detects such shifts from stability to dynamicity in Zadie Smith's depiction of writing as motion into selfhood in Alex-Li Tandem of *The Autograph Man*, a Chinese Jewish British protagonist who constantly tries to determine his own identity, to write his own self, so as to create himself auto-graphically through shifting notions of place. This motion into selfhood that characterizes transnational British literature is also of importance in Joel Kuortti's analysis of the "strategies of identification" in Saumya Balsari's project of negotiating aspects of colonial mimicry, transnational power-relations, and diasporic self-invention. While the protagonists of Balsari's strategies of identification straddle multiple movements between India, the U.K., and the U.S., Bernadine Evaristo's protagonist Lara, as E. M. Ester Gendusa illustrates, triangulate between Europe, Nigeria and Brazil in search of her roots of many generations located in the identity of her selfhood, positioned in London. Existing forms of identity politics are also insufficient for the protagonists in Chang-Rae Lee and Karen Tei Yamashita's work. Kathy-Ann Tan's essay contends that whether by the form of the detective story or through magic realism, both authors complicate the notion of borderland identities. Instead, they propose scenarios in which the protagonists can only make sense of themselves by applying transnational frameworks to their lives. Such politics of transnational identity liberate the protagonists from discussions of essentialist identity.

All six papers in this section treat movement and motion not as singular, arbitrary contradictions of identity, but recover these incidents as patterns of postmodern identity formation. In this sense, they illustrate that movement and motion become the primary metaphors of identity, both in the literal sense of migration as well as in the figurative sense of dynamic politics of identity. The concept of identity that the authors discuss echoes Stuart Hall's assertion that identity is not a fixed identity but a "production" (222) manifested in the complexity of the process of identification that individuals undertake to the same extend as communities. Thus, the politics of motion that these essays discuss redefine identity politics in a transnational context where place ceases to be the sole representational parameter of identity and movement between places becomes the central space a person's agency.

Such heuristics are also dominant in the second set of chapters, the ones that discuss "politics of belonging." While politics of motion emphasizes fluidity and, at times, contradiction, as shaping factors of the politics of transnational identity, politics of belonging denotes the interventions necessary in order to secure a sense of selfhood that can adopt such politics of motion. One of such spaces that the six essays of this section recover as location of the politics of belonging is the interpersonal relationship between the protagonist and their social environment. By emphasizing what Adrienne Rich has termed a "politics of location" of the individual protagonists, these chapters discuss the ways in which the protagonists are positioned in relation to other people.

Angling the discussion of transnational identities to the Indian American experience, Delphine Munos analyzes the post-national refiguring of homeland in Jhumpa Lahiri's work. Positioning emerging identities, Lahiri mingles the conceptions of nostalgia for the homeland with the advent of new becomings, formulating them as joint resources for identity politics of belonging. In the case of Şebnem Toplu's analysis of Hanan Al-Shaykh's work, these interpersonal relationships are shaped by the protagonists' longings and desires. Out of the genealogies of their interpersonal encounters that engender the protagonists and determine their identity quests, Al-Shaykh's novel evidences that the domestic sphere and the public sphere through which the protagonist travel, are shaped by similar patterns of power and order. Jessica Weintraub reevaluates Zadie Smith's *White Teeth*, exposing that the novel's characters posit their transnational politics of longing through a narration of dubious accidents of love and connection, considering love as a mediating and motivating source more than ethnic identity in the molding of selves in politics of transnational identity.

Several chapters in this section also animate critical conversations about the narrative strategies that account for such depictions of belonging. Caryl Phillip's *A Distant Shore* employs a specific narrative technique to communicate the protagonists' sense of loss and longing. Through an omniscient narration, the author presents the two protagonists plagued by a feeling of "unhomeliness," as Josiane Ranguin proposes. Not only the African refugee has difficulty assuming a home within Britain, but also the British character feels estranged from her home country. In their interpersonal relationship, as Ranguin illustrates, the two seem to find a common sense of identity, a sense of belonging. Also with attention to narrative form, Jopi Nyman's viewpoint brings forth the problematic of African child soldiers in fiction, focusing on Ishmael Beah's memoir, which places its narrator in discourses of violence and trauma. However, Beah's reconstructing his divided self is leveled, Nyman argues, by the therapeutic process that transforms him into the globalized world in America. Finally, Astrid M. Fellner argues for a transhemispheric approach to Canadian literature. Taking a closer look at the border texts by Canadian Latino writer Guillermo Verdecchia, Fellner investigates the focus on the North/South border zone in recent Canadian literature. Verdecchia's works engage in a performance of a cultural space that becomes the means to negotiate Canada and establish it as a realm of cultural translation, relentless ambiguity, and fertile ambivalence.

Together, these twelve essays illustrate the multiple intersections between motion and longing that shape contemporary Anglophone literatures and the politics of identity the respective authors pursue. Integral to trasnational feminism theory and practice, these politics of identity deconstruct prevalent concepts of selfhood and thus open up new channels of cross-cultural conversations. In this vein, this collection refutes common practices of commodifying literary texts by transnational authors into convenient preconceived categories of what is American/British /Canadian and what is "Other." This also means following the social imperatives of decolonizing theory in order to facilitate that kind of border-less conceptionalization that Chandra Talpade Mohanty posits in the center of anti-capitalist solidarity, one that "acknowledges that there is no one sense of border, that the lines between and through nations, races, classes, sexualities, religions, and disabilities, are real – and that a feminism without borders must envision change and social justice across these lines of demarcation and division" (2).

Works Cited

Anderson, Benedict. *Imagined Communities*. 1983. London: Verso, 2006.

Appadurai, Arjun. "Patriotism and Its Futures." *Public Culture* 5.3 (1993): 411-29.

Bramen, Carrie Tirado. "Turning Point: What the Academic Left Hates Identity Politics." *Textual Practice* 16.1 (2002): 1-11.

Fox, Jonathan. "Unpacking 'Transnational Citizenship.'" *Annual Review of Political Science* 8 (2005): 171-201.

Friedman, Susan, Stanford. "Migrations, Diasporas, and Borders." *Introduction to Scholarship in Modern Languages and Literatures*. Ed. David Nicholls. New York: MLA, 2006. 899-941.

Fuss, Diana. *Essentially Speaking: Feminism, Nature and Difference*. New York: Routledge, 1989.

Gilroy, Paul. "'It Ain't Where You're From, It's Where You're At": The Dialectics of Diaspora." *Third Text* 13 (Winter 1990/91): 3-16.

Gitlin, Todd. "The Rise of Identity Politics." *Dissent* (Spring 1993): 172-77.

Greenblatt, Stephen. "Letter in Response." *Pedagogy* 1.2 (Spring 2001): 435-37.

Grewal, Inderpal. *Transnational America: Feminisms, Diasporas, Neoliberalisms*. Durham: Duke University Press, 2005.

------. *Scattered Hegemonies*: *Postmodernity and Transnational Feminist Practices*. 1994. Minneapolis: University of Minnesota Press, 1997.

Hall, Stuart. "Cultural Identity and Diaspora." *Identity: Community, Culture, Difference*. Ed. Jonathan Rutherford. London: Lawrence & Wishart, 1998. 222-37.

Hollinger, David. *Postethnic America: Beyond Multiculturalism*. New York: Basic Books, 1995.

Howie, Gillian. "Conserving the Principle of Identity: Identity, Representation and Equivalence." *Women: A Cultural Review* 14.2 (2003): 159-70.

Lim, Shirley Geok-lin. "Where in the World Is Transnational Feminism?" *Tulsa Studies in Women's Literature* 23.1 (2004): 7-12.

Lionnet, Francoise, and Shu-mei Shih, eds. *Minor Transnationalism*. Durham: Duke University Press, 2005.

Lowe, Lisa. "The Intimacies of Four Continents." *Haunted By Empire: Geographies of Intimacy in North American History*. Ed. Ann Laura Stoler. Durham and London: Duke University Press, 2006. 191-212.

Mohanty, Chandra Talpade. *Feminism Without Borders: Decolonizing Theory, Practicing Solidarity*. Durham and London: Duke University Press, 2003.

Rich, Adrienne. *Blood, Bread and Poetry: Selected Prose, 1979-1985*. New York: W. W. Norton, 1986.

Rushdie, Salman. *Imaginary Homelands: Essays and Criticism 1981-1991*. London: Verso, 1991.

Sollors, Werner. *Beyond Ethnicity: Consent and Descent in American Culture*. New York: Oxford University Press, 1986.

Spivak, Gayatri Chakravorty. *Other Asias*. Malden, MA: Blackwell, 2008.

-----. *In Other Worlds: Essays in Cultural Politics*. New York: Methuen, 1987.

Stanley, Sandra Kumamoto. "Teaching the Politics of Identity in a Post-Identity Age: Anna Deavere Smith's Twilight." *MELUS* 30.2 (Summer 2005): 191-208.

Walkowitz, Rebecca L. "The Location of Literature: The Transnational Book and the Migrant Writer." *Contemporary Literature* 47.4 Special issue *Immigrant Fictions* (2006): 527-45.

PART ONE: POLITICS OF MOTION

CHAPTER ONE

Theorizing Experience, Locating Identity, Writing Selfhood: Lisa Suhair Majaj's and Shirley Geok-lin Lim's Transnational Life-Writing

Silvia Schultermandl

In *Who Sings the Nation-State?: Language, Politics, Belonging* (2007), Judith Butler and Gayatri Chakravorty Spivak discuss the dual meaning of the term "state" in relation to their work: *state* as a national entity with its legal boundaries and discursive paradigms versus *state* as the condition that describes the circumstances of their writing. Butler and Spivak believe that in their work on gender and postcolonial theory respectively, these two meanings are interrelated, even mutually inform each other.

> If the state is what 'binds' us, it is also clearly what can and does unbind. And if the state binds in the name of the nation, conjuring a certain version of the nation forcibly, if not powerfully, then it also unbinds, releases, expels, banishes. (4-5)

This duality of the term 'state' pertains especially to the questions of national belonging, or any other discursively conscripted sense of belonging to a community. In a U.S. context, the dual meaning of the term 'state' evokes both the question of who gets to call themselves American and which individuals will be heard in their argumentation about the national, sexual, social, and political states that they are in. Given the constructedness of these 'states,' much in line with Benedict Anderson's assertion that nation-ness is a discursive construct, an "imagined community" emerging as the product of a rhetorical project, Butler and Spivak unpack the parameters that constitute the individual states they discuss. Butler does so by raising a very important question:

> So: how do we understand those sets of conditions and dispositions that account for the 'state we are in' (which could, after all, be a state of mind) from the 'state' we are in when and if we hold rights of citizenship or when the state functions as the provisional domicile for our work? (2)

Butler and Spivak's conversation about the dual meaning of the 'state we are in' is by no means a new, or radical, intervention.[1] What is truly innovative about *Who Sings the Nation State?* is its unconventional form: the book consists of one long dialogue between the two scholars. In places, one of the two dominates the conversation to the point that it looks as if two monologues where set together consecutively. This book, Butler and Spivak's first conjoined project,[2] is a transcript of a keynote lecture Butler and Spivak gave at the Global States Conference in May 2006, hosted by the Department of Comparative Literature at UC Irvine. The format of the published version of their talk may give it the look of a nice little coffee table book, but it raises important issues about the discursive strategies that the two "speakers" perform. Because the text is indeed "only" a transcript, and not a co-authored piece, it maintains some of the discongruencies of the original joined keynote lecture: both scholars go into the areas of their expertise without making a conjoined effort of condensing their talk into a more universal claim; the contradictions and discongruencies remain in the text and are not edited out, not even for the sake of unity and clarity; and finally, the highly anecdotal and episodic form makes an overall line of argumentation difficult to discern. Hence while at first the printed product of their joined lecture may look like a hasty publication of a topical talk, its lack of an apparent coherence is a rhetorical performance that implies another important aspect: perhaps what Spivak and Butler's text shows - also on the level of its structure - is that there cannot be a coherent conversation about the dual nature of the "states" we are in. Both scholars trace their argumentation back to their own research fields – for Butler mostly in relation to her interest in Hannah Arendt and for Spivak in Karl Marx – and to their personal identity politics. This emphasis on a lack of coherence in their discussion of the Global States is a conscious choice: as Butler suggests in one section, "there can be no radical politics of change without performative contradiction" (66).

By blending scholarly interest and personal identity politics, *Who Sings the Nation State?* epitomizes a new direction in academic life writing, one that

---

[1] In fact, what Butler and Spivak coin here as a dual meaning of the term "state" can also be read as a different approach to prevalent inquiries into the contradictions of national and cultural identity. Such confrontation between two different sets of parameters that connote a person's state have a long-standing history in American literature, dating back to Hector St. John de Crèvecoeur's famous question "What, then, is the American?" as much as to Sojourner Truth's equally famous question "Ain't I A Woman?"

[2] An earlier transcription of their conversation can be found under the title "A Dialogue on Global States, 6 May 2006," in the electronic journal *Postmodern Culture* 17.1 (Sept. 2006).

several contemporary authors pursue. As do Butler and Spivak in their experimental publication, many contemporary authors acknowledge this difference between the "state" we are in and the "state we are in" in their writing. In other words, Butler and Spivak's intervention is not new in the sense that it acknowledges the discursive overlaps of the concepts of the nation state with those of the personal state,[3] but they provide a new and interesting terminology with which to approach the dual, often contradictory, nature of the 'states' of a person's identity. Already a decade before Butler and Spivak, Lisa Suhair Majaj's and Shirley Geok-lin Lim's transnational life writing has emphasized the tensions they perceive in the clash between how they define themselves and how they are being labeled in American society. In particular, both authors candidly talk about the racist and sexist definitions with which the academic societies around them seek to define them. This awareness, which Majaj and Lim address throughout their writing and scholarship in ways that Butler and Spivak's collaborative project later epitomizes, becomes tangible in the authors' espousal of identity politics that go beyond essentialism and that theorize the inherent contradictions that seem to define their identities. Because Majaj and Lim recover personal experience as a means of voicing self-hood, they employ a subversive discourse of female identity that exposes the extent to which boundaries that accept the nation-*state* as primary representational paradigm need to be challenged in order for authors like themselves to be able to articulate the *states* from which they write.

Boundaries of Arab American Subjectivity in Majaj's Work

In her autobiographical essay "Boundaries: Arab/American," Palestinian American author Lisa Suhair Majaj evokes the difference between the dual meaning of the state she is in by offering the following anecdote about a workshop on racism in which she participated:

> Workshop participants were asked to group ourselves in the center of the room. As the facilitator called out a series of categories, we crossed to one side of the room or the other, according to our self-identification: white or person of color, heterosexual or lesbian/bisexual, middle/upper class or working-class, born in the United States or in another country, at

---

[3] Besides the groundbreaking work by Benedict Anderson, a feminist revision of the concept of nationhood can be found in Caren Kaplan, Norma Alarcón, and Minoo Moallem's project *Between Women and Nation: Nationalisms, Transnational Feminisms, and the State* (1999), a collection of essays which inquires into the discursive construction of gender and nationhood.

> least one college-educated parent or parents with no higher education, English as a native language or as a second language. Although I am used to thinking of myself in terms of marginality and difference, I found myself, time after time, on the mainstream side of the room. White (as I called myself for lack of a more appropriate category), heterosexual, middle-class, born in the United States to a college-educated parent, a native speaker of English, I seemed to be part of America's presumed majority. (Kadi 65)

The experiment, with all its implied shortcomings and pitfalls, seems to epitomize for Majaj that her "identity was not merely complex, but rather an uninterpretable excess" (ibid.)

In particular, this experience leads Majaj to question the social categories that the above experiment replicates:
> And so, standing on the majority side of the room that evening, observing the discrepancy between the facts of my life and the available categories of inclusion and exclusion, I could not help but wonder whether these categories are insufficient, or insufficiently nuanced. (Kadi 66)

The contradiction between her labeled identity according to U.S. Census categories, which define Arab Americans as racially "white," and her lived identity in the face of blatant racist slurs exposes the limitations of the term Arab American itself. The duality and contradiction that she experiences at the workshop prompts Majaj to conclude that Arab American identity is an "ongoing negotiation of difference" (84). And by characterizing Arab American identity by an ongoing process instead of by a fixed status, Majaj refutes essentialist notions of Arab American identity and seeks to create agency for herself as a writer and an activist in ways that the inherent contradictions of the state she is in can be accommodated.

From her personal experience of the "distortion" which she encounters whenever she "turn[s] to the world for some reflection of [her]self" (Kadi 67), Majaj deduces that the category of Arab American identity does not provide a meaningful vector for her self-identification. In terms of the literary production that she and other authors bring forth, Majaj questions in her essay, "The Hyphenated Author," whether "there is some 'Arab-American' essence defining and binding together individual texts as part of a larger whole." The absence of a discernable location or identity, as Majaj resigns in "Boundaries," pushes Arab Americans into a cultural borderland:
> American and Palestinian, not merely half of one thing and half of the other, but both at once – and in that inexplicable melding

> that occurs when two cultures come together, not quite either, so that neither American nor Arab find themselves fully reflected in me.

Statements like the above are reminiscent of Gloria Anzaldúa's definition of borderland identities and characterize Arab American literature as located in an "ethnic borderland: a constructive space in which interethnic ties between and within different communities of color could be established and maintained" (Fadda-Conrey 187). This claiming of the cultural borderlands between two cultures, as Majaj does in the above quotation from "Boundaries," also positions her identity politics critically toward the concept of hyphenation, a staple of the identity politics emerging in the 1970s.

The identity politics that have proliferated from the 1970s onwards in both ethnic and gender studies only offer limited conceptual space in which she can locate her identity. While the entrance of the hyphen as a new category into the American cultural imaginary of ethnicity (African-American, Asian-American, Anglo-American) created a new awareness of the ethnic diversity in the United States, the categories themselves suggest somewhat easy alliances between the concepts on either side of the hyphen (Ty 2004, Appadurai 1990). While Majaj espouses the concept of hyphenation in the title of her essay, "The Hyphenated Author," she emphasizes in the essay itself that the notion of hyphenated identities cannot encompass sufficiently the complexity of Arab American identities.

> The Arab-American community, shaped by a century-long history of migration, is remarkably diverse. It includes third and fourth generation Americans as well as recent immigrants; people from different countries and different religious denominations; those who speak no Arabic and who speak no English; people who identify primarily with the "Arab" side of their heritage and those who identify primarily with the "American" side. This diversity complicates assessment of what constitutes "Arab American" identity.

For Majaj's own life, a division between her American and her Arab heritage is not possible. In fact, to call Majaj an Arab American, or Palestinian American scholar, poet and educator already glosses over the complexities of her personal trajectory: Majaj was born in the United States to an American mother with German background and to a Palestinian immigrant father, spent most of her childhood and young adulthood in Lebanon and Jordan, moved back to the United States for graduate school, has held several teaching posts in the United States as well as in Bahrain and in Lebanon, and now lives as an independent scholar in the Greek part of Cyprus with her husband and two children.

Hyphenation, even with regards to the dual meaning of the term state, cannot account for the diasporic and transnational locations from which Majaj writes. This might stem from the fact that Majaj is never just in one state, or in a state with a dual meaning as outlined by Butler and Spivak, but that she is constantly in multiple states, states, that can in fact not be separated from each other. Majaj articulates this multiplicity of states in the following way:

> I am never *just* an American, any more that I am *just* a Palestinian. Yet I am not therefore any *less* of an American, or *less* of a Palestinian. As I was rarely given the choice in the Middle East to claim or not to claim my American identity, so I am not often given the choice in my American context to be or not to be Palestinian. At best I can attempt to pass, suppressing my identity and resorting to silence. (Kadi 82, original emphasis)

Multiple Homelands in Lim's Work

Similar to Majaj, Shirley Geok-lin Lim writes candidly about the various labels she encounters as a Malaysian American scholar, writer and educator, and how these labels assign to her identities that she seeks to reposition in her writing. Like Majaj, Lim confronts contested spaces in her definition of selfhood as well as in her choice of literary practices. In the memoir *Among the White Moon Faces*, which won her the 1996 American Book Award, Lim narrates her life amidst the confinement of Malaysian and American concepts of nationhood, concepts that seem to preclude her own participation in the cultural productions of these two states. Lim positions herself critically towards the national identity politics she experienced in Malaysia:

> The "Malaysian," that new promise of citizenship composed of the best traditions from among Malays, Chinese, Tamils, Eurasians, Dayaks, and so forth, seemed more and more to be a vacuous political fiction, a public relations performance like those put on for Western tourists at state-run cultural centers. (122)

What this celebration of Malaysian identity entails for Lim's aspirations as a poet becomes evident from her statement: "In Malaysia, I would always be of the wrong gender and the wrong race" (133).

In the United States, Lim encounters a similar problematic[4]: whereas in Malaysia her ethnic roots cast her as outsider, in the United States it is her status as an immigrant. Lim summarizes this conundrum in the following way:

---

[4] This is not to say that Lim was simply "moving from one margin to another" (89), as Mohammed A. Quayum intimated in an interview question. Lim specifies that

> [M]y circumstances as an equal national citizen here [in the United States] make me part of the American mainstream, whereas in Malaysia, I would be a marginalized citizen. But my ethnic position here makes me part of a very marginal ethnic cultural community whereas in Malaysia I would remain part of a visible and vital cultural community. Citizenship rights versus ethnic community vitality: perhaps that is the dilemma in US assimilation for Asians coming to America.
> (Quayum 90)

Met by her American college students with a great deal of curiosity for the exotic culture they see in her, Lim comments on the extent to which her long hair, her accent, and her recent immigration to the United States seemed to get in the way of her conversations with students. What they saw in her first and foremost was an exotic other, and only upon second or perhaps third take did they "take [her] seriously as a mind and as a mentor" (214). Lim describes such incidents as indicative of American academia between the late 1970s and the early 1990s. Her move from Hostos Community College in the Bronx to the University of California Santa Barbara after having been passed over for promotion time and again exemplifies to Lim that "[i]t was not my gender that got in the way but my nonwhiteness" (214). Similar to Majaj's anecdote about the lack of sufficient nuances in the categories that define her identity, Lim concludes: "I needed to find another, more welcoming America in which poetry, Asian, and woman could be accepted in the same body" (225).

Lim articulates this search for "a more welcoming America," and by extension also a more welcoming Malaysia, by identifying herself as a "deterritorialized" author:

> Kuala Lumpur is definitely not MY home turf; I am not delusionary. But neither is California. [...] my work is deterritorialized, an ironic prior property for a writer to whom "home" has been such a first-order question and thematic.
> (Quayum 88, original emphasis)

This contradiction between the maintaining of a home through her writing and the absence of an easily discernable state that may constitute home allows Lim to envision herself through her texts without adhering to expectations of the publishing market or the popular readership. There is a sense of liberation implied in the transgression of the boundaries of the state that she explored and

---

the legal "states" of personhood in the United States are much less infringed upon than in Malaysia. Nevertheless, her experiences of marginality in both nation-states are similar to the point that a more general pattern of marginalization can be observed.

that permits her writing to have stayed "quirky, not attuned to a popular readership" (Quayum 85).

Nevertheless, while Lim herself considers her work to push the edges of established categories, the coercive presence of such categories determines in which way readers regard her work. In her essay "Academic and Other Memoirs: Memory, Poetry, and the Body," Lim relates an interview question that she got from a graduate student who was working on a project on women's autobiographies. The student started the interview with the following assessment of Lim's work:

> A startling number of personal-history works – including your autobiography *Among the White Moon Faces: A Memoir of Asian-American Homelands* [sic] – by women immigrants, particularly from "Third-World" countries, have been released in the later half of the twentieth century, particularly in the 1990s. (36)

In that same essay, Lim astutely points out the prevalence, and in her case, unreflected accordance of such categories of identification: "The identities encompassed in [the student's] single question include American national, immigrant, women, third-world, twentieth century, and genre – autobiography, personal history, and narrative" (36). The accordance of such categories is indicative of the ways in which Lim's work has been received in the United States, namely as an example of a proliferating canon of literary texts that are not "mainstream" and thus seem to be in need of such classifications as "women immigrants" or "Third-World."[5] Lim however counters such attempts at categorization of her work by emphasizing that "while [her] memoir is chiefly read as U.S. ethnic, it is in fact transnational, treading between at least two subjectivities, a Malaysian Chinese and an Asian American" (37).

Personal Experience as Theoretical Intervention

The search for a more encompassing concept of self-hood cannot happen for Majaj and Lim without a careful investigation of their personal experiences. Both authors undertake literary journeys into their childhood experiences in search for answers. Through this revisiting of their childhoods, Majaj and Lim offer the reader a glimpse of their many identity negotiations through memory and narrative. *In lieu* of a coherent, chronological narrative, the episodic re-

---

[5] Amy Tan refers to the categorization of "minority literatures" into various subcanons such as "women" or "immigrant" as "literary ghetto;" see Schultermandl for a detailed discussion of this ghettoization within the American canon.

count of individual experiences emphasizes their postmodern subjectivities and the contextualization of their identities with the contradictory states that they are in.

By evoking the conflicting nature of the "states" that they are in, Majaj and Lim make interesting contributions to ongoing discussions about the relevance of personal experience to the theorizing of social and material realities. This acknowledgement of the ways in which the "states" we are in and the "states we are in" dialogue with each other resonates with two distinct trends in contemporary identity theories. The first trend is an established form of essentialist identity politics that conflates, often uncritically, lived experience with adopted politics. In this vein, a person's race, ethnicity, sex, or gender, may serve as the logical explanation for his or her interest in a specific scholarly field, and may thus be deduced as the politics that are informed by the person's lived experience. By this equation, to be able to ground one's scholarly interest and academic pursuit in one's emotional reaction to lived experiences of racism, sexism, xenophobia, and homophobia, would seemingly lend a person more authority, perhaps even more authenticity, in his or her pursuit of academic goals including tenure promotion, book publications, or course evaluation. Kenji Yoshino, who reflects in a 2006 article in *The New York Times* on such influencing factors on a person's well-being in the academic world, cunningly names this practice of turning one's personal identity into one's seemingly most adamant research interest "mesearch," a form of essentialism based on the assumption that identity and practice always cohere.[6]

The second trend investigates the limitations of experience as a basis for theorization. In "Sisterhood, Coalition, and the Politics of Experience," Chandra Talpade Mohanty argues that "[t]here is a problematic conflation [...] of the biological and the psychological with the discursive and the ideological" (113) in American feminist scholarship. As far as the myth of a universal sisterhood is concerned, Mohanty assumes that discourses of and on experience can offer a key mechanism with which to reinforce essentialism (and all the implied problems therein). She characterizes the problem as follows:

> The analytic elision between the *experience* of oppression and the *opposition* to it (which has to be based on an *interpretation* of experience) illustrates an aspect of what I referred to earlier as the feminist osmosis thesis: being female and being feminist as one and the same; we are all oppressed and hence we all resist. Politics and ideology as self-conscious struggles, and

---

[6] He discusses this issue at length in his monograph, *Covering: The Hidden Assault on Our Civil Rights* (2007).

choices necessarily get written out of such analysis. (112, original emphases)

Shari Stone-Mediatore takes Mohanty's notion of experience into a different direction. While recognizing the limitations of discourses that glorify experience, she seeks to establish "an alternative account of 'experience,' one that neither naturalizes the latter nor reduces it to discourse but considers the complexities of historical experience and the reciprocal relations between experience and writing" (111). Stone-Mediatore offers a poststructuralist critique of experience which points out the dangers of over-emphasizing experience in empiricist narratives of female agency (111-16).

Both trends grow out of the field of critical multiculturalism; while perhaps ideologically different, both pinpoint the limitations of multiculturalism for the theorizing of experience. That such theorizing often relies on the adoption of categories of identification can be both invigorating and at the same time counter-productive. AnaLouise Keating, for instance, argues that a forceful claiming of the margin institutionalizes the very division between what is considered "center" and what is considered "margin" and characterizes ethnic women as essentially different from their white counterparts. As a result, Keating specifies, "the other's oppositional worldview remains locked in a dyadic relationship that inadvertently reinforces existing power structures" (23).

In an attempt to theorize the personal beyond the limitations that essentialist identity politics pose, Sara Suleri suggests that "[w]hile lived experience can hardly be discounted as a critical resource for an apprehension of the gendering of race, neither should such data serve as the evacuating principle for both historical and theoretical contexts alike" (761). Kandice Chuh, in *Imagine Otherwise: On Asian Americanist Critique* (2003), even goes so far as to suggesting that, in the specific context of the current condition of Asian American studies, critical analysis calls for a "subjectless discourse" with which to "create the conceptual space to prioritize difference by foregrounding the discursive constructedness of subjectivity" (9). Chuh identifies one of the pitfalls of contemporary Asian American studies to be too invested in the politicization of Asian American experience, thereby ultimately producing essentialist discourses that operate along principles of particularism and exclusivism rather than offering a candid investigation of the social parameters that inform Asian American cultural productions in the United States and worldwide.

Critics like the above acknowledge the concerns of feminists theorizing about experience, as well as the limitations that an un-nuanced rationalization of experience may provide. It is precisely the nuances, however, that offer a lot of interesting incentives into the politics of a transnational identity, in ways that the chapters in this collection explore. For Majaj and Lim in particular, the ways in which their personal experiences resonate in their writing not only validates the personal as a key component in the negotiation of new modes of self-definition, it also characterizes the experience of subjects that are, like Majaj and Lim define themselves in their writing, so complex that they become non-conducive to essentialist discourses, as a fundamental basis of identity theory. It is not so much a question of whether or not their experiences predetermine their scholarship, as is the main point of contention in left-wing critics of identity politics;[7] rather, experience serves as a manifestation of complex subjectivities, especially in the transnational movements that these authors continuously undertake.

By blending experience with important scholarly debates, these authors reject the notion of a "subjectless discourse," yet they do so in a way that respects the concerns put forth by Mohanty, Stone-Mediatore and Chuh. As scholars who embrace transnational feminist practices, that is, who theorize gender with a keen awareness of the discourses of power and privilege that govern global gender patterns, Majaj and Lim not only depict the experiences of the constraints of such global gender patterns, they also reflect in their writing their own status within these hierarchies.

The performance of experience through the narrative act thus complicates prevalent assumptions about history and autobiography, and invites a reconsideration of the boundaries between reality and fiction.[8] The product of their life writing, to which their scholarly, fictional and poetic publications contribute equally,[9] are not accounts of victimization by, nor are they acts of subversion against ideologies that produce global gender inequalities; they are critical reflections of the ways in which the authors themselves have been co-opted by these ideologies such as in the reception of their academic performances in the U.S. academe and in their literary texts.

---

[7] Carrie Tirado Bramen offers an interesting discussion of the various discourses that shaped contemporary identity politics in American academia.

[8] In *Ethnic Life Writing and Histories: Genres, Performance, and Culture* (2007), Rocío G. Davis, Jaume Aurell, and Ana Beatriz Delgado posit life writing as a form of self-narrative as a literary performance of personal and collective memory; and because of the performative nature of life writing, the claims to authenticity and verisimilitude, such as implied in the question of whether everything the author relates is "really true," lose their relevance. Instead, the literary choices that the author makes to perform narrative acts open up new insights into the narrative qualities of history altogether.

[9] In "Academic and Other Memoirs," Lim subsumes "history, documentary, journal, essay, even poetry" (24) under the category of life writing.

Transnational Academic Practices

At the heart of Lim's and Majaj's performance of experience is the longing for a place within American society in which they can attain a position that allows them to re-write and counter-write the categorizations that they encounter; in short, a "more welcoming America" (Lim 1994, 225). For Lim such a place within American society would allow her to write from multiple locations of subjectivity without having to claim one label over another. In her scholarly work in Asian American Studies, Lim has proposed new ways of reading Asian American literature beyond the national boundaries that U.S. multiculturalism embraces. While refusing to reject the United States as primary location of Asian American thought (1), her most recent project, *Transnational Asian American Literatures: Sites and Transits* (2006), considers "the complex, dialogical national and transnational formulations of Asian American imaginations" (2). Lim and her co-editor's book adopts a transnational scope in its investigation of the current body of Asian American scholarship and thus purports a definition of Asian American literature that "can no longer be viewed as merely a minor ethnic province of a domestic American canon" (22). Instead, *Transnational Asian American Literatures* emphasizes the multiple dynamics at play in Asian American cultural productions, dynamics that emerge due to

> the diasporic, mobile, transmigratory nature of Asian American experience, a history characterized by disparate migratory threads, unsettled and unsettling histories churned by multiple and different Asian ethnic immigrant groups each with a different language and cultural stock, different value and belief systems, and different notions of literary aesthetics, albeit most largely mediated through the English language. (1)

Similar to Lim's discussion of Asian American literature outside existing assumptions about what it means to be Asian American, Majaj attempts the opportunity to formulate identity politics that transgress premature assumptions about Arab and Arab American women. Exemplary of recent scholarship on Arab American literature, Majaj's attempt projects a keen awareness of the dangers of adopting nationalist definitions of Arab American literature on the one hand and Western feminist notions on the other. On the forefront of transnational feminist scholarship at large[10] is Majaj's collaborative work with Amal

---

[10] Together with Inderpal Grewal and Caren Kaplan's collection of essays, *Scattered Hegemonies: Postmodernity and Transnational Feminist Practices* (1994), Amireh and Majaj's *Going Global* has already reached canonical status in the field of transnational feminism.

Amireh about the messages that Western audiences read into the lives and texts of Arab American women. In the introduction to the groundbreaking collection *Going Global: The Transnational Reception of Third World Women Writers* (2000), Amireh and Majaj articulate their frustration with their encounters of the feminist spaces that are being ascribed to them in Western academia. Amireh and Majaj specify:

> Discursive, institutional, and ideological structures preempted our discourse and determined both what we could say and whether we would be heard when we spoke. If we critiqued our home cultures or spoke of issues confronting Arab women, our words seemed merely to confirm what our audiences already "knew," – that is, the patriarchal, oppressive nature of Third World societies. If we challenged this ready-made knowledge, we were accused of defensiveness, and our feminism was questioned and second-guessed. (1)

Amireh and Majaj's assertion suggests that Arab American women scholars, in their attempt to counter the invisibility and silence that they confront and by formulating the specific politics of location from which to speak as women, are conscious of a discrepancy between what they seek to articulate and what Western feminism wants them to say. One of the fallacies that Amireh and Majaj address is the practice within Western feminism to regard Third World women, including Arab American women, as culturally authentic "windows" into the Third World (*Going Global* 2). The contested position of Arab American women within feminism, as Marnia Lazreg points out in her contributing essay in Amireh and Majaj's collection, puts to the test the parameters of inclusion and definition of global feminism and its objective of projecting a sense of global equality and sisterhood among all women (*Going Global* 35).

Lim and Majaj recognize that the attempt to analyze the specific locations that are detrimental factors in their experiences of culture is concerned with the global inequalities emergent from a world order that is based on binary oppositions such as the ones that govern the divisions into Self and Other. As women, they hold a particularly peculiar place in these global inequalities. Caren Kaplan, Norma Alarcón and Minoo Moallem, for instance, observe in their project *Between Woman and Nation: Nationalisms, Transnational Feminism, and the State*, "Women are both of and not of the nation. Between woman and nation is, perhaps, the space or zone where we can deconstruct these monoliths and render them more historically nuanced and accountable to politics" (12). Lim's and Majaj's experiences with the racist and sexist practices in the American academia exemplify to which extent women seem to figure in the American cultural imaginary first and foremost as national outsiders; and because the "the nation-state sharpens the defining lines of citizenship for women, racialized ethnicities, and sexualities in the construction of a socially stratified society" (Kaplan et al. 1), to transgress the nation-state and to imagine a transnational location of the self makes attainable the more welcoming America that Lim envisions.

This espousal of transnational feminist heuristics in their scholarly and their creative work characterizes Majaj's and Lim's awareness of the global power inequalities that, time and again, stifled the development of a transnational feminist solidarity.[11] Unlike global feminism, which often tends to be confused with "an international feminism coming out of the West" (8) and is characterized by "its tendency to essentialize, homogenize, and centralize Western social and cultural concepts of women" (Lim 8), transnational feminism offers a more dynamic set of parameters, language and frameworks for a contemporary discussion of experiences of migration across times and places. And like other scholars in transnational feminism, Lim and Majaj carefully dissect the national boundaries along which identity categories have been determined and in which race can get in the way of gender, and ethnicity in the way of national belonging.

At Home in Her Text

Lim's and Majaj's creative writing exemplifies that literature can, and perhaps must, transgress prevalent concepts of the nation-state and articulate the space between the dual meanings of the state. Since physical spaces, such as nations, neighborhoods, or academic departments, operate with restrictive boundaries, Lim sees in the literature she produces a viable space from which she can transgress established categories. In her memoir *Among the White Moon Faces*, Lim revisits her life and narrates her stories from a perspective that does not seek to distinguish between her national belonging and her "felt" sense of belonging: "Setting out from a nation that denied people like me an equal homeland, I find myself, ironically, making a home in a state that had once barred people like me from its territory" (230). This influence of Lim's location in the United States also sets the tone in the poem with which she opens up the first chapter of her memoir, "Splendor and Squalor." In this untitled poem,

---

[11] Chandra Talpade Mohanty argues in her book, *Feminism Without Borders: Decolonizing Theory, Practicing Solidarity* (2003), for a more conscious adoption of a transnational feminist heuristics for the future development of feminist thought. Only when feminist scholarship is fully aware, and acts in light of the capitalist impositions on the modern global world order, can there be a sense of solidarity between women of different national origins.

which emphasizes the diachronicity of Lim's literary journey back to her childhood, Lim introduces the reader to her quest for a home:

> Years later, I lie awake
> In the deep enclosing heart of a household.
> Years later than in a crib
> Floating among the white moon faces that beam and grasp. (9)

The search for a home in and through her writing also shapes Majaj's transnational life-writing as well as her poetry. Her poem "Claims," which appears at the end of her essay "Boundaries" and condenses into the form of a poem the very aspects that Majaj theorizes in the essay itself, offers a glimpse at the possibilities literature has to perform transgressions of boundaries. Majaj concludes her poem with the following, slightly enigmatic statement: "I am neither the end of the world / nor the beginning" (Kadi 86). She thus evokes the fluid identity boundaries that geographical and geopolitical borders cannot match. And by placing a poem at the end of her essay, Majaj epitomizes in poetic form the personal experiences she theorizes in her academic and biographical writing.

Thus, while Lim's and Majaj's creative fiction certainly is being placed within categorical boundaries, even within academic environments such as ethnic and gender studies departments and curricula, their academic life-writing speaks of more encompassing concepts of self-hood. The literary performances they undertake in their work, such as the mixing of genres on the one hand and the de-construction of genre conventions on the other, underscore the need to transgress boundaries and categories. Instead, their writing and thus their performances of identity exhibit new and innovative incentives for a politics of identity that is inherently transnational.

Works Cited

Amireh, Amal, and Lisa Suhair Majaj. "Introduction." *Going Global: The Transnational Reception of Third World Women Writers*. New York: Garland, 2000. 1-25.

Appadurai, Arjun. "Patriotism and Its Futures." *Public Culture* 5.3 (1993): 411-29.

Bramen, Carrie Tirado. "Turning Point: What the Academic Left Hates Identity Politics." *Textual Practice* 16.1 (2002): 1-11.

Butler, Judith, and Gayatri Chakravorty Spivak. *Who Sings the Nation-State: Language, Politics, Belonging*. London: Seagull, 2007.

-----. "A Dialogue on Global States, 6 May 2006." *Postmodern Culture* 17.1 (Sept. 2006): n.p.

Chuh, Kandice. *Imagine Otherwise: On Asian Americansit Critique*. Durham: Duke University Press, 2003.

Davis, Rocío G., Jaume Aurell, and Ana Beatriz Delgado, eds. *Ethnic Life Writing and Histories: Genres, Performance, and Culture*. Berlin: LIT Verlag, 2007.

Fadda-Conrey, Carol. "Arab American Literature in the Ethnic Borderland: Cultural Intersections in Diana Abu-Jaber's *Crescent*." *MELUS* 31.4 (Winter 2006): 187-205.

Grewal, Inderpal, and Caren Kaplan, eds. *Scattered Hegemonies: Postmodernity and Transnational Feminist Practices*. Minneapolis: University of Minnesota Press, 1994.

Hassan, Salah D., and Marcy Jane Knopf-Newman. "Introduction." *MELUS* 31.4 (Winter 2006): 3-13.

Kadi, Joanna. "Introduction." *Food for Our Grandmothers: Writings by Arab-American and Arab-Canadian Feminists*. Boston: South End Press, 1994. xiii-xx.

Kaplan, Caren, Norma Alarcón, and Minoo Moallem, eds. *Between Woman and Nation: Nationalisms, Transnational Feminism, and the State*. Durham: Duke University Press, 1999.

Keating, AnaLouise. "(De)Centering the Margin? Identity Politics and Tactical (Re)Naming." *Other Sisterhoods: Literary Theory and U. S. Women of Color*. Ed. Sandra Kumamoto Stanley. Urbana: University of Illinois Press, 1998. 23-43.

Lazreg, Marnia. "The Triumphant Discourse of Global Feminism: Should Other Woman Be Known." *Going Global: The Transnational Reception of Third World Women Writers*. Ed. Amal Amireh and Lisa Suhair Majaj. New York: Garland, 2000. 29-38.

Lim, Shirley Geok-lin. "Academic and Other Memoirs: Memory, Poetry, and the Body." *Ethnic Life Writing and Histories: Genres, Performances, Culture*. Ed. Rocío G. Davis, Jaume Aurell, and Ana Beatrice Delgado. Münster, Berlin: LIT Verlag, 2007.

-----. "Where in the World Is Transnational Feminism?" *Tulsa Studies in Women's Literature* 23.1 (2004): 7-12.

-----. *Among the White Moon Faces: An Asian American Memoir of Homelands*. New York: The Feminist Press, 1996.

-----, John Blair Gamber, Stephen Hong Sohn, and Gina Valentino, eds. *Transnational Asian American Literature: Sites and Transits*. Philadelphia: Temple University Press, 2006.

Majaj, Lisa Suhair. "The Hyphenated Author: Emerging Genre of 'Arab-American Literature' Poses Questions of Definition, Ethnicity and Art."

Al Jadid Magazine 26.5 (Winter 1999). http://www.aljadid.com/features/0526maja.html. Accessed 15 April 2008.

-----. "Boundaries: Arab / American." *Food for Our Grandmothers: Writings by Arab-American and Arab-Canadian Feminists*. Ed. Joanna Kadi. Boston: South End Press, 1994. 65-86.

Mohanty, Chandra Talpade. *Feminism Without Borders: Decolonizing Theory, Practicing Solidarity*. Durham: Duke University Press, 2003.

Quayum, Mohammed A. "Shirley Geok-lin Lim: An Interview." *MELUS* 28.4 (Winter 2003): 83-100.

Schultermandl, Silvia. "(Breaking out of) The 'Literary Ghetto': Where to Place Asian American Writers, Or De-Essentializing Canonicity." *Hungarian Journal of English and American Studies* 2009.

Stone-Mediatore, Shari. "Chandra Mohanty and the Revaluing of Experience.'" *Decentering the Center: Philosophy for a Multicultural, Postcolonial, and Feminist World*. Ed. Uma Narayan and Sandra Harding. Bloomington: Indiana University Press, 2000. 110-27.

Ty, Eleanor. "Rethinking the Hyphen: Asian North American and European Ethnic Texts as Global Narratives." *Canadian Review of American Studies* 32.3 (2002): 239-52.

-----, and Donald C. Goellnicht. "Introduction." *Beyond the Hyphen: Asian North American Identities*. Bloomington: Indiana University Press, 2004. 1-14.

Yoshino, Kenji. *Covering: The Hidden Assault to Our Civil Rights*. New York: Random House, 2007.

-----. "The Pressure to Cover." *The New York Times*. January 15, 2006. Accessed online at http://query.nytimes.com/gst/fullpage.html?res=9C05E0D91F30F936A25752C0A9609C8B63. April 12, 2009.

CHAPTER TWO

Identity Trajectories in V.S. Naipaul's Work

Anna Izabela Cichoń

Compulsory and voluntary dislocation, mass and individual migrations, exile, expatriation, refuge and estrangement, Angelika Bammer writes in *Displacements: Cultural Identities in Question* (1994), appear as prevalent experiences in the twentieth and the twenty first centuries (xi). Military and political conflicts, religious and ethnic discrimination, colonial imposition of power and neo-colonial globalization have altered social geographies on unprecedented scale with the result that millions of people have been estranged from the places and communities of their origin. To be "an other," Bammer continues, appears as a signifier of contemporary, postmodern identity (xii). Dislocations, understood both as an actual and a metaphorical condition, of those who are uprooted and homeless, provoke questions about relations of migrants to the places they are forced to or choose to inhabit and about their construction of identity. The multiplicity of strategies—be it of acculturation and adjustment or of resistance and marginality—point to the difficulty and complexity of problems connected with self-positioning in contemporary, multicultural societies, in a world of human flux, of inter- and trans-continental relocations.

From his literary debut *The Mystic Masseur* (1957) onwards, displacement of protagonists of mixed descent and their identity problems have been central concerns in V.S. Naipaul's work. His preoccupation with estrangement to a large degree derives from his family and personal experience: his ancestors' transcontinental migration from India to the colonial Trinidad as indentured laborers at the end of the nineteenth century, and his own move from the West Indies to England in the 1950s.[1] A lack of social belonging, Naipaul writes in

---

[1] As Gillian Dooley writes, "Understanding V.S. Naipaul as a writer entails understanding him as a man. Biographical knowledge provides insight into the work of any writer, but Naipaul more than most has been directly modeled as an artist by his family and personal history" (2006, 1).

"Prologue to an Autobiography" in *Finding the Centre* (1984), has accompanied him from early childhood (37).[2]

In his creativity that spans over fifty years and includes both fiction and non-fiction, Naipaul has been responding to the topical problems that contemporary political geographies generate and has been concerned with the positioning of subjects in contact zones, where in the era of colonialism and its aftermath subjects "previously separated by geographic and historical disjunctures" now meet, "often within radically asymmetrical relations of power" (Pratt, 7). The identity formation projects of the characters he depicts in his work—colonials, former colonials, people of various racial and cultural backgrounds—are multifarious and range from search for ethnic authenticity to assimilation through mimicry to construction of multicultural selfhood to fashioning identity with no rigid national, racial, ethnic and cultural boundaries. Particular identity models Naipaul investigates do not belong to specific periods of his writing and are not simply replaced by new ones in the subsequent books: due to his method of writing that relies on reiterating themes and motifs, they recur throughout his oeuvre. Thus, Naipaul often returns to, or re-cycles, his earlier conceptions of selfhood and views them from new perspectives, giving new insight into the problem.

Authenticity, Assimilation, Multiculturalism

In this chapter I first briefly introduce various identity models discernable in Naipaul's works. Then I consider his ideas about Western civilization as horizon of transnational identity and show evolution of his attitude to self-identification based on Western paradigms in *Half a Life* (2002) and *Magic Seeds* (2004). In the closing section I discuss reasons for Naipaul's skepticism towards the novel as a genre that may reflect identities of subjects in the contemporary world of migrations and cross-cultural connections.

Pondering upon their situatedness in the environments they live in, Naipaul's uprooted protagonists strive, in diverse ways, to achieve personal integrity and to attach meaning to their existence. They find it difficult to define themselves since they are subjected to multiple pressures occurring in the rapidly changing world of social and political transformations, and their ancestral identities are challenged by external influences. The confrontation with a reality that is incomprehensible for them produces tensions that force them to look for new strategies of being. In *Miguel Street* (1957), black Trinidadian

---

[2] In *Reading and Writing* (2000) V.S. Naipaul recalls that when as a child he moved with his family from a rural area of Trinidad to Port of Spain, "[he] never ceased to feel a stranger" (14).

characters, seemingly attached strongly to their community, are as if suspended between their ethnic identities and the western models they feel attracted to via the influence of American movies of the 1950s. Torn between dreams of change and the actual impossibility of liberating themselves from their formative surroundings, they put on masks and imitate behaviors of their idols but this sort of inauthenticity and pretence deprives them of the ability to act and turns them into passive pawns who have no control of their lives. In *A House for Mr. Biswas* (1961), the protagonist renounces his Hindu subjectivity, heroically resists the oppressive colonizing forces, and attempts to set himself free from the constraints his family and environment impose on him. Desperate to preserve personal dignity and to assert his independence—symbolically expressed as his longing for a house of his own—he rejects the idea of relational selfhood and attempts to become an autonomous subject, which eventually leads to his total alienation from his immediate environment. *The Mimic Men* (1967), in turn, focuses on the hero's attempts at assimilation in the new surroundings. As an immigrant from a Caribbean country to London, the protagonist Ralph Singh desperately tries to imitate English customs, habits, values and life-style. He even mimics Western patterns of thought and emotional responses.[3] However, no matter how hard he tries to integrate, he will always be, to use Homi Bhabha's expression, "almost the same, but not quite." Like other expatriate characters in the novel, he feels he has wasted his life on a false cause, and undergoes identity crisis. Mimicry, therefore, has a devastating impact upon Naipaul's individuals, who become utter strangers, even to themselves.[4] The formation of multicultural identity, a central theme in *Guerrillas* (1975) and "The Crocodiles of Yamoussoukro" in *Finding the Center*, relies on the characters' conscious cobbling together of various kinds of cultural experiences. The protagonists, former colonials from the West Indies and Africa, come into contact with Western culture and wish to integrate their formative and new experiences as a base of a harmonious subjectivity. However, Jimmy Ahmed in *Guerrillas* and Arlette in *Finding the Center* fail to achieve a sense

---

[3] For example, Ralph Singh shares the European shame and guilt about atrocities committed against the Jews during World War II.
[4] Dagmar Barnouw in *Naipaul's Strangers* (2003), proves that sense of alienation and utter strangeness are the dominant identity traits of Naipaul himself and all of his protagonists. Rob Nixon, in turn, in *London Calling: V.S. Naipaul, Postcolonial Mandarin* (1990), demonstrates that "fashioning and sustaining an autobiographical persona who is accepted at face value as a permanent exile" (17) is Naipaul's empowering myth that he uses to legitimize his "reputation as an objective and disinterested observer" (18).

of cultural integrity. Although doubleness has a big potential,[5] in Naipaul's narratives, hybridity is often negatively marked and leads his protagonists to displacement in all of the environments, to "cultural schizophrenia," which means that a subject, British and Caribbean at the same time, eventually becomes neither British nor Caribbean.[6]

Universal Civilization as Horizon of Identity

In *A Way in the World* (1994), *Half a Life* and *Magic Seeds*, Naipaul has scrutinized yet another identity model of subjects who, for whatever reasons, constantly move from place to place, who are without allegiance to a specific culture, and who are not bound to any particular society/community. This kind of self-construction, being a response to cross-connections and imbrications of the local with global concerns, involves looking for identification determinants outside of specific locations with their social and cultural contents. It denies, as Susan Stanford Friedman writes, "organic unfolding" (19) of personhood in the process of growth and organizes identity as interactive syncretism that involves "multiple positionality" (21), often in contradictory positions. This kind of identity resists fixity and "shifts fluidly from setting to setting" (23). While such subjects, transnational subjects, live in their local environment, they still think of themselves as citizens of the world, a world with no rigid boundaries.[7]

That the nineteenth century idea of nation-states does not hold any longer in the contemporary world is something that Naipaul expressed directly already in

---

[5] In "Diaspora and Double Consciousness," Samir Dayal acknowledges the potential of doubleness when he remarks that it is "less 'both/and' and more 'a neither just this/nor just that'" (47).

[6] Interesting, that whereas in his fiction Naipaul is skeptical about the possibility of constructing multicultural identity successfully, while talking about his own experience, he admits that he has no problem with reconciling his multiple formative backgrounds: "Many things had gone to make me. But there was no problem for me there" (Naipaul 2003, 512).

[7] In *A Way in the World* (1994) several characters seem to illustrate the case in point: Lebrun, a revolutionary, born in Panama, has no permanent residence—he lives a life in transit between the West Indies, various African countries, Canada, Britain, and the United States; Blair, a post-colonial governmental adviser, does not wish to settle and is always on the move between the West Indies and Africa; the very narrator, a West Indian by birth, emigrates to the United Kingdom for education, works as a script writer in New York and holds academic positions in Africa.

the 1970s, [8] when in *In a Free State* (1971) the narrator, a homeless tramp, ponders:

> I've been to Egypt six or seven times. Gone around the world about a dozen times. Australia, Canada, all those countries [...] I've been traveling for thirty-eight years. Youth-hostelling, that's how I do it. Not a thing to be despised. New Zealand, have you been there? I went there in 1934. Between you and me, they're a cut above the Australians. But what's nationality these days? I myself, I think of myself as a citizen of the world. (9)

In Naipaul's works, transcultural identity, that is identity shaped not in relation to a specific place but to transnational concerns (like political engagement,[9] forced or voluntary migration, traveling or the writing profession, to name the author's recurrent concerns) is an intricate and problematic auto-formation project that is not free of faults. His characters preserve their own formative, hereditary identity, no matter how complex and multilayered, and confront it with the universal values. Thus, what the author scrutinizes as modern identity in the world of global migrations is a kind of self-fashioning along paradigms that appear as universal and applicable to all mankind, independently of their ethnic and cultural background. Universal values are to offer a reservoir of identifications that subjects may adopt as a core with which other identifications are as if concomitant. Universal values are to delineate a space which subjects, independently of their actual place of dwelling, may find as their own and turn into their horizon of identity: as a locus for what is meaningful, as a source of values, as that which gives direction to their lives and helps to articulate commitments, obligations, and judgments. [10] It seems that this conception is close to what Loinnet and Shih term as "transnationalism from

---

[8] When in 1975 Naipaul attended the *East Indians in the Caribbean* conference in Trinidad, he expressed his criticism of wordly cosmopolitanism, which he saw as "a product of 'despair, defeat, and usually ignorance,' the response of a man 'who has dropped out, who can't face the present and can't face his position in the world'" (Greenberg 218).

[9] It should be stressed at this point that throughout his works, Naipaul's attitude towards political activists is negative. As a conservative (Greenberg 218), he is distrustful of revolution as a cause and full of contempt for political agitators whose altruistic motivation he does not believe. As Winokur writes, "posturing Third World revolutionaries and adoring white liberals" are "the two kinds of people [Naipaul] hates most" (128).

[10] In *Sources of the Self*, Charles Taylor explains the significance of frameworks as sources of values that make it possible for subjects to position themselves in the moral space (26-30). Taylor uses the term framework interchangeably with horizon.

above" (5). This "transnationalism from above," they explain, connects up with "the utopic views of globalization, which celebrate the overcoming of national and other boundaries for the constitution of a liberal global market, the hybridization of cultures, and the expansion of democracies and universal human rights" (6).[11]

For Naipaul, universal values that "fit all men" underwrite the transatlantic civilization. He formulated his idea in "Our Universal Civilization," a lecture given on invitation from the conservative Manhattan Institute of New York in 1990. Universal civilization, Naipaul argues,

> has been a long time in the making. It wasn't always universal; it wasn't always as attractive as it is today. The expansion of Europe gave it for at least three centuries a racial tint, which still causes pain. In Trinidad, I grew up in the last days of that kind of racialism. And that, perhaps, has given me a greater appreciation of the immense changes that have taken place since the end of the war, *the extraordinary attempt of this civilization to accommodate the rest of the world, and all the currents of that world's thought.* (516, emphasis added)

What the author finds captivating about this civilization is its broad appeal, its openness and readiness to accept other modes of life, and its rejection of fanaticism:

> I find it marvelous to contemplate to what an extent, after two centuries, and after the terrible history of the earlier part of this century, the idea has come to a kind of fruition. It is an elastic idea; *it fits all men.* It implies a certain kind of society, a certain kind of awakened spirit. I don't imagine my father's parents would have been able to understand the idea. So much is contained in it: *the idea of the individual, responsibility, choice, the life of the intellect, the idea of vocation and perfectibility and achievement.* It is an immense human idea. It cannot be reduced to a fixed system. *It cannot generate fanaticism.* But it is known to exist; and because of that, other more rigid systems in the end blow away. (517, emphasis added)

There is no doubt that Naipaul's theory as expressed in his lecture on the idea of a universal civilization is not free of a personal bias. Also, in his auto-

---

[11] "Transnationalism from above" differs from "transnationalism from below" in the sense that the latter "can be conceived as a space of exchange and participation whenever processes of hybridization occur and where it is still possible for cultures to be produced and performed without necessary mediation of the center" (Loinnet and Shih 5).

biographies and interviews he keeps repeating that in Trinidad he would not have fulfilled the desire developed in childhood to become a writer. Likewise, he goes on to say, in Eastern Europe, the Soviet Union or India he would not have had the opportunity to fulfill his ambitions, either. It is specifically the transatlantic civilization, he claims, that offers opportunities for personal advancement and self-realization:

> It is the civilization, first of all, which gave me the idea of the writing vocation. It is the civilization in which I have been able to practise my vocation as a writer. To be a writer, you need to start with a certain kind of sensibility. The sensibility itself is created, or given direction, by an *intellectual atmosphere*. (504, emphasis added)

Yet, the intellectual atmosphere alone is not enough, Naipaul carries on to explain, for his concept of "universal civilization" does not involve merely a spiritual idea, but material culture as well, that is a developed infrastructure where books are marketable commodities and an author has opportunities to have his book published and distributed:

> But books are not created just in the mind. Books are physical objects. To write them, you need a certain kind of sensibility; you need a language, and a certain gift of language; and you need to possess a particular literary form. To get your name on the spine of the created physical object, you need a vast apparatus outside yourself. You need publishers, editors, designers, printers, binders; booksellers, critics, newspapers, and magazines and television where the critics can say what they think of the book; and, of course, buyers and readers. (506)

When highlighting the importance of the well developed infrastructure which makes possible the publication and distribution of books, Naipaul overly identifies universalism with the West. For him universal civilization is not a spaceless phenomenon, a set of ideas, or a source of one's cultural knowledge or identity horizon, but territorialized places, specific locations only. [12] They are the developed and affluent Western Europe and the United States, both forming the centre and providing models for political, social, cultural and economic organization. Thus in his lecture, where he apparently discusses universal values that "fit all men" and cross-cut national borders, that have general applicability regardless of real place and that may bridge the gaps be-

---

[12] Naipaul's idea of the formative role of universal civilization which is rooted in specific places only is the opposite to what Bill Ashcroft observes about the role of location in *Postcolonial Transformation,* when he writes: "[i]t is when place is least spatial, perhaps, that it becomes most identifying" (125).

tween cultures, he actually supports the conservative idea of his about the split of the world into two distinct locations: one of enlightened and rational civilization, the other backward and fanatical. What he, then, proposes in this lecture is an elaboration, though more specific and focused, on the observations he expressed three years earlier in *The Enigma of Arrival* (1987). In part, this becomes evident from the following passage, one that has been quoted broadly:

> [...] in 1950 in London I was at the beginning of that great movement of peoples that was to take place in the second half of the twentieth century—a movement and a cultural mixing greater than the peopling of the United States. [...] Cities like London were to change. They were to cease being more or less national cities; they were to become cities of the world, modern-day Romes, establishing the pattern of what great cities should be, in the eyes of islanders like myself and people even more remote in language and culture. They were to be cities visited for learning and elegant goods and manners and freedom by all the barbarian peoples of the globe, people of forest and desert, Arabs, Africans, Malays. (130)

No wonder, then, that Naipaul's antagonists fiercely attacked him after his lecture on universal civilization with accusations that he once again, in a new guise, proposed hierarchical divisions and postulated once again another version of westernization, and that his exultation over the North induced denigration of the South.[13]

---

[13] The reception of Naipaul as a neo-colonial author gained intensity when, the same year he delivered his lecture, he published the final part of his trilogy about India, *India: A Million Mutinies Now* (1990). In this book, Naipaul once again repeats the old conviction of his that India is a half-made society, a society in the making. At the same time, though, he seems to be more optimistic about the future of India because he sees India as a country that no longer rejects western values: "With the development of an intellectual life in India, people are awakening to history. They're beginning to understand where they stand in the scheme of things. It's the beginning of a new way of looking at yourself" (Winokur 119). In a patronizing manner he remarks that he is content with the direction India takes because the country has made enormous technological progress in comparison to the state it was in during his first visit twenty years back: "India's development since I went there in 1962 has been extraordinary. [...] after two generations there has been a great efflorescence of intellectual life" (Robinson 108).

Decline of Trust in Universal Civilization?

Although in *The Enigma of Arrival* Naipaul is full of admiration for the role England plays in the post-colonial world, and in his 1990 address commends the universal civilization as a horizon of identity, one may wonder why in his books the protagonists who get in contact with Western life-style and hierarchy of values cannot achieve emotional equilibrium and cannot identify themselves with any surroundings, independently of their actual residence. *Half a Life* together with its sequel *Magic Seeds* suggest two sorts of overlapping reasons for the failure of Naipaul's transnational characters. The first one seems to be Naipaul's unfading skepticism about the possibility of positive self-identification with transnational concerns. Often enough has he stated that he is distrustful of people who are constantly on the move and who never find a place of belonging. For him this is a permanent deficiency of character (Greenberg 218). The second reason that appears new and is discernable in *Magic Seeds* is evolution of his views about the current condition of Western culture and his loss of faith in its being a commendable horizon of identity.

In *Half a Life* Naipaul reiterates his old, conservative conception that in half-made societies, like in India and Africa, individuals have no prospects for personal development and that their only chance to give meaning to their lives is to emigrate to a Western country to ascend to its enlightened life-style. The protagonist of *Half a Life*, Willie Chandran, a mixed-caste Hindu, believes that he has no opportunities for a satisfying life in India. He travels to London to study but since he feels no emotional bonds with his family, he has no urge to return home. In England Willie realizes that he does not belong there either: he is "unanchored, with no idea of what lay ahead" (*HL* 58), but he also discovers that in the new place he may re-invent himself, and start a new life: "towards the end of his second term, he saw with great clarity that the old rules no longer bound him [...] Willie began to understand that he was free to present himself as he wished [...] The possibilities were dizzying. He could, within reason, remake himself and his past and his ancestry" (*HL* 60). Thus, Willie erases his old life-scripts,[14] makes up a family history, and takes advantage of the freedom, life without attachment offers. He chooses a profession that appears ennobling to him—that of a writer. When after the publication of his first book he cannot write anything else, when his new identity, or pose rather, exhausts itself, he goes to East Africa with his wife of Portuguese and African descent, and stays there for eighteen years, all the time aware that the country is not his

---

[14] In *The Ethics of Identity*, Kwame Anthony Appiah coins the term life-script for the long-term aims one attempts to achieve in life. In Appiah's term, then, Willie has no script, no narrative that he would accept as his own (2005, 6-8; 22).

permanent residence, but merely one of many stops in his life in transit. When civil war is to break out, he realizes that he does not want to get involved in a political conflict that is not his. At the end of the book he leaves for Germany to visit his sister, and to reconsider where he might belong.

In *Magic Seeds* that continues the story from *Half a Life*, his sister, "a self-appointed recruiter for the guerrillas, while living 'on a subsidy from some West German government agency'" (Dooley 133), married to a left-wing filmmaker, manages to convince him that his place in the world is "with the oppressed, the freedom fighters" (ibid.) and sends him, through her connections, to join revolutionary movement in India. She believes that "he will find the real world, not the simplified life of the prosperous West in which life's meaning has been reduced to marking time with meals and sex and shopping until death comes" (Griffiths). Yet, when he is in India, Willie finds out that the struggle he has joined is futile. The revolutionaries, for egoistic reasons, treat engagement in the movement as a self-serving, elevating activity that attaches meaning to their lives. They do not care about the villagers and exploit them in a similar way as their actual oppressors. Disillusioned with the revolution, with awareness that he is an outsider to the people he is supposed to fight for, feeling as a stranger in the country that appears completely alien to him, after traumatic experiences including imprisonment, he is rescued by his English friend under special amnesty on grounds of his alleged reputation as "a pioneer of modern Indian writing" (*MS* 174). Once again he is full of hope of regaining meaning of his life although he senses that his plan is based on pretence and usurpation: his literary reputation rests on his debut from decades ago—a collection of derivative short stories imitative of American authors. Needless to say, Willie's comeback to Western civilization does not bring regeneration but bitter disenchantment. But this is not merely because of his lack of authenticity and inability to remodel his identity.

Willie's story seems to express Naipaul's reservations about transnational life-style that may easily turn to a form of escapism. Willie renounces his duties and obligations and, at moments of crisis, he runs away with the hope that in new places his life will be easier and problems will solve themselves. The sort of transnational identity Willie adopts relies on his rejection of commitments, which, eventually, leads to his utter uprooting. Whereas in one of Naipaul's early novels, *A House for Mr. Biswas*, the title character with heroic determination strives to find some place of belonging—symbolically expressed as his ambition to live in his own house—in *Magic Seeds* the protagonist discovers in his middle age that he is, literally and metaphorically, homeless. He realizes "with the deepest kind of ache that there was no true place in the world for him" (*MS* 238). It suddenly occurs to him that he has never had a place of his own: "Never at home in India, when I was a boy. Never here in London. Never in Africa. I lived in somebody else's house always, and slept in somebody else's bed" (*MS* 185).

Naipaul's distrust of "citizens of the world" has, in fact, not waned since *In a Free State* (1971). However, his skepticism towards the sort of transnational self-identifications he scrutinizes in the sequel gains new force because of what appears as his disillusionment with contemporary Western culture, specifically, with the condition of England. In *Magic Seeds* English culture is no longer that of a developed civilization, of "universal civilization" that he praised so highly in his 1990 lecture, but of decadence, corruption, and demoralization, which manifest themselves in the characters' loss of direction in life, lack of values, inability to love and maintain meaningful relations. The ideals—"of the individual, responsibility, choice, the life of the intellect, the idea of vocation and perfectibility and achievement" (Naipaul 2002, 517)—are on the decline: friends betray each other, marriages split, fortunes are gained by fraud, intellectual elites are consumed by inertia, men are motivated by selfish reasons. "The people Willie meets in London are every bit as loathsome as the revolutionaries he met in India. They are all narcissistic snobs, obsessed with status and class, and their own agendas of revenge and oneupsmanship" (Kakutani). It seems that Naipaul has lost confidence in the universal civilization,[15] its dominant role in the world and its being a reservoir of identity models, a source of frameworks.

Genre Conventions

The various models of identity and strategies of inhabitation Naipaul depicts in his life-long work are reflected in the evolving genre conventions of his writing. "For every kind of experience," Naipaul states in *Reading and Writing* (2000), "there is a proper form" (49). In the early phase of his creativity, when as a fresh immigrant to England he felt the need to scrutinize his background, he wrote novels and short stories about the West Indies. Thus, although he had left Trinidad, through his writing, he kept returning to his roots. *The Mystic Masseur, The Suffrage of Elvira* (1958) and *A House for Mr. Biswas* were written as novels in the tradition of European prose epics with comic insights, with well constructed plots and discerning analyses of characters whose lot is related to their environment. Naipaul was to return to this form in *The Mimic Men* and,

---

[15] As Paul Griffiths (2005) remarks, "[t]he universal civilization, having caused everyone at the periphery to forget who they are and to enter sealed chambers from which there is no exit, has now, in Naipaul's view, consumed itself as well."

with a changed setting, in *A Bend in the River* (1979). Also, his experimental novel, *Guerrillas*, with its postmodern subversions and intertextual references, follows the recognizable European epic genre. What compelled Naipaul to write novels about Carribean societies was a need to come to terms with his formative background. Although in order to become a writer he had to leave Trinidad, in order to find material for his books, he had to return home and grasp the rhythms of his ancestral places and comprehend the people he had left behind. Fiction created for Naipaul a kind of safe distance that allowed him to handle experience too painful to be exposed in other forms, like autobiography or documentary. Besides, fiction permitted simplifications, like the naïve point of view of the child-narrator in *Miguel Street*, which would not be possible to have in non-fiction.

Meanwhile, the journey he made in 1960 to the Caribbean and the commission to write a book of non-fiction opened up for him a new terrain of writing—journalism, reportage and history— which he sees as both a way of learning about the world and "a strong and immediate response to the world" (Rowe-Evans 36). The travelogues about the West Indies, South America, India and Africa that followed *The Middle Passage* (1962) deal with places related to his ancestral past and hence are of personal importance for Naipaul. At the same time, with a shift towards traveling, Naipaul has been more and more skeptical about the genre of the traditional novel, claiming that the nineteenth century form has exhausted its possibilities because it cannot mediate the geo-political changes that have occurred in the modern world. "Fiction works best," he asserts in *Reading and Writing* (2000), "in a confined moral and cultural area, where the rules are generally known; and in that confined area it deals best with things—emotions, impulses, moral anxieties—that would be unseizable or incomplete in other literary forms" (49-50).[16] The novel, he continues, because of its Western, metropolitan origin, and its "metropolitan assumptions about society: the availability of a wider learning, an idea of history, a concern with self-knowledge" (50-51), fails to accommodate the "fractured and muddled" (Robinson 112) experience of contemporary migrants. In an interview, Naipaul explains the reasons of his departure from the traditional novel: "You might go on endlessly writing 'creative' novels, if you believed that the framework of an ordered society exists, so after a disturbance there is calm, and all the crises fall back into that great underlying calm. But that no longer exists for most people, so that kind of imaginative work is of less and less use to them" (in Rowe-Evans, 36).

---

[16] As Naipaul explains, "Novels, a body of work, come best out of whole and single societies" (in Robinson, 112).

That he was gradually dropping the idea of writing novels and turning to "fluid, semifictional form" (Coetzee 286), to sequences of narratives linked together not by means of psychological and social analysis coupled with an evolving plot but through the logic of their shared themes, motifs and ideas, was visible already when he published *In a Free State* and, later, *The Enigma of Arrival*. For Salman Rushdie *The Enigma of Arrival,* as a piece of fiction and documentation, is a "mediation" rather than a novel (148), in which Naipaul rewrites rural England to turn it to a place he could inhabit, to make it his home. In 1994 Naipaul wrote another unconventional piece—A *Way in the World,* a collection of nine loosely connected sections— that was originally subtitled as a sequence. That the genre affiliation of the text is hard to determine is exemplified by the history of its publication: the book was published in the UK as a sequence, and in the USA as a novel (Dooley 121). In *A Way in the World* the author reinterprets the history of the West Indies in order to scrutinize the relation between collective, historical experience of the society and individual destiny of its subjects, himself included. As Mel Gussow writes, it is a memoir as novel or a novel in the guise of a memoir. It is not always clear when real life steps aside and imagination takes over. [...] the work establishes its own form. It is not [...] a "work of history or scholarship or fiction," although [...] it has aspects of all three. [...] As close readers of his work will realize, beneath *A Way in the World* is a palimpsest of other Naipaul narratives. In a different form, he wrote about these events in books as varied as *The Loss of El Dorado* (1969), a history of the Spanish conquest, and *Mr. Stone and the Knights Companion* (1963), the first of his novels set in England. "These are books that cost me a lot of pain," [Naipaul] said. "They didn't come out well because I was a prisoner of a borrowed form. I wasn't writing my own kind of book." For "El Dorado," he said, "I borrowed the form of the history and damaged the work." The new book is his corrective.

Despite his skepticism towards novels, for his most recent narratives--*Half a Life* and *Magic Seeds*—Naipaul has as if returned to the genre he has been critical of for the past years. One may wonder why Naipaul has turned to a form he has been so distrustful of. One of the reasons might be that despite his focus on the protagonist, Willie Chandrun—a man on the move—Naipaul scrutinizes once again, by means of the metropolitan novel, the metropolitan Western culture and the role it plays in the formation of identities of translocating subjects. Another reason for Naipaul's turning to fiction is that *Half a Life* and *Magic Seeds* are texts of autobiographical value for the author: they are his fictional autobiographies where he, as it were, tests an alternative story of his life, a story of failure and personal disintegration. Willie, thus, appears as Naipaul's negative auto-portrait and Willie's vicissitudes are "a kind of cautionary tale for what Naipaul's life might have been without the impulse or discipline to keep writing in spite of early discouragement. This frightening sense of the blankness of the life he feels he narrowly missed feeds into the desolation and despair of this novel" (Dooley 131). Viewed from this perspective, *Half a Life* and *Magic Seeds* are not pure novels—they combine fiction and autobiography, not in the manner of a conventional autobiographical novel, but its reversal: they are Naiapaul's alternative autobiographies or, to use Gillian Dooley's term, "cautionary" auto-fictions.

There is no doubt that for his themes—identity formation projects, strategies of being of contemporary migrants, encounters of subjects from culturally remote backgrounds—Naipaul has worked out a form of expression that challenges traditional and hierarchical evaluations of literary forms that deems the novel the finest of genres.[17] His narratives—fiction and travel, or "books of inquiry and exploration" (Winokur 128)—are accurately described by J.M. Coetzee who characterizes his mode as that "in which historical reportage and social analysis flow into and out of autobiographically coloured fiction and travel memoir" (281). It seems that while V.S. Naipaul's attitude to literary conventions appears progressive and innovatory, his understanding of the role of the Western culture as deployed in "Our Universal Civilization" looks conservative and controversial, to say the least. While rejecting evaluations of literary forms and celebrating diversity, co-occurrence of modes, styles and techniques in his creative practice, in his lecture Naipaul ventured a conception of the world where the center was to play the role of mediator for the peripheries. However, in his recent books—*Half a Life* and *Magic Seeds*—he seems to have renounced the former idea of his that Western civilization may serve as a commendable horizon of identity.

Works Cited

Appiah, Kwame Anthony. *The Ethics of Identity*. Princeton: Princeton University Press, 2005.
Ashcroft, Bill. *Post-Colonial Transformations*. London: Routledge, 2001.
Bammer, Angelika, ed. *Displacements: Cultural Identities in Question*. Theories of Contemporary Culture, 15. Bloomington and Indianapolis: Indiana University Press, 1994.
Coetzee, J.M. *Inner Workings: Literary Essays 2000-2005*. London: Harvill Secker, 2007.

---

[17] "It is a vanity of the age (and of commercial promotion) that the novel continues to be literature's final and highest expression," remarks Naipaul in *Reading and Writing* (63).

Dayal, Samir. "Diaspora and Double Consciousness." *The Journal of the Midwest Modern Language Association* 29.1 (Spring 1996): 46-62.
Dooley, Gillian. *V.S. Naipaul, Man and Writer*. Columbia: University of South Carolina Press, 2006.
Friedman, Susan Stanford. *Mappings: Feminism and the Geographies of Encounter*. Princeton: Princeton University Press, 1998.
Greenberg, Robert M. "Anger and the Alchemy of Literary Method in V. S. Naiapul's Political Fiction: the Case of *The Mimic Men*." *Twentieth Century Literature* 46.2 (Summer 2000): 214-237.
Griffiths, Paul. "The center does not hold." *Commonweal* Feb 11, 2005. http://findarticles.com/p/articles/mi_m1252/is_3_132/ai_n14874151/ (accessed January 03, 2008).
Gussow, Mel. "V. S. Naipaul in Search of Himself. A Conversation." *The New York Times*. (24 April 1994). http://www.nytimes.com/1994/04/24/books/v-s-naipaul-in-search-of-himself-a-conversation.html (accessed September 10, 2009).
Jussawalla, Feroza , ed. *Conversations with V.S. Naipaul*. Jackson: Mississippi University Press, 1997.
Kakutani, Michiko. "Dreams of Glory Unraveling in Chaos." *The New York Times* November 30, 2004. http://query.nytimes.com/gst/fullpage.html?res=940DEEDA103EF933A05752C1A9629C8B63 (accessed June 10, 2008).
Lionnet, Francoise, Shu-mei Shih, eds. *Minor Transnationalism*. Durham: Duke University Press, 2005.
Naipaul, V. S. *Magic Seeds*. London: Picador, 2004.
-----. *The Writer and the World*. New York: Vintage Books, 2003.
-----. "Our Universal Civilization." *The Writer and the World*. New York: Vintage Books, 2003. 503-519.
-----. *Half a Life*. London: Picador, 2001.
-----. *Reading and Writing. A Personal Account*. New York: NYRB, 2000.
-----. *A Way in the World*. USA: Vintage, 1995.
-----. *The Enigma of Arrival*. London: Penguin Books, 1987.
-----. *Finding the Center*. Harmondsworth: Penguin Books, 1984.
-----. *A Bend in the River*. London: Deutsch, 1979.
-----. *Guerrillas*. London: Deutsch, 1975.
-----. *In a Free State*. London: Penguin Books, 1973.
-----. The Mimic Men. London: Deutsch, 1967.
-----. *The Middle Passage*. London: Deutsch, 1962.
-----. *A House for Mr. Biswas*. London: Deutsch, 1961.
-----. *Miguel Street*. London: Deutsch, 1959.

-----. *The Suffrage of Elvira*. London: Deutsch, 1958.
-----. *The Mystic Masseur*. London: Deutsch, 1957.
Nixon, Rob. *London Calling: V.S. Naipaul, Postcolonial Mandarin*. New York: Oxford University Press, 1992.
Pratt. Mary Louise. *Imperial Eyes: Travel Writing and Transculturation*. London: Routledge, 1992.
Robinson, Andrew. "An Elusive Master: V. S. Naipaul Is Still Searching." *Conversations with V.S. Naipaul*. Ed. Feroza Jussawalla. Jackson: Mississippi University Press, 1997. 106-109.
Rowe-Evans, Adrian. "V. S. Naipaul: A *Transition* Interview." *Conversations with V.S. Naipaul*. Ed. Feroza Jussawalla. Jackson: Mississippi University Press, 1997. 24-36.
Rushdie, Salman. *Imaginary Homelands: Essays and Criticism 1981-1991*. London: Granta Books, 1992.
Taylor, Charles. *Sources of the Self: The Making of the Modern Identity*. Cambridge: Cambridge University Press, 1992.
Winokur, Scott. "The Unsparing Vision of V.S. Naipaul." *Conversations with V.S. Naipaul*. Ed. Feroza Jussawalla. Jackson: Mississippi University Press, 1997. 114-129.

CHAPTER THREE

"Pleased to meet you!": The Paradox of Identity in Zadie Smith's *The Autograph Man*

Jonathan P. A. Sell

For better or for worse, critics and theorists alike often become pedlars of ingenious paradoxes, the enigmatic inscrutability of which is often only matched by the impenetrable opacity of their prose.[1] Studies and reflections on questions of identity have fallen particular prey to this sort of Delphic treatment. Paul Ricoeur's *Oneself as Another* (originally published as *Soi-même comme un autre*, 1990) and Julia Kristeva's *Strangers to Ourselves* (originally published as *Étrangers á nous-mêmes*, 1991) both worry philosophico-lyrically at the idea that the individual subject both is and is not his or her self. Denis-Constant Martin (1-2) has suggested how the apparently paradoxical state of affairs consisting in simultaneously being and not being oneself is possible in two senses: firstly, an other is always present in a person's narrative identity in so far as a person changes over time and the narrative must take account of those changes; secondly, the narrative identity is always different from the real identity, is always necessarily other. Martin builds on Ricoeur's work, particularly his notion of narrative identity, itself an inheritance from Hannah Arendt (Ricoeur 246). Ideas of narrative identity and of identity as narrative also inform philosopher Charles Taylor's ideas of identity (50-52), which have come to form a major part—albeit contested—of the philosophical premises underlying multiculturalism. Notions of identity as narrative or of narrative as identity tend to be driven by some hankering after a unifying teleology for a given individual's self which confer upon it some sort of "harmonic integration", to adopt John Fekete's (195) phrase. Such notions are in the last resort liberal humanist and Zadie Smith, sometimes dubbed against her own wishes the Queen of Multicul-

---

[1] This chapter is the outcome of work in progress as part of a larger research project financed by the DGI of the Spanish Ministry of Science and Technology under the title "Metáforas de la diáspora postcolonial en la Gran Bretaña de finales de siglo (1990-2005)" (code: HUM2007-63028/FILO).

turalism, has little patience with them since they are inconsistent with her own ontology of identity and, when assimilated to determinist schemes of history, tend to curtail ethical autonomy (Sell 2007, 157-63).[2]

Zadie Smith on Identity

In her first novel, *White Teeth* (1999), Smith cocks a snook at post-structuralist, grimly determinist ideas of identity, and in doing so implicitly distanced herself from postcolonial writers. In that novel, identity is neither wholly socially, culturally, ethnically, environmentally or scientifically determined; it is not a matter of the subject being bidden to play out the script of all-powerful masternarratives. Rather, in a novel which is in some senses a paean to postmodern randomness or contingency, identity is a space in which the subject is free to don and doff identities at will (Sell 2006, 33-40); the most successful players in the identity game are "social chameleons" like Millat, "able to please all of the people all of the time" (Smith 2001, 249). When a metaphysic of chance replaces another of causality, the past can be taken or left, while identity can be changed at will or left to metamorphose by chance. Identity therefore becomes irreducible to an orderly, harmonious narrative of a unified self. All a narrative of identity can hope to do is provide, instead of a long-running biopic, a snapshot at a point in time—and that, of course, means that it is no longer a narrative. As a corollary of the novel's anathema to notions of plotted identity or liberal humanist essentialism, Smith has a problem with questions of autonomy and freewill, which perhaps explains the way key decisions throughout the novel are taken on the toss of a coin. All very postmodern, all ever so slightly glib—one would like to think that there is more to identity than simply "removing a fake beard" (Smith 2001, 18)—but none of it too much of a problem for a novel which is very much action-oriented and whose bravura plotting, feisty humor and linguistic relish left critics too knocked-out to pay much attention to characterization.

In Smith's second novel, *The Autograph Man* (2002), the key is much lower: there is little plot, a dourer humor and less linguistic pyrotechnics. As the title suggests, it is a novel much more oriented towards character and more seriously preoccupied with identity. Half-Chinese, half-Jewish, Alex-Li Tandem is the Autograph Man not only because he is a professional dealer in celebrity snaps and signatures, but because he and the novel are absorbed in the problematics of how to write the self, in his particular case, of how to carry off the tricky, but not impossible (if the hint in his surname is taken), balancing act

---

[2] Dominic Head reads *White Teeth* as a multicultural manifesto, the optimism of which is questioned by Molly Thompson.

between the competing cultural selves inscribed in his hybrid first name. Those critics, chief among them James Wood in the *London Review of Books*, who questioned Smith's achievement in her second novel, did so by disparaging its central character's nullity or vacuity and probably missing most of Smith's point. For, in *The Autograph Man*, Smith homes in with unerring aim on the issue of identity. The eponymous hero, Alex-Li Tandem, is an autograph man in two senses: he makes his living from dealing in autographs and he is constantly trying to determine his own identity, to write his own self, to create himself auto-graphically.

Ostensibly, Alex-Li's identity is negotiated about two competing poles, Jewish (on his mother's side) and Chinese (on his father's), as his hyphenated forename indicates. The novel consists of a lengthy Prologue, Book One, Book Two and an Epilogue. In one sense there is a progress from the death of Alex-Li's father in the Prologue to Alex-Li's performance ten years on of the Jewish ritual of the kaddish, in honor of his dead Chinese father—a performance which might seem to write Alex-Li's identity definitively as Jewish. Book One is subtitled "The Kabbalah of Alex-Li Tandem" and each of its ten chapters is given the name of one of the Kabbalistic sefirot which polysemously refer simultaneously to divine attributes, aspects of divine power, ways in which God is made manifest, and so on. Book Two, which also has ten chapters, is subtitled "The Zen of Alex-Li Tandem," its epigraph explaining through a quotation from a work on Zen Buddhism that for the Chinese master Kakuan, "The ten bulls represent sequent steps in the realization of one's true nature." (223). The implication of this paratextual esoterism would seem to be clear: in Book One Alex-Li, in tandem with the reader, will try to inscribe his identity within the Jewish-kabbalistic scheme, in Book Two within the Chinese-Zen scheme, as if in enactment of a Jungian quest for individuation and cosmic integration.

Even though both books culminate in the achievement of a goal (the tracking down of Kitty Alexander and the performance of the Kaddish, respectively), there is never any sense of a Taylorian *telos* being achieved and thus bestowing significance on and providing closure for Alex-Li's identity. Even with Kitty Alexander sitting in his living room, "[a]lmost everything" is still wrong with Alex (344); the hunt, it appears, had been the thing, its object rendered charmless and trivial by the capture. As for Alex-Li's performance of the Kaddish, the point about it is that it is a performance, a gesture, the sincerity of which is consequently uncertain. For Smith it is patently absurd, and inhumane, to shoehorn identity into the narrative schemes of one culture to the exclusion of another, just as the universe and all that is in it cannot be identified as either Jewish or Goyish, to choose the binary around which Alex-Li fecklessly tries to categorize the phenomenological accoutrements of human existence in his unfinished and unfinishable book Jewishness and Goyishness. For Smith, identity is too myriad and adventitious to be tidied into a narrative whose end is implicit in its beginning and is reached in an orderly series of chronological steps. As in *White Teeth*, so in *The Autograph Man* deterministic narratives of identity are jettisoned as the subject is dispersed into a series of contingent gestures. Alex-Li's climactic "performance" of the Kaddish is only undertaken at the behest of his mother and the encouragement of two Jewish friends; like an earlier assumption of a Jewish identity, it is a gesture on the same level as clicking the buckle of a wristwatch strap, as Smith's epigraph to the *Epilogue* makes clear. Gesture might give a false representation of identity, but it can help us through a sticky patch, sustain us when the going gets tough. In other words, identity becomes a socially pragmatic strategy, not some essentialist quid that can be whittled down to an irreducible core; it can indeed be removed like a false beard.

In this respect, Smith's idea of identity as gesture is similar to that of the social psychologist Erving Goffman who, building on George Herbert Mead's insight that "the self is not so much a substance as a process in which the conversation of gestures has been internalized within an organic form" (178), views human interaction as a "performance" by an actor responding to environment and audience and presenting a self for pragmatic ends in what amounts to a "dramatic realization" (Goffman 28–44). It is also impeccably postmodern, among other reasons because Goffman's theories have percolated into such areas as postcolonialism and queer theory, underlying accounts of identity like Gayatri Chakravorty Spivak's "strategic essentialism," according to which we simulate a uniform but inauthentic identity to achieve particular political goals (1–16), and Judith Butler's "performativity," which contests the liberal humanist view of the self as cohesive and self-identical. That identity is realized through gesture or performance in response to people and circumstances around us is a reminder that the "crucial feature of human life is its fundamentally *dialogical* character" (Taylor 32, original emphasis) through which the individual constitutes an identity for itself in relation to George Herbert Mead's well-known "significant others." Zora Belsey in Smith's third novel, *On Beauty* (2005), is keenly aware of the performative and dialogical character of identity and doubtful of the existence of any essential, private identity once the self withdraws from social relations:

> She found it difficult, this thing of being alone, awaiting the arrival of a group. She prepared a face - as her favourite poet had it - to meet the faces that she met [. . .] In fact, when she was not in company it didn't seem to her that she had a face

> at all . . . And yet in college, she was famed for being opinionated, a 'personality' [. . .] She didn't feel that she *had* any real opinions, or at least not in the way other people seemed to have them. [. . .] was anyone ever genuinely attached to anything? She had no idea. It was either only Zora who experienced this odd impersonality or it was everybody, and they were all play-acting, as she was. (2005: 209-10)

Here the public, external "personality" is pitted against the disturbing possibility of the private, internal identity as a non-entity.

A corollary of this contingent because interactive or dialogical identity is the dispersion of the subject into disparate selves which, long before the poststructuralists, has been indicated by Mead:

> We divide ourselves up in all sorts of different selves with reference to our acquaintances. [. . .] There are all sorts of different selves answering to all sorts of different social reactions. It is the social process itself that is responsible for the appearance of the self [. . .] A multiple personality is in a certain sense normal [. . .] (1967, 142)

Long before Goffman and Mead, Thomas Hobbes had reached a similar conclusion couched in terms of Goffman's metaphor: "a person, is the same that an actor is, both on stage and in common conversation" (106); while between Hobbes and Mead, David Hume had dissolved the self into "a bundle or collection of different perceptions which succeed one another with an inconceivable rapidity and are in perpetual flux and movement" and concluded that "the identity, which we ascribe to the mind of man, is only a fictitious one" (252-59). The distinctly Humean ring of the "ragbag of weighty ideas [Zora Belsey] carried around in her brain to lend herself the appearance of substance" (2005, 210) is, if nothing else, a salutary reminder that to uphold, as Smith does, a notion of identity as discrete performances of disparate selves need not mean one is a dyed-in-the-wool postmodernist. Furthermore, Smith's view of identity as disharmonious and non-narratable is not only authorized by a considerable number of distinguished philosophers,[3] but has been instantiated in the works of a long line of novelists. Until the latter half of the last century, most people subscribed to some notion or other of ordered, meaningful reality, which motivated the search for its reflection in ordered and meaningful aesthet-

---

[3] Smith's view also has affinities with the recent "four-dimensionalist" ontology of identity which seeks to solve the time-honoured persistence question (what does it take to say that a person persists, that is to say, that the same person exists at different times?) by positing a notion of personal identity as constituted by "person stages" understood as synchronic conjunctions of temporal and spatial parts (Olson 15-16).

ic productions. As far as the genre of the novel is concerned, even the "realism" of the nineteenth-century triple-decker usually masked an idealist project, even if that project were belied by the novel's very monstrous bagginess. More particularly, characterization in the novel from, say, *Dr Jekyll and Mr Hyde* to, say, *Midnight's Children*, shows the gradual erosion of the unitary self and its dispersion or fragmentation into a cacophony of competing selves: Stevenson introduced us to Jekyll's two selves; Rushdie's Saleem Sinai to the "[c]onsumed multitudes [. . .] jostling and shoving inside me" (1995, 9). The main characteristic of this cacophony of selves is its very non-narrativity in any straightforwardly chronological, teleological, goal-driven sense. Such non-narrativity was already demonstrated with uncanny prescience in Lawrence Sterne's precociously experimental *Tristram Shandy*, an egregious example of how literary practice goes before theory. When D. H. Lawrence turned his back on "the old stable ego of character" and, with it, "[t]he certain moral scheme" (17–18) he found in the great Russian novelists of the nineteenth century, he was merely acting in fulfillment, as were also, say, Woolf and Joyce, of *Tristram Shandy*'s prophecy.

In other words, by the time Zadie Smith started writing best-selling novels, the expectation that fiction should necessarily give us recognizable characters with stable, unitary identities and in pursuit of some more or less recognizable moral goal had long since been dead and buried—even before those "problematisations" Andrew Gibson (11) associates with novelistic practice from the 1960s onwards. Yet despite the precedents set by other practitioners of the novel, Smith's characters have been described as "blurry or under-drawn [. . .] too cartoonish" (Lasdun), "insufficiently imagined" (Hanks), "clumsily-drawn stereotypes" in novels "without living, breathing, developing characters" (Colin). Doyen of professional critics, James Wood formulated a particularly dyspeptic argument against *The Autograph Man*, according to which "Alex-Li Tandem, is a dreary blank, an empty centre entirely filled by his pop-culture devotions," a "nullity [. . .] simply an absence" (2002, 3; 9), and consequently, Smith's novel is "a text incapable of ever stiffening into sobriety" (3) and has "no moral centre" (6). Elsewhere, in relation to *White Teeth* Wood diagnosed "an excess of storytelling" in contemporary novels as "shrouding a lack [. . . of] the human," as stemming from "the crisis of character, and how to present it in fiction" (2000). If that "human" is the liberal humanist's version of it, then its absence need not be sorely missed. As for the crisis of character, perhaps it is not so much a problem of writers' representations as of readers' reluctance to interrogate their continued faith in inadequate narrative conventions.

So for Smith, identity is not the determinists' straitjacket but a space we can play in, the contours of which change from one moment to the next in response to the subject's relation to the context he or she happens to be in at any particular time. Successful players of the identity game include Millat in *White Teeth*, whom the narrator characterizes as a "social chameleon" able "to please all of the people all of the time" (269). The subject may, of course, also please itself, as Alex-Li may opt to foreground, say, his Jewishness (as noted earlier) or his Englishness. Actors or social chameleons thrive in a contingent world which calls for the "gamesmanship and good manners displayed by those adept at ideological bricolage" (Gaonkar 7). This underscores the possibility that with regard to the self, what should be considered is not how its story unfolds to a crowning, sense-making conclusion, but the process of that unfolding. For, not being historically, scientifically or culturally determined, identity cannot be made coterminous with a narrative which has a beginning in the past and develops tidily and diachronically towards an end in the future. On the collective scale, this is what Alsana in *White Teeth* learned from her discovery in the encyclopedia that Westerners were Indo-Aryans like herself: "you go back and back and back and," she says, "[I]t's still easier to find the correct Hoover bag than to find one pure person, one pure faith, on the globe" (236). On the individual scale, this is why Zen or Kabbalistic narratives never sit comfortably with Alex-Li's sense of his own self. For Smith emplotted or teleological narratives do not succeed in bringing concord to identities which are diachronically heterogeneous in a haphazard universe of constant flux, where people are permanently "on the hop" and identity is never more than a particular configuration of gestures at a given moment in time; or, as she puts it more poetically in *On Beauty*, "the daily miracle whereby interiority opens out and brings to bloom the million-petalled flower of being here, in the world, with other people" (211).

Transnational Identity?

If *White Teeth* lays the ghost of postcolonialism (Sell 2006, 29; 33) and Smith herself resists being pigeon-holed as a multicultural writer, might she and her works more accurately be regarded as transnational? *White Teeth* is perhaps the least obviously transnational of Smith's novels. Yet, in its post-postcolonial fashion, it jettisons the deterministic master narrative of gloomy post-structuralism by teasing diasporic subjects away from their roots in historical trauma and focuses on the here-and-nowness, the in-the-face buoyancy of multicultural London (which is not the same as multicultural Britain whose many peripheries are too engrossed in basic issues such as employment and housing to have time for the celebratory multiculturalism of the relatively buoyant metropolis); it revisits traditional postcolonial sites and tropes—the Pakistani waiter, the multi-ethnic bar, educational conditioning—only to find them inadequate repositories for the new energies circulating in a society where the past of the latest generations is no longer synonymous with the pain and false promises of immigration; and, though spatially bound to the metropolitan area of Greater London (apart from lengthy flashbacks to World War II Bulgaria and colonial Jamaica), it inscribes that ongoing, self-renewing process of hybridization—of cross-border activity, communication, praxis or self-fulfillment—on the postmodern level of the mini-narrative which is designated by the term "transnationalism." Neither Britain nor London serve as benchmarks of identity to be aspired to or rejected; rather they are recognizable spaces that provide convenient limits within which to circumscribe, for the purposes of the fiction, the endless and numberless chains of adventitious collisions which engender the sort of diversity that makes a mockery of passports, flags and notions of geo-politically determined citizenship. If the older generation represented by Samad is still afflicted by the bug-bears of assimilation, of racial prejudice and still put faith in the powers of socio-cultural conditioning to groom stable, acceptably monocultural individuals, the younger generation of the Iris Bowdens and the Millats are much more open to more fluid, non-essentialist, non-national or ethnic conceptions of identity.

Smith used part of her earnings from *White Teeth* to fund a sojourn in the United States. Thus, the Caribbean-English compound of her genetic identity received an infusion of that transnational, trans-Atlantic *gheist* which makes itself manifest politically in the "special relationship" between the United Kingdom and USA, culturally in the shared diet of Hollywood movies and TV drama and comedy series,[4] and, idealistically, in Caryl Phillips's yearning for a non-bureaucratic, supra-national identity mapped—ironically—onto the coordinates of the slavers' "golden triangle." That same *gheist* inspires *On Beauty* which traces the ups and downs of the Belsey family: Howard, the English academic teaching at a U.S. East Coast university, his African-American wife, and their three teenage children.

Meanwhile, it is probably not coincidental that Book Two of *The Autograph Man* follows its author across the Atlantic to New York as Alex-Li tracks down Kitty Alexander, the chief object of his autograph-collecting obsession. There,

---

[4] As the standard fare on TV sets, in cinemas and in theatres across Europe is, in this sense, "trans-Atlantic", the term may soon come to mean no more (and no less) than Western; by which time novelists seeking to accrete added layers to their identities will have to go considerably further than hopping across the pond. But by that time it may also be equally true that, due to the rising *latino* population in USA and the steadily eroding hegemony of white Anglo-Saxons both there and in UK, "trans-Atlantic" will denote a quite different cultural-social-ethnic reality.

at the breakfast buffet of his hotel, Alex-Li confronts a metaphor for the smorgasbord of transnational identity: in addition to boiled eggs "in their china cups, pretty as Buddhas," "half a pig" and scrambled eggs, there is "porridge [...] sat on a piece of tartan" (Scottish), "[t]hin slices of waxy Dutch cheese, Italian baloney or German Hams, conserves claiming Cornwall in *ye olde* earthenware jars, Philadelphia cream cheese, melted Swiss chocolate, fluffy Caribbean ackee or twelve hot English kippers," not to mention, among other goodies, "maple syrup" (North America), "croissants" (France), "bagels" (Jewish)[5] and smoked salmon (Norwegian? Scottish?) (233). More importantly, Alex-Li's feckless attempts to classify all aspects of existence as either Jewish or Goyish, as well as the helpless inadequacy of his own hyphenated forename to set the seal on his identity, clearly position the novel as questioning the capacity of simplistic models of hybridity—typified in the practice of monohyphenation—to address the real, multifarious, motley nature of identity where not only blood and place of birth play a part, but also what clothes you wear, what TV programs you watch, what music you listen to and what brand of energy-drink you buy. This skepticism regarding binaries or the yoking together of the heterogeneous by means of a textual symbol, is characteristic of transnational theory and a hallmark of Smith's approach to identity. Alex-Li's own genealogy is considerably more complex than the Jewish and Chinese components of his hyphenated name might suggests. At one point he ponders some photographs of his Czech and Russian ancestors on his mother's side and concludes, in confirmation of Smith's presentism, that the sort of people who store family mementoes are "the types who follow ominous noises into the dark cellar, who build their very homes on top of Indian burial grounds. People from movies. Everyone in these photographs is dead, thought Alex wearily. Tiring, all of it" (2003, 35). For Smith, as, famously, for Paul Gilroy, what counts is not "where you're from" but "where you're at;" and this too is a basic tenet of transnationalism. At the same time, Smith's view of identity as a performance transforms it into a dynamic process of ongoing production consonant with a transnational model of identity, while Adam's kabbalah scheme of Alex-Li's identity removes it from the ambit of national, ethnic or cultural affiliations, locating it instead in a network of personal affinities.[6]

---

[5] In fact, Smith metaphorically converts the bagels from Judaism to Buddhism, their "yang [having been] split conveniently from their yings".

[6] It is to that kabbalah that I should not like to return in more detail.

The Paradox of Identity in *The Autograph Man*

Among Smith's novels, the issue of identity is interrogated with greatest vigor in *The Autograph Man*, a novel consumed with the trappings of and obsessions with celebrity. Smith suggests that compliance with externally imposed or attributed identity is a performance, each particular element of which is a gesture—this last a recurrent word in the novel. Even though, as mentioned above, the idea of identity as a dramatic realization is reminiscent of the theories of Erving Goffman and Judith Butler, and even though the idea of playing to externally constructed scripts is redolent of critical discourse analysis, I think Smith's insights into the gap between identity as the externally generated, public projection of a persona and the private experience of a more or less coherent and unified self may just as well have their origin in her own experience as a reluctant media personality in the wake of *White Teeth*'s rampant success. Her own dissatisfaction with the scripts written for her is echoed by Alex-Li's abhorrence of telephone answering machines, expressed in theatrical language:

> These beeps still gave Alex stage fright. He seemed the only man left who felt that way about it. He despised the performance aspects. Anyone who is able to leave a successful answering-machine message is a kind of actor. (58).

Crucially, the culturally-coded performance of the kaddish into which Alex-Li is cajoled by friends and acquaintances is preceded by an epigraph from Peter Handke's *The Weight of the World*:

> Suppose I weren't allowed the gestures people make when they don't know what else to do: clicking the buckle of my wristwatch strap, unbuttoning and rebuttoning my shirt, running my hands through my hair. In the end I'd have nothing to sustain me, I'd be lost. (415)

When at a loss about what to do, we always have the option of making a gesture to prevent us losing ourselves. The critical point here is that, as Zora Belsey realized, gestures are necessarily directed at somebody, they imply a social context. And this quotation prefaces what to Alex-Li's friends is his climactic performance of his identity, and what to him is his reluctant compliance with an externally imposed script. His public performance of the kaddish is in compliance with Jewish tradition and allows Adam to fill in the missing space on his kabbalah of Alex-Li's identity, where he "stuck Li-Jin [Alex-Li's father] in the empty sun-faded spot, midway between - and elevated above - the popular philosopher Ludwig Wittgenstein and the popular writer Virginia Woolf" (413). For Adam, Alex-Li's identity is now happily constructed. But the Epilogue itself shows that Alex-Li merely pays lip-service to the Jewish script, complies with, but is not committed to, the ritual. By having Alex-Li recite the words of the kaddish, Smith can show us that his own mind is actually elsewhere, on the rabbi picking at the skin of his right thumb, on a friend rubbing his nose with a knuckle, on his girlfriend straightening her skirt, and so on. The performance, then, of externally imposed identity is socially useful, it can get us out of a fix or help in our relations with friends and acquaintances; but far from being our own self, it is our self as written by others and is therefore not us but an other.

This conscious disjunction between our identity as we ourselves experience it and the identity we perform for the benefit of others, or for our own benefit in our relations with others, with authority or with society at large is analogous to the difference between the subjective and objective cases in grammar. Nowhere is it expressed with more telling concision than in Philip Sidney's sonnet where he bids Stella, impervious to whatever charms his subjective identity might possess but a practiced sympathizer with fictional personages, not to take him for what he actually is but to attend instead to his narrated self: "I am not I, pity the tale of me" (149). To gain benefit in the public domain of social intercourse, the subject converts itself though the production of a narrative identity or performance of a script into an object accessible to hermeneutic interpretation and consequently available for, and capable of, social praxis: oneself reconstitutes one's self as another. In the early modern period, such "self-fashioning," to adopt Stephen Greenblatt's phrase was a political expedient reflected in the extreme paradox of Viola's and Iago's identical assertions that "I am not what I am" (*Twelfth Night* 3.1.39 and *Othello* 1.1.65, respectively [Wells and Taylor]), which brings us to the paradox of identity referred to earlier. We can be and not be ourselves at one and the same time when, for example, performing our external identity, our social persona, while being conscious that it is not our private self. As I suggested earlier, Smith's own predicament as reluctant media persona may have alerted her to the paradox inherent in the shortfalls between external and internal identities.

However that might be, *The Autograph Man* reiterates a quizzical motif of that paradox to such an extent that it becomes a trope of identity. The motif first appears in a quotation from private individual Archibald Leach, more famous to the public as Hollywood personality Cary Grant: "*Everyone wants to be Cary Grant. Even I want to be Cary Grant*" (58, original emphasis). It reappears later when Alex-Li observes how Bogart's big-headedness (in the literal sense) meant that "he looked like a caricature of *himself*" (137, original emphasis). Thus Bogart is simultaneously himself (with his real big head) and not himself, but an other, a caricature of himself. Again, at an auction, one autograph-collector suggests to another that "You should ask that the writer lady makes you this bloke in a book who organizes an auction and then buys his place in, er ... wait - no, yeah, in a book as a character who organizes an auction and then buys his place in a book and asks ..." (114).

At what point does the second autograph-collector cease to be himself and become the bloke in the book; and to the members of the public reading the book, who is the real autograph-collector? But this particular paradox of identity is illustrated most acutely in Adam's kabbalah of Alex-Li, composed of autographs of famous people that Adam has bought from his friend and stuck on the wall. By the novel's close, there are ten autographs in all: Ludwig Wittgenstein, Virginia Woolf, Franz Kafka, James Stewart, Fats Waller, John Lennon, Betty Davis, Muhammad Ali, Li-Jin (Alex-Li's father, as mentioned above) and Alex-Li Tandem himself. Earlier in the novel, Alex-Li has presumed "his own inclusion [...] is a joke," while nonetheless admiring his friend's collection, "the most perfect he has ever known. Small, selfless, almost entirely arbitrary" (128). In the context of the present discussion, that "selfless" is a bundle of semantic energy: on the one hand it is recognition on Alex-Li's part of his friend's efforts to make sense of, to give a shape to, his own self; on the other it also connotes his awareness that his self is somehow missing from the kabbalah, even though Adam has included him as part of it. As for the kabbalah itself, it too may be interpreted in a variety of ways. It could, for example be taken as his friend's attempt to give form to Alex-Li's self by building a composite narrative—or collage—of Meadian "significant others". It could also be read as a Freudian scheme of Alex-Li's kathetic interiorization of the love-objects he is reluctant to acknowledge as lost; the inclusion of himself in this psychic seraglio would then be an explicitation of how the melancholic's psyche—and Alex-Li is a decidedly melancholic type—falls prey to a suicidal narcissism when the id continues to lust after the love-objects the ego refuses to surrender up (Freud 452-54; 472-75). However that might be, Smith alerts us to the very paradox of identity as enunciated by Sidney, Viola and Iago, theorized by Hobbes, and elaborated by Ricoeur and Kristeva. Oneself is inescapably an other when included in any narrative, script or kabbalistic scheme of identity. And that paradox is reduced to the level of a gag, something trivial—or unsatisfactory—enough to be laughed off.

It is a paradox consistent with transnationalist conceptions of identity and congenial to the generally postmodern dispensation that presides contemporary cultural studies. Yet it also bears a curious affinity with English modernist statements regarding identity and fictional character. The presence of Wittgenstein and Woolf in the same kabbalah hints tantalizingly at the extended circle of the Bloomsbury group which, in addition to Wittgenstein, included such thinkers as G. E. Moore, an influence on aspects of modernist aesthetics, and Bertrand Russell, occasional correspondent of, among other, E. M. Forster, one of Smith's self-confessed literary idols. The motifs of paradoxical identity I have cited together with the inclusion of Alex-Li himself within the set of sefirots which constitute Alex-Li are close analogues of Bertrand Russell's famous paradox, which may be expressed as follows:

> Some sets [...] are members of themselves and some are not. For instance, the set of horses is not a member of itself since it is a set and not a horse, whereas the set of non-horses is member of itself [because it is not a horse]. [The question then arises] [i]s the set of all sets which are not members of themselves, a member of itself? If it is [a member of itself] then it is not [a member of itself]. If it is not [a member of itself] then it is [a member of itself] (*Dictionary of Philosophy* 287-88).

The cognitively bewildering effect of reading this quotation—an effect which enacts the more seriously bewildering impasse of Russell's paradox itself—is akin to the bewilderment experienced when one is made conscious of the ontological discrepancy between a subject's social-external and private-internal identities. Which is the real identity? Is the social identity a merely useful, if accidental, adjunct or, somehow or other, a sort of essential excrescence of the private self?

It should be noted that a subject's social identity may be constituted by others (in which case, there will be as many such identities as others which constitute it), as is the case with Adam's kabbalah of Alex-Li's identity, but it may also, as Goffman made plain, be constituted in the subject's dramatization of its own self for external consumption. Book Two of *The Autograph Man* portrays Alex-Li in active pursuit of his own identity whereas Book One had shown him as the passive object of his friends' attempts to construct it for him. For Alex-Li, Kitty Alexander is his own most significant other; but when he smuggles her back to London, it is as a rather embarrassing and certainly unself-fulfilling adjunct. Alex-Li is patently, and distressingly, not what he had hitherto cultivated as his most salient defining characteristic: the only sense in which Kitty Alexander helps Alex-Li to find himself is by demonstrating that he is not her, or more precisely, that she is not a necessary, let alone sufficient, condition for his own self to be recognizable as him. There is an interesting parallel here with the early modern iconographical practice of indicating the identity of the subject of a painting by providing that subject with an instantly recognizable attribute. The difficulty arises when the attribute is foregrounded to such an extent that it is taken to be the painting's subject at the expense of the true subject. Thus E. H. Gombrich (26-30) famously argued that the painting known for centuries as "Tobias with angel" should more properly be referred to as "The Angel Raphael" since the latter was identified through reference to his adjunct Tobias, who was in turn identified through reference to the fish held in his hand. Without the fish there would be no Tobias, and without Tobias there would be no Raphael. Would there, then, be no Alex-Li without Kitty Alexander? Smith seems to think not: the elderly Hollywood heart-throb, who admittedly once played a kitsch Hollywood version of Chinese, may well give a sense to Alex-Li's life (a Taylorian goal in relation to which Alex-Li may spin out the narrative of his own identity), but that sense is not to be confused with Alex-Li himself. Once more, one's identity is not to be confused with whatever representational techniques or hermeneutic strategies are brought to bear in order to give it meaning.[7]

But to return to my point, in *The Autograph Man*, Smith subjects identity to a neo-Modernist scrutiny, putting to one side notions of hybridity[8] and liminality and returning to earlier notions of the ambiguity which inevitably attaches to identity once it is admitted that identity is inevitably socially constituted. Such externally presented or projected identity—the performance of gestures in compliance with social, externally composed scripts—is what Smith's novelistic mentor E. M. Forster would term "human intercourse [...] as a social adjunct [...] a makeshift." For Forster, "perfect knowledge" of other people "is an illusion. But in the novel we can know people perfectly [...] In this direction fiction is truer than the evidence, because it goes beyond the evidence" (1962, 70). Alex-Li's performance of the kaddish is identity as "social adjunct"; the "evidence" satisfies his friends and earns him social approval; but "beyond the evidence," Smith the novelist can show her readers the real Alex-Li, chafing at the mask, glancing around at the world outside the ritual, carrying on regardless of any script. Meanwhile, second-generation modernist William Empson's remarks on the social aspect of literature might well serve, *mutatis mutandis*, as an account of the pragmatic function of compliance with external identities: "So that literature, in so far as it is a living matter, demands a sense, not so much of what is really there, as of what is necessary to carry a particular situation 'off'" (276). Empson then proceeds to address the issue of "Character,"

---

[7] Smith's third novel, *On Beauty* (2005), is, as Smith herself states (ix), among other things "a novel inspired by a love of E. M. Forster" and a *"hommage"* (original emphasis) by means of which she hopes to repay her indebtedness to him. This intertextual encounter with her literary identity's own adjunct offers interesting parallels with Alex-Li's pursuit of Kitty Alexander, but any consideration of them falls outside the scope of this chapter.

[8] Laura Moss takes *White Teeth* to inscribe "everyday hybridity;" Elaine Childs, in contrast, detected "hybridity anxiety" in the same novel.

which he contrasts to "Looks" in a relation parallel to that between "Meaning" and "Pure Sound":

> The fundamental source of pleasure about Looks is an apprehension of Character; a change in one's knowledge of the Character alters (by altering the elements selected) one's apprehension of the Looks. The Beauty resides in the Sound and the Looks; but these, being aesthetic constructions, are largely distillations (solutions into forms immediately conceivable) from the meaning and the Character.
>
> As to say that the Meaning (rather than the Sound) is what matters about poetry, so it seems very intellectual and puritanical to say that Character (rather than Looks) is what matters about people [...] (277)

Changing "Character" for "the Self" and "Looks" for "Gestures", we would have an elegant statement of Smith's position regarding external, socially constructed identity. It is useful and, in most cases, is not only the closest we will get (outside fiction) to knowing a person's identity, but also all we need to know.

This ties in with the novel's Prologue which revolves around a wrestling match between Big Daddy and Giant Haystacks, the good and the bad guy respectively. Just before the bout ends in Big Daddy's predictable victory, the novel's narrator steps in and provides the following comment:

> And of course it's ridiculous, but the thing is, they are not here to express genuine feelings, or to fake them and dress them up natural like on TV - they are here to demonstrate actions. And all the kids know that. Any fool can tell a story - can't they? - but how many can demonstrate one, e.g., This is what a story is, mate, when it's stripped of all its sentiment. This afternoon these two hulking gentlemen are here to demonstrate Justice. (38)

There is here a contrast between "story" and "demonstration." "Story," like narrative identity, like positional scripts, like TV does not deliver an unmediated view of the real: what seems natural is a fake. "Demonstration," on the other hand, which may be something like Goffman or Butler's performance stripped of all context-oriented intentionality, seems to provide the illusion of transparency, of "what-you-see-is-what-you-get. Applied to identity, it is as if Smith yearns for an identity correlative with Empson's "looks," an identity which, purely phenomenological, is transparent, unproblematic, and does not call for any digging beneath the surface appearance. Elsewhere in the novel identity is similarly pared down to surface, to demonstration when, for example, three women in Alex-Li's underground carriage "laughed frenziedly, jiggling on the hand-straps, demonstrating what *three women having fun* looks like" (77, original emphasis).

Such an identity is probably not a very serious proposition—about as plausible, in fact, as the half-hearted postulation of an international language of gesture. *On Beauty* ends with Howard Belsey's unintentionally silent PowerPoint presentation of a series of Rembrandt's paintings. Zadie Smith appears to be on the point of renouncing her own art, hamstrung by its dependence on words—which always spring from elsewhere than from immediate, demonstrable and unmediated reality—in favor of the surfaces and textures of oil on canvas which have the capacity to freeze gestures in time. Yet of course, Smith's ecphrasis of Rembrandt's *Hendricjke Bathing, 1654* is as mediated as any other assemblage of words: when Smith writes Hendrickje "*seemed* to be considering" and "[she] looked away, *coyly*" (442-43, my emphasis), her own subjectivity is intervening in the transcription of the painting. In the absence of any such untrammeled, transparent identity, it is the job of novels like Smith's to, in the words of Forster, "give us the illusion of perspicacity" (1962, 71). But not, necessarily, of "power," for it is the privileged insight into Alex-Li's mind during the rite of the kaddish which reminds us that the individual subject is its own redoubt against those who would oblige it to perform their scripts.

"Pleased to meet you!"

The early modern parallels that have been adduced to clarify Zadie Smith's views on identity should warn us against pigeon-holing her either as a transnationalist writer or a neo-modernist writer on the strength of those views alone; they should also warn us against finding novelty in either transnationalist or modernist views of identity which may better be regarded as historically conditioned revivals of much older conceptions.

Paradox is a popular trope of postmodern fiction and criticism; much postmodern fiction and criticism in turn has its theoretical roots in the epistemological ambiguity and paradox laid bare by philosophers like Russell and Wittgenstein. But paradox enjoyed its social and cultural heyday in, once again, the early modern period; and it is to that period that I should like briefly to return. If paradox had originally been a trope which praised the unpraiseworthy (Lausberg 240), in early modern English rhetoric and cultural practice it became associated with any device—for instance, the oxymoron, the imprese and the Metaphysical yoking of heterogeneous ideas—the elucidation of which called for the extreme exercise of wit. In other words, paradox engendered an intellectual response in the interpreter, and it is some such cerebral effort which we nowadays most often associate with the trope.

Yet the early modern interpreter would have found in the resolution of paradox a pleasure which compensated the hard mental work. The emotive payout of the tropes is often lost on modern interpreters, and this is a shame. In the context of a view of identity such as Zadie Smith's—whether it be termed transnational, neo-modernist, perspectivist, performative, or whatever—which is sensitive, on the one hand, to that disjunction between private and public, internal and external, selves that underlies the paradox of simultaneously being and not being one's self, and celebrates, on the, the imbrication of the private in the public, the inter-relatedness of the individual and society or, in Smith's less political, more human term, "company," it does one good to be reminded of the pleasures of social intercourse. It is when we begin to peel away the identity society at large, certain others, or we ourselves have scripted for a particular individual and start instead to become acquainted with someone who is not what we took him or she to be; it is when, in short, we become exposed to the paradox of another's identity as we come, gradually, to get to know them, that pleasure may take hold. It is then that the formula "Pleased to meet you!" may be transformed from a simple cliché into a positive and open stance towards being in the world and, most importantly, being in it with other people. That, I would suggest, is the infectious, upbeat attitude which underwrites all of Smith's novels and transcends sectarian models of identity.

Works Cited

A Dictionary of Philosophy. London: Pan, 1979.
Butler, Judith. *Gender Trouble: Feminism and the Subversion of Identity*. New York: Routledge, 1999.
Childs, Elaine. "Insular Utopias and Religious Neuroses: Hybridity Anxiety in Zadie Smith's *White Teeth*." *Proteus: A Journal of Ideas* 23.1 (2006): 7-12.
Empson, William. *Seven Types of Ambiguity*. New York: Meridian Books, 1955.
Fekete, John. *The Critical Twilight*. London: Routledge, 1977.
Forster, E.M. *Aspects of the Novel*. Harmondsworth: Penguin, 1962.
Freud, Sigmund. Extract from *The Ego and the Id* in *The Essentials of Psychoanalysis*. Harmondsworth: Penguin, 1986.
Gaonkar, Dilip Parmeshwar. "Introduction: Contingency and Probability." *A Companion to Rhetoric and Rhetorical Criticism*. Ed. Walter Jost and Wendy Olmsted. Oxford: Blackwell, 2003. 5-21.

Gibson, Andrew. *Postmodernity, Ethics and the Novel. From Leavis to Levinas*. London. Routledge, 1999.

Gilroy, Paul. "'It Ain't Where You're From, It's Where You're At': The Dialectics of Diaspora." *Third Text* 13 (1990/91): 3-16.

Gombrich, E. H. *Symbolic Images: Studies in the Art of the Renaissance II*. Oxford: Phaidon, 1972.

Greenblatt, Stephen. *Renaissance Self-Fashioning*. Chicago: University of Chicago Press, 1980.

Hanks, Robert. "Zadie Smith: A New Chapter". *The Independent* (5 June 2002). Last accessed 1 Dec. 2006 at <www.findarticle.com/p/articles/mi_qn4158/is_200220605/ai_n12618770>

Head, Dominic. "Zadie Smith's *White Teeth*: Multiculturalism for the Millenium." *Contemporary British Fiction*. Ed. Richard J. Lane, Rod Mengham and Philip Tew. Cambridge: Polity Press, 2003. 106-119.

Hobbes, Thomas. *Leviathan*. Ed. J. C. A. Gaskin. Oxford: Oxford University Press, 1996.

Hume, David. *A Treatise of Human Nature*. Ed. L. A. Selby-Bigge. 2nd edition revised by P. H. Nidditch. Oxford: Clarendon, 1978.

Lasdun, James. "*On Beauty* by Zadie Smith." *The Guardian* (10 September 2005). Last accessed 1 Dec. 2006 at <www.book.guardian.co.uk/reviews/generalfiction/0,,1566399,00.html>

Lausberg, Heinrich. *Manual de Retórica Literaria*. Trans. José Pérez Riesco. 3 vols. Vol. II. Madrid: Gredos, 1966.

Lawrence, D. H. "Letter, D. H. Lawrence to E, 5th June, 1914." *D. H. Lawrence: Selected Literary Criticism*. Ed. Anthony Beale. London: Heinemann, 1967. 17-18.

Martin, Denis-Constant. "The Choices of Identity." *Social Identities* 1.1 (1995): 5-21.

Mead, George Herbert. *Mind, Self, and Society*. Chicago: Chicago University Press., 1967.

Moss, Laura. "The Politics of Everyday Hybridity: Zadie Smith's *White Teeth*." *Wasafiri* 39 (2003): 11-17.

Olson, Eric T. "Personal Identity." *The Stanford Encyclopedia of Philosophy*. Ed. Edward N. Zalta. Last accessed 2 Feb. 2005 at <www.plato.stanford.edu/entries/identity-personal>

Ricoeur, Paul. *Time and Narrative*. Vol. 3. Trans. Kathleen Blamey and David Pellauer. Chicago and London: University of Chicago Press, 1988.

Rushdie, Salman. *Midnight's Children*. London: Vintage, 1995.

Sell, Jonathan P.A. "Chance and Gesture in Zadie Smith's *White Teeth* and *The Autograph Man*: A Model for Multicultural Identity?" *The Journal of Commonwealth Literature* 41.3 (2006): 27-44.

-----. "Autonomy and Contingency in the Novels of Zadie Smith." *The Ethical Component in Experimental British Fiction since the 1960s.* Ed. Susana Onega and Jean-Michel Ganteau. Newcastle: Cambridge Scholars Publishing, 2007.

Sidney, Sir Philip. *Selected Poems.* Ed. Katherine Duncan Jones. Oxford: Oxford University Press, 1973.

Smith, Zadie. *White Teeth.* Harmondsworth: Penguin, 2001.

-----. *The Autograph Man.* Harmondsworth: Penguin, 2003.

-----. *On Beauty.* London: Penguin, 2005.

Spivak, Gayatri. *The Post-Colonial Critic: Interviews, Strategies, Dialogues.* Ed. Sara Harasym. New York: Routledge, 1990.

Taylor, Charles. *Sources of the Self: The Making of Modern Identity.* Cambridge, MA: Harvard University Press, 1989.

Thompson, Molly. "'Happy Multicultural Land'? The Implications of an 'excess of Belonging' in Zadie Smith's *White Teeth*." *Write Black, Write British: From Post Colonial to Black British Literature.*" Ed. Kadija Sesay. Hertford: Hansib, 2005. 122-140.

Wells, Stanley and Gary Taylor, eds. *The Oxford Shakespeare: The Complete Works.* 2nd edition. Oxford: Clarendon Press, 2005.

Wood, James. "Human, All Too Human." *The New Republic Online* (24 July 2000). Last accessed 1 Dec. 2006 at <www.powells.com/review/2007_08_30.html>

-----. "Fundamentally Goyish." *London Review of Books* (3 October 2002).Last accessed 5 May 2004 at <www.lrb.co.uk/v24/n19/print/wood02_.html>

CHAPTER FOUR

Transnational Identity and Saumya Balsari's *The Cambridge Curry Club*

Joel Kuortti

> "With its rows of small houses, ethnic food stores, hair salons, curry houses, Internet cafés, bookmaker, health shop and dry cleaners, Mill Road was the city's pumping heart."
> – Saumya Balsari, *The Cambridge Curry Club*

Saumya Balsari's novel *The Cambridge Curry Club* (2004) explores the range of possible transnational, diasporic positions critically, problematizing seemingly self-evident identifications: colonial mimicry, persistent adherence to unchanging tradition, or unquestioning celebration of hybridity. In "The Postcolonial and the Postmodern: The Question of Legacy," a discussion of the difficulties of cultural translation, Homi K. Bhabha comments on how the various transnational forms of cultural transformation – "migration, diaspora, displacement, relocation – [make] the process of cultural translation a complex form of signification" (191). I will be discussing the ways in which Balsari's *novel* engages with such significations, rather than the more general position of transnational, diasporic writers.[1] It should be noted that here transnational diaspora is understood in the restricted socio-historical sense that is reflected in the novel itself. Further dimensions of contemporary transnationality would include exilic, refugee, and other comparable wretched subaltern positions.[2]

Balsari's story is set in a charity shop IndiaNeed on Mill Road in Cambridge, UK in the early twenty-first century. Its movement among transnational subjects takes place in the context of the history of Cambridge from the coloni-

---

[1] For a discussion of transnational authorship, cf. Inderpal Grewal, 35–79.

[2] See Gayatri Chakravorty Spivak, "Diasporas Old and New: Women in the Transnational World," 3–5. Transnational issues are important in *transnational feminist studies* which seek to "destabilize rather than maintain boundaries of nation, race, and gender. Transnational is a term that signals attention to uneven and dissimilar circuits of culture and capital," cf. Inderpal Grewal and Caren Kaplan.

al Roman settlement to the Oxford riots in 1209 leading to the establishment of Cambridge University,[3] from Oliver Cromwell's transient existence in the city[4] finally to the contemporary Indian community, with new immigrants moving in and the second generation moving out to the United States. The transnational movements are various and cross over each other. In the novel, these movements are discussed in terms of diaspora which is formulated by Durga, one of the main characters, in the following way: "Diaspora isn't only about displacement; it's a progression, a moving to a new location of the liberated self" (46). Thus, the problematic quality of diasporic positionality, often described even as traumatic, is complemented with a perception of its liberating potential.

One of the issues of diasporic existence is naming, and it emerges as an important theme in the novel. In my article, I will first look into this issue of designation and how it reveals post-colonial tensions in the transnational context. Secondly, as these tensions seem to challenge various strategies of identification, I will look at these strategies and how they vary between the different characters of the novel. The characters negotiate questions of identity in different ways. There is certainly an element of fear attached to the contestation of identity: fear of losing traditional values, fear of the Other – be it the English jungle, wild sex, or evil influences in general – that has an effect on the diasporic subjects. The result is an intriguing view on the challenges to the construction of identity – a new transnational identity with multiple ethnicities, identities, and strategies of survival.

Name Calling

The Cambridge Curry Club narrates incidents during one October Thursday in IndiaNeed.[5] The main characters are four married women who work in the shop: sixty-year-old Eileen Watts from Northern Ireland,[6] fifty-seven-year-old

---

[3] From the point of view of the colonial/post-colonial educational setting, it is interesting that the story should take place in Cambridge, as it designates the colonial "home" of Cambridge Overseas Examinations that began in 1862, see Anthony P. R. Howatt and H. G. Widdowson, *History of English Language Teaching* (301).

[4] Cromwell (1599–1658) came to Sidney Sussex College in 1616 for a year, and in 1640 he was the Long Parliament MP for Cambridge, yet his contacts remained shallow, unlike with Oxford, see Antonia Fraser, 19–20 & 60–61.

[5] Except for the Epilogue which captures further developments during the following weeks.

[6] The character of Eileen, as a part of the Irish transnational experience, would invite an analysis of her own. Although the story is a post-9/11 one, it makes no reference to that tragic incident or to international terrorism in general, except in passing to the violent situation in Northern Ireland when Eileen appears with a toy gun

Swarnakumari Chatterjee from Kolkata, forty-seven-year-old Heera Malkani Moore from Hyderabad, and twenty-nine-year-old Cambridge graduate Durga Prabhu who was born in London and grew up in Britain and India. The story about the day is interwoven with sketches from the past of each of the women as well as other characters. Together, these storylines build up – among other things – a perceptive analysis of identificational strategies through issues such as naming.

Even though the novel tells the stories of the four women quite democratically, there are two key features through which issues of identity are focalized. First of all, there is Durga who as a Cambridge graduate had done "an MPhil in Modern Society and Global Transformation, Social and Political Sciences" (142). While not autobiographic, Durga's character reads like the author's *alter ego* and is used as a critical, theoretical, sardonic voice throughout the novel. It is also through Durga that a critique of naming is explicitly expressed. [7] She thinks that "[a] name was nothing," it has no meaning apart from signifying the person it designates (89). Thinking about the cultural meaning of her own name, she further wonders: "Was a name an identity, an anonymous cloak or a terrifying emptying of self?" (ibid.).[8]

The second focalizing feature is the confrontation between Heera and the shop owner, "[t]he director of the board of the charity, Diana Wellington-Smythe," who "was mockingly nicknamed 'Lady Di' by her staff" (8). While Mrs Wellington-Smythe is generally projected as a condescending colonial manager, in places her own story sheds considerate light on the development and behavior of her character. However, on top of her suspicions about the employees, she is also very indifferent and even unsympathetic towards Heera and refers to her persistently as "Helen." Heera protests constantly against this misnaming: "How many times have I told her my name's not 'Helen' [...] I don't understand – what's this *English problem with names*?" (88; emphasis added). Here the question of naming is interpreted by Heera in terms of nation-

---

hidden under her apron and "she recalled an assailant's attack on her brother in a Belfast alleyway" (105). Furthermore, Eileen "was fiercely proud of her heritage" as an Irishwoman and was "[a]nnoyed by Durga's appropriation of the Diaspora to signify Indian sub-continent migration alone" (41); Eileen is also connected to the transatlantic diaspora through a family connection as in her childhood her "exhausted father ran away and jumped aboard a ship called *Providence* bound for New York" (7).

[7] Cf. Joel Kuortti, 137–146.

[8] For more on Durga in Hinduism, cf. Abhijit Dutta, *Mother Durga: An Icon of Community and Culture* (2003).

al or ethnic identity:[9] the English in their colonial superiority cannot or will not make the effort of getting the names of other – ethnic, immigrant – people, right. Correspondingly, Mrs Wellington-Smythe calls Swarnakumari "Sara," but she is indifferent: "If they can't say my name, they can't, *na*?"; to which Durga replies critically: "Or won't?" (89).

It is not, however, only the English that are presented as having this problem with the proper use of names.[10] In Heera's opinion, authenticity is lacking also in the parlance of diasporic Indians: "Talking of names, funny how Asians born here just can't pronounce Indian words the way we do" (90). It is not only the "outsiders" who cannot perform but also the "insiders" are divided on this, according to their exposure to authentic cultural experience. This complexity is further dispersed into a transatlantic context. The Chatterjees' Bengali family friends, the Banerjees have a daughter Madhumita living in California. She had married an Albanian classmate Gjynejt. He is known by many (Albanian) names: to his parents he is 'Gjelosh', to his friends 'Haxhi', and to Madhumita 'Ferrok.' All this is very perplexing for Shyamal, Swarnakumari's husband. Furthermore, as this "Gjynejt – Gjelosh – Haxhi – Ferrok" was "addicted to ketchup, he had been nicknamed 'Heinz' by his American classmates" (63). Shyamal finds this choice of name a relief, for "Heinz was a German or Austrian name, it could even be Swiss. It sounded respectably Western and European" (63).[11]

Just like Balsari's text indicates, where the colonial subjugation has resulted in patronizing attitudes, the post-colonial position is no less troubled. Where South Asians, and colonized people in general, present a designation problem for the colonizer, similarly the post-colonials seem to struggle with the names of the Other – here especially an Eastern European Other. In her analysis of

---

[9] Compare this with the way Gogol Ganguli's name is treated in Jhumpa Lahiri's *The Namesake* (2004).

[10] One review comments on Balsari's own mix-up with Durga's name (89): "In this context, Balsari makes a faux pas, which gives the discussion on naming an unintended, and unfortunate dimension. Durga, as the mythical goddess, is not Durgashtini but Durgatinashini, the one who destroys evil" (see Anusua Mukherjee, "In a Mad, Mad Shop."

[11] Another transatlantic figure in the novel is Roman Tempest, an American teacher coming to teach a Mphil course in American Literature in the university, and falls in love with Durga; their introductions portray them in ironic literary overtones: "'I'm Roman Tempest'[…]. 'Then I must be Indian Storm'" (142). Cf. Matthew Arnold, 227. In this context, "Indian Storm" could as well be claimed to refer to the American Indian Storm Dance as to the Indian diaries of the legendary war correspondent Sir William Howard Russell, where he describes how he "had the first idea of an Indian storm" (393).

post-colonial fiction, Mita Banerjee comments: "In its portrayal of Eastern Europeanness, postcolonial fiction depicts ethnicity as it was depicted prior to the emergence of postcolonial literature" (316). All this shows that there is no easy solution to be applied because the propensity for misrepresentation does not unquestionably stop at the post-colonial fault line but finds new forms in the transnational situation. The directions of contact, influence, and signification are, indeed, not singular, rigid, or stable.[12]

In the novel the issue of names is expressly linked to questions of identity when a photographer from *The Cambridge Evening News* comes to the shop to take photographs. He had agreed on the matter with the director and asks the four women in the shop: "Which one of you is Diana Wallington-er-Smith?" (181). Durga mocks the photographer's comment for cultural blindness and sums up his inaptitude in naming in highly erudite, academic manner as follows:

> Do you think any of us could be Diana Wellington-Smythe? Such a deliberate *transposing* of the postcolonial subject would not only be *aesthetically unappealing* but necessitate an *inapposite dismantling* of notions of self, ethnicity, race and class, thus bringing it into *hybrid discontinuity*. (181; emphases added)

The photographer's answer to Durga's comment – echoing his initial uncertainty about the right form of the name – in face of such a perceptive post-colonial reading of his seemingly innocent interrogation is an enigmatic "Er . . ." (181). This "Er" functions as a filler word connoting both hesitation[13] and acknowledgement of making a mistake, *erring*. Durga's learned retort – complete with a sarcastic comment on the *aesthetic* disagreeability of such accidentally implied mixing – reflects on what Homi Bhabha has termed *colonial mimicry*.[14] Durga questions the sheer possibility of ethnic, lower-class, immigrant (Indian) women even trying to imitate a white woman, and pass as a white upper class English woman. Durga's immediate humorous, ironical response to the photographer's idea (and his consequent speechlessness) corresponds explicitly with the novel's explorative take on questions of transnational identity: if the immigrant women were to "be" Diana, it would result in "*inapposite dismantling*,"

---

[12] The transnationalism discourse too easily mirrors the colonial past, while there are other, "minor transnationalisms" taking place all the time, as Françoise Lionnet and Shu-mei Shih remind us: "The transnational [...] is not bound by the binary of the local and the global and can occur in national, local, or global spaces across different and multiple spatialities and temporalities" (6).

[13] See Martin Corley, Lucy J. MacGregor and David I. Donaldson, 658–668.

[14] Homi K. Bhabha, (1994, 85–92).

or inappropriate fragmentation of identity, as it would mean such a hybrid mixture that would do away with identificational signposts.

Heera continues Durga's bookish critique by commenting matter-of-factly that "she won't like you messing with her name, by the way. It's Wellington-Smythe" (181). The photographer is downright unable to get the name right even after being reprimanded of "messing with" it. In his further question he changes it (perhaps *willingly*) once more to Willington-Smith (182), echoing Heera's critique of the "English problem with names," only now in terms of class, not ethnicity. The evidently middle class assistant photographer – who speaks colloquial English – is clearly either not familiar, comfortable, or agreeable with such aristocratic upper class names as Wellington-Smythe. Later on Heera, too, gets her moment of retaliation when she deliberately mispronounces the director's name on the phone as "Daina" (210); earlier on she had already talked angrily and dismissively about her to the other women as "That La Di Da woman" (97), and Durga enigmatically as "Lady Go*di*va" (86; emphasis original).

True enough, 'Daina' or Mrs Wellington-Smythe has a colonial heritage. Her father had been born in Shimla, India where his father had served in the military, and she herself had visited India at the age of twenty four. She had grown up in her grandfather's home which had been full of Indian antiques and artifacts. On her own visit, however, "India and a people's raw display of emotions left her wary of the depths of dark, warm eyes" (87). Despite this internalized suspicion, Mrs Wellington-Smythe puts up the charity shop India-Need "twenty years later as [an] apology to the country of her father's birth" (88). The proclaimed philanthropic purpose of the charity is to help various villages in Rajasthan. Once more, it is Durga who explicates what a charity shop really means: "A symbol of the Diaspora, failed dreams and of what we can't have or hold any more, a domain of collective hope and renewed, recycled life" (195). It is indeed in the choice of the image of the charity shop where a major contesting of identity takes place: whether it signifies imperialist and colonial or transnational and post-colonial identities.

While Durga portrays the shop in terms of transnational diaspora, Heera is offended by Mrs Wellington-Smythe's accusations and criticizes vehemently her objectives: "Such a bloody hypocrite, setting up this shop to impress her fancy friends like that Vicky woman and calling it IndiaNeed! Tell me, does India need her?" (188). Here in the two readings of the seemingly philanthropic objectives – in the two conflicting interpretations of the term *need* – collide and result in questioning of the foundation of the whole enterprise. This collision is further ridiculed as Diana's friend Vicky Bartlett insinuates that Diana has been planning to shut down the shop and start another charity "to protect a rare species of Indonesian fox" (95). The unproblematized passage from human to animal, from Indian villagers to Indonesian foxes as recipients of charity, is presented in a deeply Orientalist and imperialist manner, and gives a final lie to the pretense of altruistic, philanthropic basis of the endeavor.[15]

The subaltern eats

The women of the charity shop begin gradually to notice their colonised position. Heera had dedicated herself to her work in the shop fiercely, which was "a quality Diana Wellington-Smythe astutely exploited" (19–20). Her reward is, however, mere suspicion. Heera traces also another significant complaint when she comments that "every day we eat cold lunch just because Lady Di says the shop should not have food smells. We are not allowed to eat warmed-up Indian food in here" (188). This restriction appears as yet another racist colonial residue in Britain where the *goras*, the white Britons, hunger for Indian curry – "you know how these goras are – they always want to go for an Indian" (190) – , but do not want their environment stained with the colonials or with their smells.

A similar comment about food smells had previously been made to Swarnakumari by her husband on her arrival to Britain from India decades earlier: "No Indian cooking smell should go to the neighbour" (48). When Heera realizes the unqualified injustice of the situation, she is resolute about effecting a change in the matter:

> All that nonsense about Indian food smells! I know I should have told her right away from the beginning, but from next week we'll use a hot-plate, all right? I'll tell her straight on her face if she says anything, 'You call us your "Curry Club", don't you, so then we *are* going to eat our Indian food.' Let it smell, who cares? *Arre*, in fact, if we started serving Indian snacks in here, the customers would come running *because* of the smells. (188; emphases original)

Heera's protestation is, indeed, justified as Mrs Wellington-Smythe does condescendingly call the women in the shop her "Cambridge Curry Club." When Heera voices her grievance over the food issue, Durga's reply is layered with both colonial and post-colonial terms and innuendos: "The natives are getting

---

[15] See Gayatri Chakravorty Spivak, "The Bionic Episteme," lecture at the WALTIC Congress, 29 June–2 July 2008, Stockholm.

restless. Mutiny. The subaltern speaks" (189).[16] The mutinous speaking, speaking against, is here taking the form of eating, which is not insignificant from the gender point of view.

In addition to these considerations, a comment could be made on the way names reveal cultural incongruity, or misidentification that causes protests. This comes up when Heera thinks about proper names for restaurants when she suggests the women go together for a lunch. She remembers a time when she had visited an Indian restaurant in London: "A place called 'Curry in a Hurry'. First of all, what a name! *Arre*, how can you have curry in a hurry?" (190). Here, 'curry' and 'hurry' just do not go together, and Heera protests against such cultural misrepresentation.

Also Heera's and Mrs Wellington-Smythe's conflict provides grounds for dissent. As the shop's manager, it is Heera who mostly deals with Mrs Wellington-Smythe, talking to her frequently on the phone (18, 52, 85, 193, 210). The confrontation between them escalates when Mrs Wellington-Smythe begins to suspect Heera for the thefts that have been taking place in the shop (193). Heera is infuriated: "She suspects me! Who the hell does she think she is?" (194–195), "bloody thieves run around in this world doing dishonest things, but no, Lady Di has to catch me instead!" (196). While Mrs Wellington-Smythe does indeed hold some stereotypical suspicions of poor immigrant women like Heera and is convinced of their corruption (38), there is also an element of understanding towards her. As the narrative moves through various points of view in different chapters, Diana's fears, hopes and views are represented, too. Furthermore, Swarnakumari "You know the word 'understand.' It means to 'stand under', to feel how it must be inside the other person's skin. We must try to understand Mrs Wellington-Smythe. I think she has some problems. She is not looking happy – something is wrong" (195). The seemingly univocal judgmental position is deconstructed and an alternative view is suggested.

As it happens, towards the end of the novel, the women manage to catch the thief pestering the shop. This does not, however, provide a neat closure for the story as the thief manages suddenly to escape. Durga interprets the incident in theoretical terms, ironically as is typical for her interjections:

> It frequently happens that the signifier slips and evades the grasp of the signified in a poststructuralist site of unintentional fallacy. It must be remembered that we live in a society of

---

[16] Durga's words refer especially to the Indian Mutiny (a.k.a. Sepoy Mutiny) of 1857, and to Gayatri Chakravorty Spivak's 1988 essay "Can the Subaltern Speak?" on (the possibility or otherwise of) subaltern, post-colonial women's agency.

> simulacrum, free of connection to reality. One should therefore
> desist from further discourse. (213–214)

Using the thief as a site of metaphorical focal point, Durga concludes that reality and language are slippery and signification an endlessly deferred process. In face of this deferral, Durga does not, however, desist from further discourse, although on the other hand she "was accustomed to the silence that invariably followed her observations" (16). Here, the novel seems to suggest that critical theory, necessary in itself, unavoidably fails in communication, and the theorist, or the author, is in no superior position to explain the everyday reality compared to any other participants.

Strategies of Identification

The incidents leading to the subaltern "mutiny" are embedded in at least three different discernible strategies of identification. The strategies the different "natives" in the story apply for their identification in the diaspora vary from traditionalism to mimicry and to the embracing of hybridity. These strategies do not appear as definite, clear-cut entities but are present in various combinations and to varying degrees in the characters' outlook. All these stances are also looked at critically and problematised in their contexts.

1 The traditionalist strategy

The *traditionalist strategy* appears in the novel most clearly as a nostalgic yearning for home in India as is the case with Heera's friend Barry who "ached to leave it all and return to India" (32). However, even Barry has made concessions as he enjoys his whisky and uses the name Barry instead of the original Bhagat (26).

Traditionalism is most clearly adopted by Swarnakumari. Hailing from a Brahminic Bengali family, she vouches for Indian religious and cultural traditions and roots (6). For her, tradition functions manifestly as a survival strategy in hostile Britain. She challenges the critically indisposed Durga on this issue: "Tell me, Durga, who are you without your roots, *hanh*? It's because of our roots that we can survive in this society" (46). Swarnakumari is convinced that simply by being from a good Indian family, like herself, one is saved from the perils of the modern world such as homosexuality (13), interracial sex (45), and drugs (210). Durga, who contests her sarcastically on all these points, had herself been "whisked away from the temptations of drugs, cigarettes, sex and rock'n'roll" when her parents had premeditatedly decided to move back to India from London when she was thirteen – in order to infuse into her "a dose of roadtested middle-class Indian values" (148). This project does succeed to an extent as she enters an arranged marriage, although the couple then moves to Britain. Furthermore, she develops a highly critical stance towards given values and attitudes.

Durga is very critical of the tendency to hold on to tradition and regards it in generational terms, asking,

> what's with you first-generation Indians, anyway? You came here thirty years ago with a suitcase you never unpacked. It's all about tradition, family, culture, honour, isn't it? Why are you so keen on carrying on tradition? It's as if you're scared – you have to obey, or else. But does tradition exist? Is it real for us to taste, smell, feel and hold? (45)

The metaphor of tradition as luggage that Durga employs here is one that is used by many postcolonial writers such as Salman Rushdie.[17] Durga's "diasporic question" of the reality of tradition – does tradition taste, smell, feel – takes the issue beyond mere nostalgic memory to the level of corporeality, although no definite answers are forthcoming.

Swarnakumari's husband, aware of her Brahmin sensibilities and upper-caste upbringing, had, for his part, "ensured her protection from the *evil influences of British society*, endorsing her reluctance to venture out of the home" (66; emphasis added). In her protected reverence for religious traditionalism, Swarnakumari had however developed a matching reverence for the British aristocracy and royalty, for which Heera gently criticizes her. When Swarnakumari arranges the shop's display window with the Queen's photograph, Heera says: "Just look at Swarna, how that woman bends ... she can bend for England!" (5). On the other hand, Heera's position relating to England is differentiated when she makes fun of her cousin Viju who on his first visit to England had worn ridiculously warm clothes and carried an enormous amount of medication with him. She comments: "Was he preparing to go into an *English jungle*, or what?" (91; emphasis added). This reference to England as a *jungle* – together with "the evil influences of British society" – is a hilarious reversal of the colonial attitude in the transnational context. This attitude, so integrally built in the Orientalist ideology, is further emphasized through Swarnakumari's fear of overt sexuality (45), sexual perversity (5), homosexuality (13), and pollution (96).

---

[17] See e.g. Salman Rushdie, *Shame* (New York: Picador, 1983), p. 86.

2 The mimicking strategy

The *mimicking strategy* in the novel, then, appears in a much more embedded way than traditionalism. The transnational subjects have adopted various aspects of British way of life into their everyday lives, whether it is Barry's adopted new name (26), Mallika's musical preferences (80), or Shyamal's choice of white bread and Earl Grey tea instead of "the nostalgia-inducing vapours of ginger tea laced with cardamom" (56–57). Avtar Brah has written on dilemmas of diasporic attitudes for old and new homes in the transnational space:

> On the one hand, "home" is a mythic place of desire in the diasporic imagination. [...] On the other hand, home is also a lived experience of a locality. Its sounds and smells, its heat and dust [...] all this, as mediated by the historically specific of everyday social relations. (192)

Here Brah emphasizes the importance of contextual specificity of diasporic experience in forming new identities. Using such contextualized specificity, Durga further problematizes the strategy of mimicry for passing: "Give the immigrant net curtains and he simply blends, like the tea packet labels that say *Product of more than one country*. But to blend or not to blend into the diasporic cuppa – that is the question" (42–43; original emphasis).

Choosing a strategy for 'homing diaspora' – to make one's new transnational locality home – is complex like Durga's pseudo-Hamlet's question insinuates. The transnational diasporic immigrant, as another "product of more than one country", may or may not choose to use net curtains to make home but "to blend or not to blend" remains the question for her or him. One has to make do with that made-up home. And home, as Brah attests,

> is intrinsically linked with the way in which the processes of inclusion or exclusion operate and are subjectively experienced under given circumstances. It relates to the complex political and personal struggles over the social regulation of "belonging." (194)[18]

3 The hybrid strategy

The blending that Durga contemplates in the tea package example is not like the kind of hybridity acknowledged in the *hybrid strategy*. The metaphor used in the blending of different teas implies a compulsory, set package one either

---

[18] Here Brah is talking about *diaspora space* in which the struggle for belonging affects both those on the move and those "staying put" (181).

accepts or rejects. It is comparable to the choice between tradition or mimicry, struggling, as Brah puts it, "over the social regulation of 'belonging.'"

What I mean by hybridity here is rather a more transformative process that problematizes essentialist notions of identity (Kuortti and Nyman 3). In this view, it is not just any mixture of cultural ingredients but its transnational post-coloniality "implies a markedly unbalanced relationship" between the various aspects of an identity (ibid. 2). Even though herself not a prime example of a hybrid strategy, Durga once more voices the issues, this time counterbalancing tradition and hybridity:

> "Don't you see that you seize upon 'Indian culture' out of desperation and fear? Fear of erosion and erasure of identity. Why not welcome the churn of East-West encounters instead, take the plunge into the flow and see what happens? Diaspora isn't only about displacement; it's a progression, a moving to a new location of the liberated self." (46)

The result of this "churning" process is a new location – in Bhabha's terms in *The Location of Culture* "the third space of enunciation" – where one's identity is not simply this or that but something else (218).

Constructing a Transnational Identity

As I have tried to show through my discussion, the characters of Balsari's novel *The Cambridge Curry Club* negotiate in different ways the questions of identity. There is certainly an element of fear of the Other – in the form of English jungle, wild sex, or evil influences– that has an effect on the transnational people. There is certainly an element of losing traditional values. From the gender point of view it seems that this anxiety is particularly (but not exclusively) experienced by women. One dimension where this struggle over identity is present is naming. By problematizing simplistic positions, the novel contrasts different attitudes, practices and ideologies.

The result is an intriguing view on the challenges to the construction of a new transnational identity with multiple ethnicities, identities, and strategies of survival.

Works Cited

Arnold, Matthew. "Obermann Once More." *New Poems*. London: Macmillan, 1868, 220–242.
Balsari, Saumya. *The Cambridge Curry Club*. London: BlackAmber, 2004.

Banerjee, Mita. "Postethnicity and Postcommunism in Hanif Kureishi's Gabriel's Gift." *Reconstructing Hybridity: Post-colonial Studies in Transition* Eds. Joel Kuortti and Jopi Nyman. Amsterdam: Rodopi, 2007. 309–324.

Bhabha, Homi K. *The Location of Culture*. London: Routledge, 1994.

-----. "The Postcolonial and the Postmodern: The Question of Legacy." *The Cultural Studies Reader*. Ed. Simon During. 2nd edition. London: Routledge, 1999. 189–208.

Brah, Avtar. *Cartographies of Diaspora: Contesting Identities*. New York: Routledge, 1996.

Corley, Martin, Lucy J. MacGregor and David I. Donaldson. "It's the Way That You, Er, Say It: Hesitations in Speech Affect Language Comprehension." *Cognition* 105.3 (December 2007): 658–668.

Devi Mahatmyam, The. Trans. P. R. Ramachander. Hindupedia.com. Available at <www.hindupedia.com/en/Devi_Mahatmyam_Text#Chapter_3:_Killing_of_Mahishasura>. Accessed Nov. 20, 2009.

Dutta, Abhijit. *Mother Durga: An Icon of Community and Culture*. Kolkata: Readers Service, 2003.

Fraser, Antonia. *Cromwell: The Lord Protector*. New York: Grove Press, 2001.

Grewal, Inderpal. "Becoming American: The Novel and the Diaspora." In Grewal, *Transnational America: Feminisms, Diasporas, Neoliberalisms*. Durham: Duke University Press, 2005. 35–79.

Grewal, Inderpal and Caren Kaplan. "Postcolonial Studies and Transnational Feminist Practices." *Jouvert* 5.1 (Autumn 2000), para. 3. Available at <http://english.chass.ncsu.edu/jouvert/v5i1/grewal.htm>. Accessed 30 Nov. 2009.

Howatt, Anthony P. R. and H. G. Widdowson. *History of English Language Teaching*. 2nd ed. Oxford: Oxford University Press, 2004.

Kuortti, Joel "Nomsense: Salman Rushdie's *The Satanic Verses*." *Textual Practice* 13.1 (1999): 137–146.

Kuortti, Joel and Jopi Nyman. "Introduction: Hybridity Today." In *Reconstructing Hybridity: Post-colonial Studies in Transition* Eds. Joel Kuortti and Jopi Nyman. Amsterdam: Rodopi, 2007. 1–18.

Lahiri, Jhumpa. *The Namesake*. Boston: Houghton Mifflin, 2004.

Lionnet, Françoise and Shu-mei Shih. "Introduction: Thinking through the Minor, Transnationally." In *Minor Transnationalism*. Ed. Françoise Lionnet and Shu-mei Shih. Durham: Duke University Press, 2005. 1–23.

Mukherjee, Anusua. "In a Mad, Mad Shop." *The Telegraph* (Calcutta) (July 25, 2008). Available at

<www.telegraphindia.com/1080725/jsp/opinion/story_9584893.jsp>. Accessed Nov. 20, 2009.

Rushdie, Salman. *Shame*. New York: Picador, 1983.

Russell, William Howard, Sir. *My Diary in India, in the Year 1858–9*, vol. 1, 4th pr. London: Routledge, Warne & Routledge, 1860.

Spivak, Gayatri Chakravorty. "The Bionic Episteme." Lecture at the WALTIC Congress, 29 June–2 July 2008, Stockholm.

-----. "Diasporas Old and New: Women in the Transnational World." *Revolutionary Pedagogies: Cultural Politics, Instituting Education, and the Discourse of Theory*. Ed. Peter Pericles Trifonas. New York: Routledge, 2000. 3–29.

CHAPTER FIVE

Transnational Axes of Identity Articulation in Bernardine Evaristo's *Lara*

E. M. Ester Gendusa

Bernardine Evaristo's first novel *Lara* (1997) subversively intervenes within the traditional circuits via which British national identity is shaped, reproduced and transmitted. Its innovative features – in terms of genre, style and motifs – can be fully appreciated when examined in the light of an interpretative frame whose theoretical perspectives originate in that intersection area where feminist critique and (post-)colonial studies productively conflate.

Dating back to the 1980s, this theoretical merging – which resulted in one of the most recent academic fields – has not always seen its strands relate harmoniously. Indeed, the hermeneutic domain has been, at times, conflictual, when one takes into consideration, on the one hand, the debate over whether the analytic category of gender or that of race should be of prominence when analyzing women's oppression and, on the other, the black feminists' effective argument according to which Western feminism runs the risk of obscuring the multiplicity of the material realities affecting the everyday lives of the different groups of women around the world.

It is, however, undeniable that the two abovementioned areas of critical discourse share a certain number of interconnections – in relation to both their historical development as bodies of thought and to their major theoretical tenets. Both deriving from coherent political movements developed between the late 1960s and late 1970s in Britain and in the United States, within the academia, feminist theory and (post-)colonial studies are informed by a common concern, that of dismantling the phallogocentrism of Western discourse and the (symbolic) hierarchies pervading the binary oppositions on which it is constructed.

Recently, their critical interweaving has produced innovative as well as thought-provoking perspectives. According to Bill Ashcroft, Gareth Griffiths and Helen Tiffin,

> Until recently feminist and post-colonial discourses have followed a path of convergent evolution, their theoretical trajectories demonstrating striking similarities but rarely intersecting. In the last ten years, however, there has been increasing interest not just in their parallel concerns but in the nature of their actual and potential intersections – whether creatively coincident or interrogative. Feminism has highlighted a number of the unexamined assumptions within post-colonial discourse, just as post-colonialism's interrogations of Western feminist scholarship have provided timely warnings and led to new directions. (233-34)

When applied to Evaristo's *Lara*, the interrelated interpretative categories of gender and race allow to demonstrate that the innovations characterizing the novel in terms of its content deconstruct and recast the symbolic assumptions on which Englishness is constructed since they reveal themselves to be a way to interrupt the transmission of gender-biased and racist cultural models which inform the representations of the national character as elaborated within English official discursive practices. In considering the variable of gender, the divisive character of such discourses – configuring 'second-class' citizens – is well illustrated by Lynne Segal, who persuasively links welfare politics to the interconnected statist rhetoric in her *Why Feminism?* where she contends:

> Since the 1980s [...] there has been a huge expansion in low-waged, insecure jobs in Britain [...]. This has occurred alongside continuing attacks on welfare benefits, including the specific targeting of state assistance for single mothers and the disabled [...]. The rolling back of social welfare has in turn incited a renewed emphasis on the importance of traditional family life and, in particular, fathers' rights and responsibilities. Women, overall more engaged in the work of childcare and nurturing, suffer specifically, or disproportionately, from welfare cutbacks and paternalistic rhetorics. (201-02)

In privileging the analytic category of race, instead, Heidi Safia Mirza asserts that: "To be black and British is to be unnamed in official discourse" (3). Mirza further suggests that "The construction of a national British identity is built upon a hegemonic white ethnicity that never speaks its presence. We are told that you can be either one or the other, black or British, but not both" (3). In her examination of the official acts issued by the British government and regulating nationality – from the *British Nationality and Aliens Act* of 1914 to the 1981 *Nationality Act* –, Maria Helena Lima also underlines the progressively exclusivist nature of British national discourse (51-52).

Against this backdrop Evaristo's writing strategies in terms of style, and especially the formula of the novel-in-verse – chosen to defy the rigidity of the Western logocentric canon – acts as the stylistic underpinning of a narrative fabric which becomes the site of a symbolic revision of British history – colonial and otherwise – thus alerting attention to its status as a "representational construct" (Ermath 56).

Writing from the perspective of a metropolitan woman novelist of mixed origins, Evaristo sets her peculiar verse-novel primarily in a (post-)colonial London that witnesses the novel's eponymous protagonist (and major focus of perspective) overcoming her identity split and attaining a personal sense of self throughout a progressive – though conflictual – process of identity formation/negotiation. The result of autobiographical projections, Lara, a young Anglo-Nigerian woman, thus becomes a vehicle through which the marginal counterpart of the British hegemonic identity model is voiced and given visibility.

The oppositional nature of the resulting identity figuration epitomized by Lara can only be fully appreciated if the analytic category of gender is given prominence in the context of an interpretative paradigm where it is inextricably interwoven with that of 'race.' Such a theoretical interweaving provides a grid in the light of which Evaristo's novel proves to be constructed on a three-fold conceptual frame.

First, Evaristo contests a supposed homogenous as well as discrete vision of English national identity which British cultural and political practices still perpetuate. In so doing, she simultaneously puts into perspective the mono-cultural view on which such a vision rests and, consequently, she imaginatively recuperates the microcosms of a colonial past which the official archive has purposely obscured and with which, in the novel, the metropolis necessarily comes to terms.

The 'gender' axis of the theoretical grid informing the present analysis helps to illustrate the second conceptual movement underpinning the novel. Indeed, the above mentioned recuperation of cultural contexts is neither a simplistic nor a celebratory process, as it exposes complex levels of subordination. In fact, the novel gives a voice to those female figures whose presence has been symbolically expelled from the process of history-making as it is articulated within the dominant discursive constructions of Britishness. Important in this respect is Evaristo's representation of the sexual assault perpetrated by the male colonizer on the colonized woman. Moreover, this being the opening scene of the novel, it allows the writer, *inter alia*, to cast light on and denounce the violence pervading the colonial scene and the gender relations at play in it.

Evaristo's sensitivity to gender can be also detected in her treatment of the dynamics regulating the relationships between the sexes within London's immigrant communities of Nigerian descent. Far from adopting a gender-neutral stance, Evaristo explicitly reveals the existence – within these groups – of unbalanced gender relations which cause the women belonging to these communities to be confined to subaltern and disadvantageous positions with respect to the male members. It thus follows that in Evaristo's creative shaping of the (post-)colonial nation – which in the novel comes to be typified by London – a revision of the traditional categories of national identity is rendered more problematic by the author's critique of those male-dominated gender dynamics that the metropolis perpetuates, even accelerates.

Finally, after underlining not only the racialized nature of British nationalist discourses but also the patriarchal (and matriarchal, as in the case of Edith, Lara's maternal grandmother) biases informing certain processes of metropolitan ethnic identity construction,[1] Evaristo shapes a peculiar hybrid identity. The novel projects the image of a metropolitan female character of mixed parentage who, after acknowledging the split in her identity – caused by the multifaceted legacies of colonialism –, tries to overcome this division after the discovery of her family origins and the articulation of a plural cosmopolitan sense of self. The deriving newly-acquired self-awareness tends to be, on the one hand, the first stage along the route to her social empowerment and, on the other, it reveals itself as the symbolic premise for a notion of (post-)colonial nation where persisting patriarchal regimes of power and racial forms of subordination, if not overturned, are made visible and potentially opposed.

Evaristo's novel outlines Lara's personal development from her adolescent concerns to her pursuit and problematic acquisition of a personal as well as national identity, along a trajectory which witnesses her becoming an adult through her first encounters – whether perturbing or invigorating – with the opposite sex and through a triangulation leading her from England and the Mediterranean area to Nigeria and, finally, to Brazil.

Being of Black Nigerian and White English parentage, in the London of the 1960s the adolescent mixed-race Lara falls victim to an essentialized dominant discourse which questions her right to lay claim to British citizenship. Mirrored in this discourse are social practices that condemn Lara to continually defer any cultural belonging to British society, so echoing the ostracism inherent in those

---

[1] It is important to remember that the depiction of family gender relations in *Lara* is particularly articulated. Indeed the novel does not eschew to expose Edith's matriarchal attitudes. Edith – Lara's maternal grandmother – initially disapproves of her daughter's marriage with a man of colour (Lara's Nigerian father) and, later on in the novel she will resent her grand-daughter having a dark skin.

attitudes which her father himself had been faced with when first arriving in London from Nigeria in the 1950s. Telling in this respect is the following dialogue between Lara and her English best friend Susie:

"'Where'you from, La?' Susie suddenly asked
one lunch break on the playing fields.' 'Woolwich.'
'No, silly, where are you from, y'know originally?'
'If you really must know I was born in Eltham, actually.'
'My dad says you must be from Jamaica,' Susie insisted.
'I'm not Jamaican! I'm English!' 'Then why are you
coloured?' (Evaristo 65)

It follows that if in the aftermath of colonialism immigrants from the ex-colonies suffered from a traumatic de-territorialized experience in the metropolis, their children – as the dialogue shows – were and still *are* attributed a racialized identity which continues to label them as outsiders. Consequently, it is the legacy of colonialism that surfaces in Susie's words as she and, later on in the novel her boyfriend, racially abuse Lara. Susie's attitude bears witness to the girl's introjection of a narrative of the 'nation' which, while echoing the colonial encounter, proves to be pervaded by a stereotype representation of the racial Other linked in the imagination to the colonial space within a metonymic relation, notwithstanding his/her being born in Britain. As a consequence, the deriving essentialist configuration of 'Britishness' comes to embrace exclusively white citizens and inevitably alludes to a set of racialized power relations that are linked to physical appearance. As the previous quotation indicates, in Susie's delineation of the British national character Lara is consequently de-territorialized and, as a result, perceived as not belonging to the 'nation.' A possible explanation for this can be found in Avtar Brah's suggestion that

[i]n racialized or nationalist discourses this signifier can become the basis of claims – in the proverbial Powellian sense – that a group settled "in" a place is not necessarily "of" it. [...]
In Britain, racialized discourses of the nation continue to construct people of African descent and Asian descent, as well as certain other groups, as being outside the nation. (5)

In addition to that, Lara's positioning within the nation is further problematized in that not only is she of Nigerian descent, but she is also of mixed-race background, as she is a Nigerian-English young woman, being born of a Nigerian father and an English mother of Irish descent. The deriving identity *in-betweenness* clearly emerges from the following quotation:

Home. I searched but could not find myself,

> not on the screen, billboards, books, magazines,
> and first and last not in the mirror, my demon, my love
> which faded my brownness into a Bardot likeness.
> Seasons of youth stirred in my cooking pot, a spicy
> mix of marinated cultures, congealed into cold, disparate
> lumps, untended, festered. (Evaristo 69)

Lara's words implicitly allude to the social power of perception in the reproduction of symbolic racialized configurations of identity. As we shall see later on, far from exclusively affecting the public imaginary, such a cultural construction intervenes in regulating the relationships between the ethnic groups peopling the nation.

At this point of the analysis, it is important to stress one of the conceptual strengths of the novel which is its sensitivity towards the articulation of gender dynamics within the immigrant communities in London. In fact, far from limiting herself to unveiling the persistence of a "racialized" difference for Lara, Evaristo, also shows that in the metropolis the girl is subjected to a two-fold discrimination: that is, in terms of gender and in terms of race.[2] This is a pivotal theoretical axis of the novel when we consider that in engaging with the dynamics through which the category of difference manifests itself and affects the members of immigrant communities, Evaristo eschews any kind of gender-blindness. Correspondingly, the complex process of identity negotiation and location put into practice by Lara is also explored from a gendered point of view.

In the novel, Lara is exposed to a double subordination, originating from racial as well as gender inferiorizing relationships. In other words, white English people's racist attitudes – of which Lara is a victim – are paralleled by patriarchal gender relations within the Nigerian community. As the object of racial abuse and a victim of hierarchical power dynamics between the sexes permeating her own ethnic community, Lara experiences tensions both outside and within her own family. Interrelated inferiorizing race and gender dynamics confine her to a subaltern subject position with respect to both her Nigerian father, who does not hesitate to have recourse to violence and actually batters the young Lara, and, later on in the novel, to Josh, her Nigerian boyfriend. In particular, the latter, in urging Lara to assume a submissive role within the

---

[2] From the 1980s onwards, the urgency of studying the analytic category of gender in its complex interaction with that of race has been resolutely expressed by Black feminists both in the United States and in Britain. Within the American context, bell hooks, Chandra Talpade Mohanty and Angela Y. Davis deserve a particular mention, while among the Black British feminists Hazel Carby, among others, have provided noteworthy contributions to the debate.

couple, shows a gender biased perspective Lara disapproves of and, consequently, cannot share, as we shall see.

This results in Lara being initially trapped within a conflictual identity *in-betweenness* which prevents her from fully identifying with the British group and which also hinders any identification with the members of London's Nigerian community. In fact, while the former ostracizes her as not being fully white, the latter does not hesitate to exercise forms of internal gender discrimination, implying physical violence and the presupposition of Lara's having to conform to a pre-conceived role of loyal keeper of the ethnic culture. Before betraying her with another woman, Josh will ultimately tell her:

'You'll not marry a Nigerian if you can't obey me' [...]
'You don't even know what
Jollof rice is, let alone how to cook it. You're strictly
a fish fingers and mash girl. You'll make a sorry wife.' (Evaristo 90)

The foregrounding of divisions of a gendered nature within the Nigerian community is what makes Evaristo's *Lara* of particular value. In line with the theoretical assumptions and political positions of black feminist theorists and writers who, from the 1980s onwards, have elaborated in their critical interventions as well as in their creative works the notion of "double colonization" suffered by black women in formerly colonized countries and which originates from their being victims of both racial and patriarchal discriminations, Evaristo's novel shows that an analogous phenomenon is replicated in the metropolis and continues to affect women belonging to immigrant communities.[3] Hence, the literary representation of the (post-) colonial woman living in London offered by Evaristo – in reproducing the reality of such a situational context – is far from being pacificatory. In fact, Evaristo's *Lara* manages to highlight the fact that metropolitan (post-)colonial women are engaged in a twofold struggle deriving from the intersection of a positive claim to heterogeneous as well as distinctive ethnic peculiarities on the one hand, with the urgency of feminist emancipation on the other.

Thus, in refusing to portray London as an unproblematic site of experience, Evaristo offers a complex image of the metropolitan space which becomes the starting point of Lara's identity search and the contradictory site where the social positioning of her multilayered self may occur. Such a multi-layered articulation of London's urban space can be explored in the light of the analytic

---

[3] The notion of "double colonisation" is illustrated – among others – by Susheila Nasta who argues that it is "brought about by history and male-dominated social and political systems" (Nasta xviii).

perspective informing John McLeod's *Postcolonial London* (2004), where the critic argues that:

> "On the one hand, London is the location where the British Government and so many state agencies have their national headquarters, circumstances that assist in the city's imaginative fashioning almost as a synecdoche for the nation. On the other hand, [...] London's transcultural facticity has made possible new communities and forms of culture indebted to its history of "peopling" which in turn come to pose a considerable challenge to the pastoral articulation of English national culture as representative. In this conception, London can be considered a profoundly disruptive location, incubating new social relations and cultural forms which conflict with the advocacy of a national culture or the pursuit of cultural nationalism. (18)

Consequently, London is conceptualized as both the heart of the former imperial nation and as a new multicultural as well as potentially subversive space. This two-fold qualification of the metropolis finds its parallel in Lara's personal experience. If she is initially denied the right of abode in the metropolis, being a victim of a nationalist racism centered on color, she eventually starts to experience London as the very first terrain of her identity search and consequent personal development. In order to overcome her alienation so as to try to attain a sense of identity wholeness, Lara feels she has to reconstruct her family history and, as a consequence, she starts asking her father about his Nigerian roots. However, faced with his self-induced amnesia of the past (which is to be interpreted as a traumatic legacy of his own diasporic experience) and deprived of any possibility of straightforward self-identification with white Londoners, she sets out on a personal journey into those London areas mostly peopled by immigrants of African or African-Caribbean descent. However, following the disappointment caused by Josh's sexist attitude, she leaves London and starts to travel on the physical level across nations – thus criss-crossing the European, African and American continents – and, on the imaginative level, across the generations of her ancestors. These multiple displacements make it possible for Lara to retrace the fabric of her family's multicultural heritage and to inscribe herself in the ensuing network of belongings that she herself establishes.

On a wider level, Lara's journeys – in time and space – and her recuperation at the same time of her family past also generate for London itself the possibility to recuperate its symbolic bonds with its colonial past and to engage with the latter dialogically. As a consequence, in Evaristo's novel, unlike what used to happen in the colonial 'centre/margins' polarity, London, rather than being perceived as the hegemonic focus of exclusionary discursive practices, comes to occupy a decentralized position within the complex web inscribed by the multiple relationships existing between the metropolis itself, former colonial capitals and Eastern European countries visited by Lara in the course of the novel. Thus, the ensuing image of London constructs itself not only on its conflictual internal reconfigurations – mainly due to the progressive arrival of (im)migrants from England's ex-colonies (such as Lara's father) – but also in relation to Lara's multiple routes and through the recuperation of her ancestors' life stories.

The novel's fabric is thus interspersed with first-person narrations by some of the men and women peopling Lara's family history, but, since it is in fact her grandparents or great-grandparents who intervene in the narration as autonomous voices, the young woman is not given direct access to most of these stories. Although this narrative articulation testifies to how complex the appropriation of a usable past for the post-colonial metropolitan woman may be, it is, however, thanks to this literary device, that Evaristo's *Lara* pursues a twofold aim: on the one hand, on the content level, it contributes to disrupt traditional Western master narratives by giving a voice to minor historical actors who, otherwise, would remain silent; on the other hand, as far as the stylistic level is concerned, it manages to challenge the canonical logocentric literary matrix by interrupting and fragmenting its traditional flux. In addition, the deliberate choice of writing a verse-novel allows her to break the fixity of Western traditional literary genres whose boundaries thus undergo a productive cross-fertilization. In the novel, their permeability is to be seen as the stylistic underpinning of Lara's overcoming of a divided self following her refusal of the white/black dichotomy initially informing her subject position.

In *Lara* the opening voice is that of Tolulope, the protagonist's paternal great-grandmother. The slave woman, who dies in a Brazilian plantation, relates the unspeakable violence she has suffered, the circumstances of her death, which follows her being brutally raped by the owner of the plantation, and her subsequent symbolic rebirth. In giving a voice to Tolulope, Evaristo not only gives expression to a segment of history that the Western metropolis tends to erase through willful strategies of cultural exclusion, but she also succeeds in symbolically inscribing her novel's protagonist within a network of relational as well as new emotional connections linking her female ancestors across different generations. Thus the delineation of a female genealogy allows Evaristo – together with other post-colonial women writers – to reconstitute – if only through her textual practice – a historical past which the colonial archive as well as Western historiography have programmatically obscured by means of imperialistic cultural practices, but also to assert the urgency for metropolitan (post-)colonial women to reclaim an egalitarian self-definition in terms of gender relations within the ethnic community to which they belong. Hence this 'voicing' of Tolulope is to be interpreted as a narrative strategy aimed, on the one hand, at casting light onto women as both victims of and active agents in the process of History-making[4] and, on the other, at reversing gender homogenizing tendencies which pervade both official Western discourse and male-dominated post-colonial counter-discourses centered on the conceptualization of the new metropolitan ethnic identity.

In so doing, Evaristo manages to complicate the simplistic system of oppositional binaries such as Western self/ethnic Other and male/female, thus foregrounding not only the gendered nature of racialized discourses, but also the equally problematic gender-blindness of some post-colonial political and cultural practices. What can be considered to be one of the merits of the novel is that it actually complicates the aforementioned binary oppositions as well as the single categories they consist of, thus showing, for example, the internal heterogeneity of signifiers such as 'woman' and 'man.' When exposing forms of internal gender discrimination against the female members of the Nigerian community, not only does Evaristo confront the issue of "double colonization" – which, on the social level, inevitably proves a double oppression – but she also deliberately avoids celebratory terms to portray immigrant communities: in highlighting their inherent contradictions she thus shows just how pervasive forms of gender subordination may be and, consequently, how differently racialized discourses affect men and women. Regarded in this light, for postcolonial women writers literature becomes an instrument with which to "repudiate the 'patriarchal appropriation of power over the Word'" (Nasta xxv).

In the novel, the thematic issues analyzed so far are interwoven with specific formal strategies – including the hybridization of genres and styles – which reinforce its oppositional nature compared to the fixity of the Western literary canon. Thus, 'permeability' becomes a key characteristic in *Lara,* whose stylistic fabric originates, on the one hand, from the conflation of fictional prose and poetry and, on the other, from processes of transcodification (from the oral code to the written one). Against this background, Evaristo's peculiar prose-poetry and her use of the oral first-person narrative mode, which recalls the practice of story-telling, prove particularly suitable to dismantle the authority of Western unifying paradigms and patriarchal symbolic structures through productive processes of literary syncretism.

---

[4] The intentional use of the term "History" is here meant to underline the constructed nature of the official historical records as the result of hegemonic discursive practices and as opposed to the multifaceted totality of socio-cultural experiences lived by marginal groups.

The multiple hybridizations of the novel are paralleled by continuous intersections of different temporal levels which, being the result of a precise ideological tension, deliberately aim to disrupt one of the most cherished Western signifiers, that is, the highly celebrated notion of a unilateral linear progressive timeline as the quintessential symbol of the advancement of Western rational civilization. Thus, Evaristo's narrative mode inevitably interrogates and questions Western canonical literary tradition and revisits the past in the light of what has been displaced or silenced, so as to insert it into an active process of continuous reappraisal: lost voices and previously unwritten stories related to the colonial past – English and otherwise – are thus brought back to life and accorded a new dignified value as historical evidence.

Moreover, this manipulation of time levels and the deriving temporal fragmentation also reflects the conflictual nature of Lara's problematic search for a reintegrated as well as multilayered subjectivity. In more specific terms, as John McLeod suggests:

> Her travails between different pasts and places are echoed in the structure of *Lara* which similarly moves unexpectedly back and forth across history and nation, plaiting together different strands of culture and ancestry into a linked yet by no means homogenizing narrative which approximates to the transcultural character both of Lara and contemporary London. (178)

Emblematic of this significant coherence between the novel's thematic choices and narrative strategies is the abovementioned female genealogy linking Tolulope and Lara, where the novel's permeability in terms of temporal levels and of cultural axes becomes most manifest. In particular, Tolulope's story could be read as a kind of anticipation, in embryo, of Lara's experience. In fact, Lara's initial multilayered subordination in terms of gender and race – originating from her being a woman of Nigerian origins living in present-day London – might recall Tolulope's double inferiorization as a black colonized woman. This parallelism clearly reinforces Evaristo's emphasis on the legacy of imperialist practices affecting immigrants' daughters in the contemporary post-imperialist multicultural metropolis.[5] A further development of the analogy linking the two women across time and space is made possible by Tolulope's rebirth through water, as it anticipates Lara's self-recovery the final stage of which will take place along the Amazon River.

However, having said that, it is imperative to underline that Evaristo proves particularly sensitive to the historical and cultural specificity characterizing the contexts where Tolulope and Lara respectively live. Lara's subordination is

---

[5] The emphasis on the specificity of Tolulope's colonial context is a way for Evaristo to elude the contested homogenizing allegory of the 'Third World Woman'.

thus accounted for by her social and material realities being different to those of her great-grandmother. In fact, the young woman's inferiorization is determined by contemporary racist and ethnic discriminations and, consequently, its overcoming – albeit not an unproblematic one – is made possible by the political awareness originating from Lara's ultimate context-specific 'location' within the conflictual space of a future-oriented cosmopolitan London.

Central to the completion of her self-discovery are the multiple journeys, which eventually take her to Turkey, Nigeria and Brazil, along a route that symbolically – although only partially – retraces that of the slave trade. Her travels lead her to the awareness that her innermost sense of self lies in the manifold intersections of her family roots, which she interrogates and reinterprets in a personal way. In this sense, the recuperation of her family's untold stories should not be interpreted as a nostalgic cultural practice and, similarly, her process of identity formation does not entail any quest for a primordial archetypal Nigerian or Brazilian past or for any cultural essence with which she might intend to identify herself in exclusivist terms. Instead, as Mark Stein puts it:

> In line with Fanonist thinking, Lara is [...] intent on working through the memory of slavery, and thereby both acknowledging and leaving behind ancestral historical experience. Her travels have led her to encounter her ancestors in order to dis-identify herself from them, to underscore her separateness and her difference. (81)

This active negotiation enables Lara to proclaim a personal identity which, far from being a monolithic one, is, on the contrary, *in progress* or, to use a term recalling the numerous aquatic images pervading the novel, *in flux,* and which originates from a multilayered sense of belonging, from the awareness of being the fruit of several cultural interconnections and transnational diasporic inscriptions.

However, such a multi-layeredness is not to be understood in terms of a continuous deferral of identity articulations or collections of fragments resulting in a sterile collage of Lara's self. On the contrary, it has to be interpreted as a critique of discourses of fixed origins and, more important, as a political attempt to pose a challenge to exclusivist visions of the British 'nation' and of a presumed 'pure' British character. What is more, though enriched with the import of her family's cultural traditions, Lara's identity, at the end of the novel when she is back to London, proves to be firmly located in the metropolis and marked by the materiality of this situational context. As Sebnem Toplu puts it, "Lara's complex intercultural identity merges stronger with what she has always felt like; she *is* English" (11, original emphasis). But Lara's deriving sense of self and of national belonging inscribe a revised notion of Englishness: a national category which is enriched by multiple cultural interconnections. Significantly, however, her identity negotiation does not result in a straightforward totalizing identification with other non-English cultural entities, but at the same time it entails a cultural pluralism from which it nourishes itself.

Against this background, what is particularly important is that the recreation of symbolic liaisons between Lara and her ancestors allows Evaristo to trace an alternative figuration of the contemporary mixed-race subjectivity of the metropolis, which inevitably results in a transformed city cartography. Evaristo thus explores, and consequently unveils, new multilayered forms of the subjectivity of metropolitan women are the bearers of heterogeneous as well as of complex sets of experiences. In this respect, highly indicative of the interconnectedness of the emotional and diasporic affiliations forging her personality is the cultural syncretism she experiences in Brazil along the River Amazon where she listens to Catholic hymns and African drums played in an Indio church.

In light of this redefinition of the female metropolitan identity, mainly founded on a personal re-creation of multiple historical as well as existential connections, following Elleke Boehmer we can say that Evaristo may well be included in a specific group of authors, that is

> A second generation of more strictly speaking diasporic writers (children of migrants) such as Hanif Kureishi, Zadie Smith, or Monica Ali – [who have] produced definitions of the postcolonial as almost invariably cosmopolitan. It is a literature that is necessarily transplanted, displaced, multilingual, and, simultaneously, conversant with the cultural codes of the West: it is within Europe/America though not fully of Europe/America.
> (230)

Lara's being 'conversant' with multiple cultural systems is not, however, a simplistic form of syncretism, as it is complicated by its author's sensitiveness to interconnected relations of subordination. Indeed, at the end of the novel, Lara's persona comes to be defined by overlapping cultural belongings and in the light of multiple axes of differentiation among which gender is given priority. Moreover, as seen before, far from being so overwhelming as to overdetermine her personal experience and trap it in the dynamics of an exclusivist search for lost origins, the recuperation of her multiple attachments allows Lara to overcome her initial sense of alienation in the metropolis. Her deriving metropolitan positionality proves to be imbued with diasporic traits that she has absorbed and re-created in a personal way while combating *unbe-*

longing and that can be fully appreciated if analyzed in the light of Brah's notion of 'diaspora.' As Brah asserts:

> Diaspora should be understood in terms of historically contingent 'genealogies'. [...] Diasporas are also potentially the sites of hope and new beginnings. They are contested cultural and political terrains where individual and collective memories collide, reassemble and reconfigure. (180, 193)

Back in London from the Brazilian rainforest, Lara has acquired a deep self-consciousness and is ready to experience the metropolitan space as a place where sociosymbolic changes may occur. More precisely, as Patricia Murray puts it, the novel's protagonist "Begins to discover, or rather reproduce, her own version of post-colonial London; a new hybrid identity that challenges the inevitability of a divided and racist capital to suggest, instead, a positive diasporic space" (38-46).

Thus, Evaristo contributes to subvert traditional exclusionary representations of London's space which, as a consequence, now comes to be conceptualized as potentially subversive. Moreover, as a result of Lara's renewed location in London, Evaristo's intervention within traditional Western narrative practices entails a willful re-writing of the metropolis's history which, founded on a productive re-inscription of previously silenced voices, paves the way to possible social transformation.

Finally, the unveiling of Lara's mixed cultural background and her inscription within a female genealogy become instrumental to Evaristo's twofold undoing of the illusory fixity of hegemonic identity models. Indeed, Lara's ultimate acceptance of the multiple cultural belongings converging in her identity is not synonymous with an uncritical celebration of a harmonious fusion of cultures to be found in London, as this potential projection is further complicated by the author's attention to the gender nexus which informs power relations and leads Lara to refuse any identification with patriarchal identity patterns.

Evaristo's novel thus proves a complex and articulated intervention in present-day narrative practices intended to re-mould the normative notion of Britishness by deconstructing the presumption that it should be identified exclusively with 'whiteness'. Instrumental to such deconstruction is the renewed image of a cosmopolitan London that the novel offers, if only in partially projective terms. In turn, such projections demonstrate that London, as a consequence, proves not only the product of real life experiences, but also a fictional reality, that is the result of literary practices which actively intervene in the delineation of the national image. More specifically, in McLeod's words:

Postcolonial London does not denote a given place or mark a stable location on a map. It emerges at the intersection of the concrete and the noumenal, between the material conditions of metropolitan life and the imaginative representations made of it. It is as much a product of "facticity" as a creation of the novels, poems and other texts. (8)

Lara, then, as an example of gender as well as (post-)colonial "'theory' located in 'creative' texts" (Ashcroft et al. 2), allows its author to destabilize commonsensical meanings and to deconstruct established forms of consciousness associated to the traditional notion of British identity by critically examining dominant models of hegemony and actively intervening in the mechanisms of representation so as to engender processes of cultural transformation.

Indeed, *Lara* proposes a kind of identity politics through which the metropolitan female mixed race subject, thanks to a productive (although problematic) recuperation, acceptance and reconciliation with the transnational axes of her family past, overcomes her initial contradictory sense of uprooting and starts to positively address her being *both* Black *and* English.

At the very end of the novel, following the acquired self-awareness of her multifaceted Englishness, Lara – who is now conscious that "future means transformation" (139) – projects herself onto London's cosmopolitan space whose gendered and racial mechanisms of socio-political exclusion have been exposed and can be – at least potentially – resisted. Indeed, it is from this space that she lays claim to her right of citizenship in what she assertively calls "*my* island" (140, emphasis added).

In conclusion, Evaristo's novel, while eschewing and opposing exclusivist identity configurations, delineates a 'multi-ethnic-accented' mode of citizenship. However, the latter, although plural, cannot be deemed as vaguely cosmopolitan, being as it is deeply rooted in the English socio-cultural context to which Lara feels to belong. And, in addition, it is also forged out of an inextricable interconnection with the gender axis of positionality. In that sense, Evaristo seems to share Rosi Braidotti's concern when the feminist theorist warns that:

> What is needed, among other things, is a sense of accountability, responsibility and, ultimately, belonging. [...] Being a citizen of the world may appear attractive at first, till one thinks more carefully about the historical exclusion of women form the right of citizenship. (253)

In compliance with the Black feminist project, as formulated by Mirza, who contends that "to valorize our 'different' experience means we have to locate that experience in materiality" (20), Evaristo never loses sight of the contingent racist as well as patriarchal power relations at play in the metropolis, and she also succeeds in representing each structure of subordination as being inscribed within the other.

In reaction to this gender-race nexus of power relations which articulates her subject position, Lara ultimately expresses her sense of belonging to England as a mixed race subject and as a young woman. Thus, the novel contributes to shape a new definition of Englishness which comes to be extended to a female citizen with a family background involving transnational ethnic influences. In fact, it is this mode of citizenship that Lara consciously claims and appropriates, after attempting – not in unproblematic terms – to reconcile her plural cultural belongings.

In this respect, Evaristo's novel can thus be seen as part of a specific change occurring within British cultural practices as highlighted by Lola Young, who mentions "a process of becoming embedded in British culture whilst re-constructing and re-defining what 'British' means" (13). Indeed Evaristo's *Lara* delineates a transnational mode of citizenship that queries the traditional interrelated inscriptions of race and gender which have to be held responsible of the construction of homogenizing female national identities, as suggested by Norma Alarcón, Caren Kaplan and Minoo Moallen, who contend in *Between Woman and Nation* (1999) that "it is through racialization, sexualization, and genderization that the nation is able to transcend modernities and to become a timeless homogenized entity" (7). On the other hand, the transnational motif in *Lara* is not only able to forge – within a context-related arena – new historicized and inclusive identity paradigms, but it is also conversant with a space of agency which, in turn, constructs itself, in line with Black feminist politics, on the elaboration of these new multiple signifiers of the metropolitan female self-hood which necessarily alter the coercive equilibrium of the nation-state.

Works Cited

Alarcón, Norma, Caren Kaplan, and Minoo Moallen. Introduction. *Between Woman and Nation: Nationalism, Transnational Feminism, and the State*. Ed. Norma Alarcón, Caren Kaplan, and Minoo Moallen. Durham: Duke University Press, 1999. 1-16.

Anderson, Benedict. "Imagined Communities." *The Post-Colonial Studies Reader*. Ed. Bill Ashcroft, Gareth Griffiths, and Helen Tiffin. London and New York: Routledge, 2006. 123-25.

Ashcroft, Bill, Gareth Griffiths, and Helen Tiffin. "Feminism". *The Post-Colonial Studies Reader*. Ed. Bill Ashcroft, Gareth Griffiths, and Helen Tiffin. London and New York: Routledge, 2006. 233-234.
Bohemer, Elleke. *Colonial and Postcolonial Literature*. Oxford: Oxford University Press, 2005.
Brah, Avtar. *Cartographies of Diaspora. Contesting Identities*. London and New York: Routledge, 1996.
Braidotti, Rosi. *Nomadic Subjects*. New York: Columbia University Press, 1994.
Ermath, Elizabeth Deeds. *Sequel to History: Postmodernism and the Crisis of Representational Time*. Princeton: Princeton University Press, 1992.
Evaristo, Bernardine. *Lara*. Tunbridge Wells: Angela Royal, 1997.
Lima, Maria Helena. "The Politics of Teaching Black and British". *Black British Writing*. Ed. Victoria Arana and Lauri Ramey. Basingstoke: Palgrave Macmillan, 2004. 47-62.
McLeod, John. *Postcolonial London. Rewriting the Metropolis*. London: Routledge, 2004.
Mirza, Heidi Safia. Introduction. *Black British Feminism*. Ed. Heidi Safia Mirza. London: Routledge, 1997. 1-28.
Murray, Patricia. "Stories Told and Untold: Post-Colonial London in Bernardine Evaristo's *Lara*." *Kunapipi* 21.2 (1999): 38-46.
Nasta, Susheila. Introduction. *Motherlands*. Ed. Susheila Nasta. London: The Women's Press, 1991. xiii-xxx.
Said, Edward. *Culture and Imperialism*. London: Vintage, 1994.Segal, Lynne. *Why Feminism?*. Cambridge: Polity, 1999.
Stein, Mark. *Black British Literature: Novels of Transformation*. Columbus, OH: Ohio State University Press, 2004.
Suleri, Sara. "Woman Skin Deep: Feminisms and the Postcolonial Condition." *Colonial Discourse and Post-colonial Theory*. Ed. Patrick Williams and Laura Chrisman. New York: Columbia University Press, 1994. 244-56.
Toplu, Sebnem. "'Where are you from originally?': Race and Gender in Bernardine Evaristo's *Lara*." *InterCulture*. Dec. 2004. Web. 17 Feb. 2007. http://www.fsu.edu/~proghum/interculture/pdfs/toplu%20race%20and%20gender.pdf
Young, Lola. Foreword. *Write Black, White British*. Ed. Kadija Sesay. Hertford: Hansib, 2005.

CHAPTER SIX

"All the difficult names of who we are": Transnational Identity Politics in Chang-Rae Lee's and Karen Tei Yamashita's Fiction

Kathy-Ann Tan

The rise of new forms of identity politics (in which religious convictions and ethnic affiliations play an ever increasing role) in the last two decades has challenged and reconfigured traditional notions of belonging and citizenship. In efforts to rethink existing definitions of identity in a globalized present, critics have gradually moved away from the notion of "single root identity"[1] (*identité racine unique*, or identity as an exclusive and unique product inherited from one's ancestral roots), putting forth instead that of "rhizome identity" (*identité rhizome*).[2] The latter does not comprise one single root of culture inherited from the individual's past, but posits identity as a process of multiplicity informed by multiple nodes and roots of different cultural encounters that the present still interlaces together.

The age of global mobility has also led to the phenomenon that multiculturalism is no longer the exception but the norm. Every major city in the world

---

[1] See Édouard Glissant's *Poetics of Relation*, especially the chapter titled "Poetics" (23-36).

[2] Glissant draws on the idea of the rhizome that Deleuze and Guattari first posit in *A Thousand Plateaus*. In the latter, Deleuze and Guattari identify six defining characteristics of the rhizome: connection, heterogeneity, multiplicity, signifying rupture, cartography and decalcomania. It is the last two principles that are particularly useful to my conceptualization of a transnational identity politics. The principles of cartography and decalcomania refer to the method of mapping rather than tracing, of being "open and connectable in all of its dimensions, [...] detachable, reversible, susceptible to constant modification" (13), even "reworked by an individual, group, or social formation" (14). Transnational identity politics, I would argue, can be described precisely by such processes of constant interaction between various cultural and sociological forces at the level of the individual, group or social formation which result in the individual's continual process of negotiation with, and adaptation to, her/his environment.

now has its minority groups, and governments spend a percentage of their budgets on integration programs for immigrants young and old. This has led to the much-criticized feel-good multiculturalism that actually glosses over the distinctions between different cultures and is hence a masked form of racism.[3] In a move to adopt a less flawed view of multiculturalism, therefore, the term "transnational" has increasingly been gaining currency to delineate a system of exchanges across the globe where hybridization and diasporic identities are produced and performed without the controlling force of a dominant culture.

Global Mobility and Identity Politics

To come back to an issue already brought forth in the introduction to this collection of essays, how, then, can we define identity politics within the wider framework of a transnational approach to notions of the production and dissemination of culture? I suggest that there are two ways of doing this. The first involves a closer look at the current role of the nation-state and if it still continues to inform notions of identity politics on a global scale. The second entails an examination of the very factors themselves that contribute to cultural production in the contemporary era.[4] Both methods also shed light on the phenomenon of migration and mobility that characterizes the present age.

The debate surrounding the role of the nation-state is currently in a phase of polarization. On the one hand, there are the critics who argue that the nation-state is now in decline, dead, or even, as Kenichi Ohmae, leading

---

[3] Feel-good multiculturalism is best illustrated by the cross-cultural romance depicted in the recent wave of Asian-British films such as *Bend It Like Beckham* (2002) and *Ae Fond Kiss* (2004). In the former, Jesminder, an Indian Sikh girl falls in love with her white Irish football coach and ends up with him against all odds. In the latter, Casim, a Glaswegian DJ of Pakistani Muslim origin also ends up with Roisin, an Irish music teacher in a Catholic school. The film also opens with a sequence in which Casim's younger sister, Tahara, stands up for her Muslim, Pakistani, Glaswegian identity, as well as her right to support the Glasgow Rangers. See Ellen Dengel-Janic and Lars Eckstein's discussion. Rajeev Balasubramanyam strongly insists that multiculturalism is a form of propoganda and that multiculturalist propoganda is used as a means of social control in Britain.

[4] Linnea Marie Hasegawa aptly summarizes the relationship between literacy and cultural production in her unpublished dissertation, "Articulating Identities: Rhetorical Readings of Asian American Literacy Narratives." She argues, "[b]ecause literacy is not just about the ability to read and write, but about who can participate in cultural production and nation-building, literacy—as a way of gaining legitimacy or access to social and political power—becomes even more essential (and problematic) for those who are denied access on the basis of gender, race, national origin, class, etc" (2004, 4).

spokesperson for this camp, claims, "altogether irrelevant" (91).⁵ That is, in a world of increasing acceleration of the speed at which people, goods and information traverse the globe, where communication is nearly instantaneous, national borders and barricades have now become obsolete. Similarly, Susan Stanford Friedman, in her article "Migrants, Diasporas, and Borders," argues for a paradigm shift from nation-based models of identity politics to transnational models emphasizing the global space of ongoing travel and transcontinental connection" (906). On the other hand, there are critics who argue that identity politics is still inescapably entwined with notions of citizenship and the nation-state. Frans Schuurman, for example, argues that "the nation-state as the locus of an emancipatory struggle and as the frame of reference for the construction of a collective identity is still important (and will remain so for the time being)" (75). Indeed, despite increasing emphasis on concepts of global governance, individuals are still identified by means of documents like passports that indicate one's place of birth, nationality, and citizenship. Even in supra-governmental structures like the European Union, only slightly over half of the population identify themselves as European alongside their national identities, signifying allegiance first and foremost to the nation-state.⁶

One way of escaping this dualism is to regard both extreme viewpoints as ends of a continuum in which, at any one time, an individual can inhabit a variety of positions along that scale. It is here that Pierre Bourdieu's famous notion of the "habitus"⁷ (introduced by Marcel Mauss as early as 1934) is useful in thinking about the criteria according to which one is located in this continuum. Commonly defined as a system of "dispositions" embodied by the individual agent in response to the determining structures of class, family, educational background, as well as other external socio-political conditions,

---

⁵ See also Kenichi Ohmae's *The End of the Nation State* (1996).

⁶ The website for the Public Opinion Analysis sector of the European Commission carries out Eurobarometer surveys which address major topics concerning European citizenship. In a survey from 2004, 58% of respondents were likely to identify themselves as being European alongside their national identities. There were discrepancies between individual countries too; Luxembourg proved to be the country where the most number of citizens were willing to describe themselves as European (78% of the population), whereas the British were least likely to do so (40% of the population). The Eurobarometer surveys can be found at:
http://ec.europa.eu/public_opinion/index_en.htm.

⁷ Bourdieu's much-debated concept of habitus is originally defined in *Outline of a Theory of Practice* (1972) as a "system of durable, transposable dispositions, structured structures [...] which generate and organize practices and representations that can be objectively adapted to their outcomes without presupposing a conscious aiming at ends."

Bourdieu's "habitus" implies that identity is a series of dispositions that might be ultimately less a political than a cultural phenomenon, although the fields of politics and culture should not, and cannot, be wholly separated. This would certainly tie in with the resurgence, in the last two decades, of interest in cultural studies and its integration into a transdisciplinary mode of literary analysis, one that borrows from sociological and anthropological fields of research, among others.

If one accepts that the central thrust of transnational identity politics in an age of globalization is therefore positing identity as a series of dispositions that are informed by ways of cultural production, then the quest for accruing and acquiring cultural, social and symbolic capital (Bourdieu) is one that is reflected back on the transnational individual's attempts to accumulate cultural, social and symbolic knowledge because it confers power, status, but most importantly, because it renders the possibility of global mobility itself, as well as recognition of one's acceptance as a member of the transnational community. Moreover, new forms of identity politics can only come into being when there are enough individuals who regard these as worthy of equal status and recognition on a global platform. New forms of identity politics can also only come to fruition if older, established binaries are collapsed and replaced with new terminologies signaling the importance of dynamic exchange and reciprocity across the globe.

Instead of demarcating the binaries of the "global" and the "local," for example, it has become customary to speak of a "glocal" (Robertson) imaginary that participates in acts of border-crossing. The notion of hyphenated identity[8] (which demarcates two primary cultural affiliations) as appropriated, though heavily debated, by minority groups in the United States, has also been replaced by that of the diasporic citizen, which partakes in "complex strategies of cultural identification" (Bhabha 292) which can never be reduced to a mere distinction between the home and the host cultures. In a similar vein, critical discourse has increasingly moved away from speaking of a politics of globalization, toward a professedly more dynamic, less Eurocentric and universalist, transnational approach, which proffers "a space of exchange and participation wherever processes of hybridization occur and where it is still possible for cultures to be produced and performed without necessary mediation by the center" (Lionnet and Shih 5). Migration and mobility have become the key slogans of a new, liberatory identity politics, in an era where the self is acknowledged to be

---

[8] The term "hyphenated," incidentally, was first used in a derogatory sense as early as 1890, and obtained currency in president Theodore Roosevelt's speeches during the World War I, most commonly in reference to German American and Irish American citizens whose political allegiances were most commonly called into question.

less an assembled product than a dynamic process that includes both continuity and discontinuity (Stuart Hall).

If this is the current consensus on identity politics in a time of global mobility, however, then why are authors like Chang-Rae Lee and Karen Tei Yamashita still categorized and read as Asian American writers? Why, despite the commonly used term "global citizen," do we still shy away from using that of "global writer," or, indeed, that of "global reader"? Is this indicative of a fear of generalizations and universalizations, or a rather stubborn, even neo-conservative, preference for retaining those labels that indicate our roots, the places of our birth and the countries we subsequently call "home"? In order to disentangle some of these issues, it is necessary to scrutinize the very definitions of self and belonging that remain central to our negotiations of identity politics.

In the following, I will attempt to do this via an examination of two novels by diasporic writers – Chang-Rae Lee's *Native Speaker* (1995) and Karen Tei Yamashita's *Tropic of Orange* (1997) –, focusing on the extent to which the construction of a transnational identity politics in these novels critiques and refashions current assumptions of the field.[9]

Chang-Rae Lee's *Native Speaker*

Narrated in the first person, Chang-Rae Lee's first novel, *Native Speaker*, tells the story of Henry Park, a second-generation Korean American who, after experiencing the death of his seven-year old son and the departure of his wife Lelia (a New Englander of Scottish descent), suffers increasing bouts of identity crisis. He works as a spy for a detective agency, "Glimmer and Associates," whose immigrant, multilingual employees offers its clients "ethnic coverage." Henry is assigned the task of spying on John Kwang, an ambitious first-generation city councilman, and ends up working as a volunteer in Kwang's political campaign. Kwang's career, however, starts to take a dip at the height of the Black/Korean conflicts raging across New York City. With multiple boycotts, fires, vandalism, crowds of chanting blacks opposing heavily armed Koreans, Kwang finds himself in a stalemate where he cannot publicly

---

[9] I hasten to add a disclaimer at this point. While exploring how the female/mother narratives in both novels represent a force that destabilizes the masculine idea of "border" might be most fitting in line with the overarching scope of this collection of essays because it adds a new dimension to existing perspectives of transnational feminism, this shall not be the object of inquiry in this essay as existing criticism has already focused on this topic. See, for example, Florence Hsiao-ching Li's article.

express his sympathy for either side. When a Korean storeowner shoots and kills a black man, black groups hold demonstrations that break out in violence and destruction. Then one of the other volunteers, a dedicated Spanish student named Eduardo Fermin, is accidentally killed in Kwang's office due to a fire, and investigations reveal that it was a case of arson commissioned by Kwang himself because he had found out that Eduardo was a spy. Kwang never finds out Henry's "real" identity, however, and Henry, who increasingly comes to like and admire Kwang, ends up turning in evidence of Kwang's *ggeh*, or Korean money club, and Kwang's career ends up in shambles. The lack of a unified narrative voice in the novel is pertinent; the text shifts from passages of lyrical self-reflection and recollection to terse, clipped speech in the vein of a spy-detective, noir thriller.

It is tempting to interpret *Native Speaker*'s central motif of espionage as a fitting metaphor for the Asian American immigrant's tendency to observe quietly instead of partaking in the action, for the feeling of being an outsider on the fringes of society looking in, longing for a sense of belonging. However, as Sur-yon Kim adroitly points out, *Native Speaker* has often been misread by critics who conclude that the protagonist is an Asian American seeking to assimilate himself into American society, and therefore that the novel seeks to accurately portray the Korean American immigrant experience. Instead, Kim sees the novel as a *Bildungsroman* that narrates the story of Henry Park, his quest for identity and his struggle to define himself. Placing emphasis on the subplot of the novel, which follows the story of the subject Henry is sent to spy on, first-generation Korean American city councilman John Kwang, and the demise of his political career, as well as Henry's reconfiguration of his own identity in relation to that of Kwang's, Kim argues that Lee "is writing the story of every person caught up in a web of politics that try to define culture and enforces to culturally delineate an individual according to such political rules" (n.p.).

I would agree with Kim's interpretation of the novel, and argue that Lee does not seek to accurately portray the Asian American experience as a whole, because there is no single unified or generic story that can be portrayed or recorded in the first place. Instead, stories exist in the plural, and even the task of accurately depicting a life is called into question in the novel. This is illustrated in the task that accompanies each of Henry Park's assignments – to write a report on the person to whom he is assigned:

> Typically the subject was a well-to-do immigrant supporting some potential insurgency in his old land, or else funding a fledgling trade union or radical student organization. Some-

times he was simply an agitator. Maybe a writer of conscience. An expatriate artist.

We worked by contriving intricate and open-ended emotional conspiracies. We became acquaintances, casual friends. Sometimes lovers. [...]

Then we wrote the tract of their live*s*, remote, unauthorized biograph*ies*.

I the most prodigal and mundane of historians.

(18, emphasis added)

Unable to speak of, or come to terms with, his childhood past and his rigid Korean upbringing ("[o]ur mode at the firm was always to resist history, at least our own" (28)), Henry externalizes his need to reconstruct his own past, the "tract of [his own] life" by casting himself in the role of historian in order to write other people's histories and biographies. These biographies are placed neatly in juxtaposition to the "chosen narratives" or "legends" that Henry and the other private detectives create for themselves in their assumption of an alter-ego for their task:

The legend was something each of us wrote out in preparation for any assignment. It was an extraordinarily extensive "story" of who we were, an autobiography as such, often evolving to develop even the minutiae of life experience, countless facts and figures, though it also required a certain truthful ontological bearing, a certain presence of character.
(22)

The irony of the situation, of course, is that Henry himself does not possess the "certain truthful ontological bearing" and "certain presence of character" that are pre-requisites to writing the legend, at least not during the period that he works with "Glimmer and Associates." It is even arguable if Henry attains this by the end of the novel, when he has wrapped up his assignment and reconciled himself with his wife, working as her speech therapy assistant.

To come back to Bourdieu's notion of the "habitus" and my extrapolation of this concept in the form of identity as a series of dispositions that are informed by transnational modes of cultural production, one could perhaps read *Native Speaker* as a novel that illustrates this very notion. In producing reports on well-to-do immigrants whose personal and political integrity are questionable, "Glimmer and Associates" cater to their clients who are largely "multinational corporations, bureaus of foreign governments, individuals of resource and connection" (18). As Henry explains, "We provided them with information about people working against their vested interests. We generated background studies, psychological assessments, daily chronologies, myriad facts and extrapolations. These in extensive reports" (ibid.).

One could read the reports as a literal manifestation of transnational cultural production, and interestingly, it is through the act of putting together a primer on John Kwang that Henry gradually confronts his own identity as a second-generation Korean American in the light of his strict Korean upbringing.

Performing Serial Identity

Perhaps the most unique aspect of *Native Speaker* is the way in which it incorporates the archetypal quest for identity and self-knowledge into the narrative framework of a spy/detective story. Early on in the novel, Henry says to the reader, "[o]ur work is but a string of serial identity" (33). The term "serial identity" is used to denote literally, a series of identity, such that an individual's identity at any given point in time is traceable or associable to his/her identity in a prior appearance in the past. The phrase "serial identity
theft," of course, is more commonly used to denote the practice of adopting multiple false identities, and is fitting in line with the detective story elements of *Native Speaker*. Each time Henry Park is assigned a subject to spy on, he must not only adopt an alter-ego and thus enact a form of "serial identity theft," but the "legends" or detailed fictional autobiographies of each alter-ego he impersonates are themselves versions traceable or associable with the 'real' person he is – he might use his own name, for example, or disclose information about his wife or dead son.

The performative aspect of identity, as theorized by Judith Butler among others, is also a central theme in the novel. Henry's emotional reticence, his ability to hide behind a mask and thus perform a role, which is precisely what his job as a spy requires him to do, is closely linked to his strict Korean upbringing. His mother, for example, "believed that displays of emotion signaled a certain failure between people" (31) and to his father, a Confucian of high order, "the world [...] operated on a determined set of procedures, certain rule of engagement" (47). Henry's own mixed feeling of disillusionment yet acceptance with the inheritance of his legacy, his upbringing, is signaled in his ruminations about the centrality of the family in a traditional Korean context:

> I know all about that fine and terrible ordering, how it variously casts you as the golden child, the slave-son or daughter, the venerable father, the long-dead god. But I know, too, of the basic comfort in this familial precision,

> where the relation abides no argument, no questions or qua-
> rrels. (6-7)

The adherence to performative gender roles and the venerability of the patriarch in Korean culture and Confucian thought is thus unquestioned, even for second-generation immigrants.[10]

Even Henry's mother partakes obediently in this reification of patriarchal values. In an incident in Henry's childhood, his mother chides him for asking his father about his grocery store:

> "Don't shame him! Your father is very proud. You don't
> know this, but he graduated from the best college in Korea,
> the very top, and he doesn't need to talk about selling fruits
> and vegetables. It's below him. He only does it for you,
> Byong-ho, he does everything for you. Now go and keep him
> company."(56)

Henry's mother's insistence that Henry, as a dutiful Korean son, should respect his father's rank and position and not embarrass him by asking him about a job that is beneath him reflects, as Tim Engles has pointed out, the Korean concept of *nunchi* (42). Literally translated as "eye measure," *nunchi* refers to the heightened sensitivity developed by individuals of a society to the discernment of rank and class, which subsequently determines the markers of recognized social status in conversation. As such, *nunchi* is therefore a cultivated skill that is vital for effective inter-personal communication in Korean "high context culture."[11]

Another example from the novel serves to illustrate this concept of *nunchi*. Ahjuma, a woman brought over from Korea to look after, cook and clean for Henry and his father when Henry's mother passes away, is regarded by Henry's wife Lelia as a cryptic mystery, a woman whose exterior and facial expressions are as inscrutable as her own husband's. When she learns that Henry does not know Ahjuma's real name, Lelia is shocked, and even more so to learn that it is not a matter of great concern to Henry:

> It was the truth. Lelia had great trouble accepting this stun-
> ning ignorance of mine. That summer, when it seemed she
> was thinking about it, she would stare in wonderment at me

---

[10] For an informative study on the patriarchal system in Korea, how it is changing in the twenty-first century and how family politics is being realigned as a result, see Boo Jin Park.

[11] Cf. Edward T. Hall's *Beyond Culture* (1976). The term "high context culture" refers to a (more often than not, Eastern) culture's tendency to cater toward small close-knit groups that celebrate the group over the individual, maintaining and fostering a strong sense of tradition and history.

> as if I had a gaping hole blown though my head. I couldn't blame her. Americans live on a first-name basis. She didn't understand that there weren't moments in our language – the rigorous, regimental one of family and servants – when the woman's name could have naturally come out. Or why it wasn't important. At breakfast and lunch and dinner my father and I called her "Ah-juh-ma," literally aunt, but more akin to "ma'am," the customary address to an unrelated Korean woman. But in our context the title bore much less deference. I never heard my father speak her name in all the years she was with us. (68-69)

This passage signals the great and irreconcilable cultural divide between Henry's Korean and Lelia's American upbringing. While Henry regards "Ahjuhma" as a polite form of address and does not pry into the nature of her relationship with his father, Lelia wants to know more about the woman, is not satisfied until she confronts her one day in the laundry room and even constructs a story for her and her journey to the United States.

In its depiction of Henry and Lelia's heated disagreement about Ahjuhma, *Native Speaker* is, I would argue, a novel that does not fall into the trap of a feel-good multiculturalism. The cultural divide between them is not eliminated in the archetypal plot of a cross-cultural romance plot and throughout the novel the reader is reminded that Lelia leaves Henry because of her inability to understand, and put up with, his emotional reticence any longer. The lack of feel-good multiculturalism in the novel is also represented by the circumstances that lead to the death of Henry's seven-year old son, Mitt, in a playground accident (a dog pile) gone horribly wrong. The incident is foreshadowed by incidents of racial abuse Mitt suffers in the suburban American neighborhood:

> One afternoon Mitt tugged at my pant leg and called me innocently, in succession, a chink, a jap, a gook. I couldn't immediately respond and so he said them again, this time adding, in singsong, "Charlie Chan, face as flat as a pan" [...] One day Mitt came home with his clothes soiled and said that they had pushed him down to the ground and put dirt in his mouth. Lelia, who up to now had been liberal and assured, started shrieking angrily about *suburbia, America, the brand of culture we had to live in*, and packed Mitt up the stairs to scrub his muddy face, telling him all the while how wonderful he was. (96, emphasis added)

Lelia's misgivings about surburbia, America and the brand of culture in which her family has to live, reflect the ethnic and political tensions in New York

City. De Roos, the Democrat mayor of the city, a "careerist, a consummate professional [... who] knew how the game should be run against an ethnic challenger: marginalize him, isolate him, acknowledge his passion but color it radical, name it zealotry" (36), does little to alleviate matters. In the face of increasing Black/Korean tension, he tries to play off one ethnic group against the other, whereas John Kwang's attitude is different because he actually describes in detail and does not attempt to play down the mistrust that each group has of the other.

Kwang's strategy of securing the ethnic vote is reflected in his strategies in dealing with the electorate. His assistants are taught phrases like "hello," "goodbye" and "please wait a moment" in Korean in order to properly greet the large numbers of Korean constituents who come to the Flushing office. Soon, it is not only the Koreans and most of the Chinese who vote for Kwang, but Southeast Asians and Indians, Central Americans, blacks from the Caribbean and West Indies and Eastern Europeans:

> He [Kwang] gave cash bonuses for the top five people registering the most voters each month, bonuses for pledged future votes, bonuses for signing up immigrants for naturalization. It was like a church drive but at all hours, the whole body of us spread through the district [...] This his daily order: do the good duty, go out into the street, go into the stores, stop them in the alleyways. Just get in a word. In ten different languages you say *Kwang is like you. You will be an American.* You have a flyer with his fine picture and his life story beneath. Show them that. If you tell them the story of their lives they will listen. (143, original emphasis)

However, playing the ethnic card is not always the easiest thing to do. When Black/Korean tensions start escalating in the city, Kwang confesses to Henry over dinner one evening:

> The NAACP [National Association for the Advancement of Colored People] has invited me to certain forums but I feel token there. Everybody is hesitant, cautious. They study me carefully. I can see they're not sure if I'll promote an agenda that suits them. I can support social programs, school lunches, homeless housing, free clinics, but if I mention the first thing about special enterprise zones or more openness toward immigrants I'm suddenly off limits. Or worse, I'm whitey's boy. (194-95)

This passage clearly shows that, despite its changing ethnic demographics, New York City remains home to deep-seated racial prejudice and xenophobia.

Despite the fact that Kwang supports several political initiatives at grassroots level to support the fostering of bilingual education in the form of tax vouchers and the subsidy of native language study outside of schools, and earns recognition among the largely immigrant electorate for doing so, the ingrained mistrust that minority groups have of politicians comes to the fore in a series of incidents that leave Kwang's personal life and political career in shambles.

Kwang himself remains, in the vein of a spy-detective novel, a mysterious figure. His ineffability is reflected in a passage in the middle of the novel, where Henry even speaks of him as a "necessary invention" (140):

> I do not know the first or last iota of him. [...] I know only that I will never see him again, and that anything I can say or offer by way of his present life might well be taken as reductive and suspect. [...] The fact is I had him in my sights. I believed I had a grasp of his identity, not only the many things he was to the public and to his family and to his staff and to me, but who he was to himself, the man he beheld in his most private mirror. (ibid.)

As time goes on, Kwang begins to lose his grip on his job and his private life, as rumors are spread about his excessive use of street money and underage volunteers. He begins drinking heavily and indulges in sexual liaisons with Sherrie Chin-Watt, his PR secretary, a second-generation Chinese American and Berkeley Law graduate. When he is finally caught in a car accident with an underage hostess at an exclusive drinking establishment that he frequents, Kwang's career is effectively over. He then goes into hiding after the accident, and a part of Henry feels a sense of relief at his disappearance. What Henry fears, interestingly, is seeing the "expression of self-loss and self-doubt on a face that [he has] known as almost unblemished, resolute" (328) should Kwang ever resurface. As he admits to himself, "I am here for the hope of his identity, which may also be mine" (ibid.) Kwang's reputation is irreversibly destroyed, however, when many of the members of his *ggeh* are revealed to be illegal immigrants, as is the underage Korean hostess with whom he is found in the car.

Significantly, Henry narrates the story of Kwang's downfall in retrospect and describes it as the falling away of a series of masks:

> Through events both arbitrary and conceived it so happened that one of his faces fell away, and then another, and another, until he revealed to me a final level that would not strip off. The last mask. And what I saw in him I had not thought to see, but will search out now for the remainder of my days. (141)

Interestingly, although Kwang's masks are stripped away one by one, it does not make Henry's task of writing his report on Kwang any easier. On the contrary, Henry realizes that he cannot write the primer on Kwang that his boss is expecting, a realization that also triggers the turning point in Henry's own quest for identity:

> But one night last week, after a full day of escorting him to district meetings and fundraisers, I realized that Kwang presented a profound problem for me. I couldn't write the usual about him. [...] I could not picture him. [...] Certainly, a strange thing is happening. My recollection and sight are focusing elsewhere now. I am seeing a different story. [...] The teller, I know, can keep his face in the shadows only so long. We want him to come out, step into the light, bare himself. (204)

This is also the moment when Henry realizes that his entire life has been formed of "necessary fictions" (206). At this point in the novel, the relationship between John Kwang and Henry Park is at its most complex, and also at its most porous. They seem to understand each other, yet in a way that allows for the fact that they might never cross paths with one another again.

When Kwang invites Henry to dinner one evening after a long day's work, for example, Henry begins talking about his father. He does not go into detail, nor does he have to explain anything, for Kwang seems to understand his background immediately:

> I didn't have to tell John Kwang the first thing about my father and our life [...] Simply, it felt good not having to explain any further. To others you need to explain so much to get across anything worthwhile. It's not like a flavor that you can offer and have someone simply taste. The problem, you realize, is that while you have been raised to speak quietly and little, the notions of where you come from and who you are need a maximal approach. (182)

The Korean way of raising a child "to speak quietly and little" is something both Kwang and Henry share first-hand experience of. In a parallel to Henry's ineffability (literally, an incapability of being expressed in words) and hence his reticent and coded Henryspeak, there is something as indescribably strange about Kwang's speech that Henry cannot pin down. To Henry, Kwang's accent is almost impeccably American, revealing no trace of his Korean roots, and Henry cannot help but feel at one point that "although I had seen hours of him on videotape, there was something that I still couldn't abide in his speech. I couldn't help but think there was a mysterious dubbing going on" (179). The last image interestingly signals the performance of identity not only on a physical, but also on a linguistic, level. Kwang is, unlike Henry, a non-native speaker of English. His American accent, therefore, has been acquired, learned and practiced to the point of perfection such that his speeches sway not only the Korean and East Asians but also the Spanish and Mexican voters. In an interesting parallel, language acquisition to the point of native speaker standards is also something that Henry's wife, Lelia, is engaged in.

Articulating Identity

Henry Park's wife, Lelia, works as a speech therapist for children. The children she sees have various articulation problems due to physiological defects or learning disabilities. The ones that Henry develops a particular affinity for, however, are the non-native speakers who "came to her because they had entered the first grade speaking a home language other than English" (2). These are the ones that Lelia helps the entire day to "manipulate their tongues and their lips and their exhaling breath, guiding them through the difficult language" (ibid.).

Ironically, although Lelia spends her time teaching her young patients how to speak her native language accurately, she is unable to voice her criticisms of Henry by speaking to him, writing him a parting letter instead in the form of a much-deliberated list of who he is in her opinion. The list reads,

[Y]ou are surreptitious
B+ student of life
first thing hummer of Wagner and Strauss
illegal alien
emotional alien
genre bug
Yellow peril: neo-American
great in bed
overrated
poppa's boy
sentimentalist
anti-romantic
_____ analyst (you fill in)
stranger
follower
traitor
spy (5)

Upon cleaning out the bedroom, Henry finds another scrap of paper under the bed on which is written in Lelia's handwriting, "False speaker of language." He deciphers the list as a series of "idioms, visions of (him) in the whitest raw light, instant snapshots of the difficult truths native to our time together" (1). He proceeds to destroy the original list, "prefer[ing] versions of things, copies that aren't so precious" (4). Henry, likewise, cannot tell Lelia the details of his job, and resorts to elliptical and cryptic replies that Lelia exasperatedly terms "Henryspeak" (6).

The novel's recurring motif of lists manifests itself again in the Kwang subplot of the novel. The personal and biographical information of every voter and potential voter is kept in a series of folders, an electronic database, in Kwang's office. As Henry recounts,

> [w]ith this body of files we could sift and sort through the population of the district by gender, race, ethnicity, party affiliation, occupation. We had names and birthdates of their children and relatives. Data on weekly income, what they paid in rent, in utilities, if they were on public assistance, how long. If they had been victims of crime. Their houses of worship. The languages they spoke, in rank of proficiency.
> The list always growing, profligate. Almost biblical. (177)

Every Friday, Kwang would take a list of entries home to memorize by heart. Drawing a clear parallel with Henry's own tendency to commit everything to memory that he sees and reads, Kwang's memorizing is described as "more a discipline for him, like a serious craft or martial art, a chosen kind of suffering involving hours of practice and concentration by which you gradually came to know yourself." (177) This early episode in the novel is paralleled with another, more sinister one, toward the end of the novel, when Henry finds out that Kwang is running a clandestine *ggeh* whose members are largely illegal immigrants. When Henry is given the task of coordinating and accepting money from the various members of the illegal *ggeh*, he describes:

> I do the same thing every night. I enter the giving in vertical rows. [...] I have steadily become a compiler of lives. I am writing a new book of the land.
>
> Like John Kwang, I am remembering every last piece of them. Whether I wish it or not, I possess them, their spouses and children, their jobs and money and life. And the more I see and remember the more their story is the same. The story is mine. [...] I work so hard that one day I end up forgetting the person I am. (279)

The way Henry commits each entry into his memory ("my memory is fantastic, near diabolic. It arrests whatever appears before my eyes. I don't memorize anymore. I simply see" [178]) and the merging of all the different stories and backgrounds of the illegal immigrants together in a mirroring of Henry's own life brings him a step closer to his final act of selfrealization.

Ironically, it is a final act of betrayal (Henry's betrayal of Kwang's trust and his turning over of the financial sheets of the *ggeh*, which have not been declared to the tax authorities) that brings about Henry's final moment of self-awakening. "In every very act of betrayal dwells a self-betrayal, which brings you that much closer to a reckoning," Henry thinks (314). At the end of the novel, the story has come full-circle. As Henry hands over the incriminating evidence of Kwang's illegal money club, he realizes that he has done exactly what his father had done all those years ago: "My ugly immigrant's truth, as was his, is that I have exploited my own, and those others who can be exploited. This forever is my burden to bear" (319-20). The burden that Henry ends up having to bear is much larger than he first imagines. When the INS (Immigration and Naturalization Service) reveal that they have
rounded up all the suspected illegal immigrants and their families at their residences, with the intention of deporting most of these people, Henry realizes that his father may be one of them. The end of the novel sees Henry reconciled with his wife Lelia, and working as her assistant when she tours round summer schools teaching English as a Foreign Language to children. Henry is ironically now the "Speech Monster," donning a green rubber hood and gobbling up kids when they do not speak but cowering when they repeat the phrase of the day and articulate it correctly.

Ultimately, *Native Speaker* demonstrates the difficult, yet necessary, process of articulating a viable transnational identity politics, for it is only in doing so that the Asian American immigrant is able to critique the ways in which the dominant culture constructs him/her as the Other. Or as Linnea Marie Hasegawa argues, this is a strategy which allows the Asian American writer to "discursively (re)construct the self and make claims for alternative spaces in which to articulate their identities and to interrogate narratives that have placed them outside of the nation" (14). As Henry Park himself says in a passage that addresses the reader directly,

> [b]ut I and my kind possess another dimension. We will learn every lesion of accent and idiom. [...] We are your most perilous and dutiful brethren, the song of our hearts at once furious and sad. For only you could grant me those lyrical modes. I call them back to you. (320)

Karen Tei Yamashita's *Tropic of Orange*

"Standing on the map of my political desires/ I toast to a borderless future." So begins one of the epigraphs to Karen Tei Yamashita's third novel *Tropic of Orange*. The lines are a quote from fellow writer and social activist Guillermo Gomez-Pena's poem, "Freefalling Toward a Borderless Future" (from *The New World Border*), and indicate at the very outset the themes of border-crossing and biopolitics (in Agamben's sense of the term in *Homo Sacer*) in a globalized era where low and high culture come together and hip-hop coexists with classical music. In the novel, borders are continuously shifted, crossed, broken down and redrawn. Using elements of magical realism, news speak, film noir, hip hop and Chicano culture, *Tropic of Orange* explores issues of global migration, the exploitation of immigrant labor and corporate multiculturalism, and transnational identity, all set against the seemingly borderless sprawl of Los Angeles (a "techno-industrial mega-metropolis of migrating people," in Yamashita's own words [Glixman, n. p.]) and New Mexico.

Tropic of Orange represents a timely call to revise and challenge assumptions about identity politics. Its examination of border culture and border transgression is enacted within a narrative mode which itself blurs the boundary between the fantastical and the real. By extrapolation, I would argue, Yamashita's novel should also be read not solely within the context of Asian American literature, as has been largely the case so far, but within a wider framework of border and social theory. More specifically, the construction of a transnational identity politics in this novel also critiques and posits a viable alternative discourse to the feel-good multiculturalism that has pervaded much contemporary literature.

The plot of the novel is as follows: An orange falls to the ground in the garden of a ranch house in Mazatlán, Mexico owned by Gabriel Balboa, a Mexican-American reporter for a big L.A.-based newspaper. The magical orange, through which the Tropic of Cancer passes in the form of a thin silvery thread that stretches "farther in both directions, east and west, east across the highway and west toward the ocean and beyond" (12), is picked up by a mysterious old man (Arcangel) who carries it northward to the U.S. border, literally dragging the Tropic of Cancer with it. The stretching northward of the latter anticipates a new cartography of borders and geographical boundaries (Li, 152).

As Rafaela Cortes, the Mexican caretaker of Gabriel's ranch house, and her son Sol, follow Arcangel and the magical orange, strange things start to happen as the gradual spatial displacement of the Tropic of Cancer leads to time-space compression in the space between Mazatlán and Los Angeles. Streets bend and stretch, and oranges are quarantined for fear of being poisonous, hence multiplying their value on the black market. In the midst of the apocalyptic frenzy, Gabriel's girlfriend Emi, a Japanese American television reporter who is "so distant from the Asian female stereotype – it was questionable if she even had an identity" (19), rushes around trying to cover the events live. One of the news stories features Manzanar Murakami, a homeless issei (first-generation Japanese) immigrant and former heart surgeon, who spends his days on the overpass of the downtown Harbor Freeway orchestrally conducting the traffic to symphonies he hears only inside his own head. Others include live coverage of a tanker truck collision and the spillage of thousands of gallons of fuel, and the taking over of cars and buses by the homeless, who make squatter-style homes out of these vehicles. Two more characters make up the plot. There is Buzzworm, a "Big Black seven-foot dude, Vietnam vet, an Afro shirt with palm trees painted all over it, dreds, pager and Walkman belted to his waist, sound plugged into one ear and two or three watches at least on both his wrists" (27), who becomes Gabriel's street-wise informant during the apocalyptic chaos Los Angeles finds itself in. Then there is Bobby Ngu, Rafaela's boyfriend and Sol's father, a "Chinese from Singapore with a Vietnamese name speaking like a Mexican living in Koreatown" (15), who also finds himself caught up in the apocalyptic frenzy on a mission to find his wife and son.

Content vs. Hypercontexts

The apocalyptic chaos of the novel's plot finds its counterpart, however, in the order of the novel's intricate formal structure. One "Table of Contents" works in a more traditional linear mode of reading whereas the second forces the reader to read "hypercontextually," which results in a series of possible permutations as to the actual sequence of how the chapters are read. If one reads the novel in temporal sequence, for example, one would read the chapters in the "correct" numerical order, i.e. one to forty-nine, as depicted in the first illustration. However, if one were to follow the grid in the second illustration, with the days of the week running horizontally and the seven characters of the novel running vertically along the margins of the grid, then the resulting reading process(es) would be very different indeed. If one were to read "hypercontextually," then, and piece together Rafaela Cortes' story first, one would end up with the following sequence of chapters: one, ten, eighteen, twenty-four, thirty, thirty-eight, forty-five. Alternatively, if one decided to read all the chapters that have Mexico as a setting first, then the sequence would read: one, ten, twenty-four, thirty-eight, thirty-two, seven, eleven, twenty-one, twenty-three. This playful offering of different possible combinations of reading the novel indicate not only the postmodern element of the text, but also represents the potential for subverting any one authoritative interpretation of the text.

The novel is thus split into forty-nine chapters, each assigned to one of the seven days of the week. Each day of the week ends up with seven chapters, narrated from the point of view of the novel's seven protagonists who are either living in or traveling en route to Los Angeles. Accordingly, the character's intertwined stories take place over the course of a week, simultaneously in locations from Mazatlan to Los Angeles. However, the order of the novel's formal structure does not simply hold in the plot's chaos. Or, as Johannes Hauser has accurately observed, "chaos and order in the text are not simply opposite poles" (2006, 4). Rather, they should be seen as "parts of the representation of a reality which challenges the reader with a specific aesthetic simultaneously shedding light on the ruptures and coherences of global migration and economics" (ibid.).

"Soft" Borders, Ethnic Nostalgia and Feel - Good Multiculturalism

In comparison to Henry Park, the male protagonist of Chang-Rae Lee's *Native Speaker*, and his attempts to shed the vestiges of his unhappy childhood and strict Korean upbringing, Gabriel Balboa's nostalgic efforts to return to the past are encapsulated in his passion for old-fashioned notebooks, film noir, and his vintage car, as well as his spontaneous decision to buy a house in Mazatlán, Mexico, where his grandmother used to live (an act which signifies the acquiring of cultural capital because Mazatlán is, for him, a space endowed with cultural memory). Gabriel's comic efforts of bringing trees that flourish in a Californian climate to Mazatlán, only to see them die, reflects the futility of his attempts to carve out an imagined, and utopian, space for himself, a space imbued with exoticism, in line with his "erotic tastes of chili pepper and salty breezes" (5).

Yamashita's satirical account of Gabriel Balboa's displays of ethnic nostalgia are matched by the instances in the novel which critique the element of feel-good multiculturalism rampant in large metropolises such as Los Angeles. At one point in the novel, Emi says to Gabriel while they are eating in a sushi bar, "Cultural diversity is bullshit [...] It's a white guy wearing a Nirvana T-shirt and dreds. That's cultural diversity. [...] I hate being multicultural" (128). When the white woman sitting next to her, dressed in a silk blouse, wearing handcrafted silver and with two ornately-lacquered chopsticks holding her hair together, patronizingly swivels around to berate Emi, declaring,

> I happen to adore the Japanese culture [...] I adore different
> cultures. [...] I love living in L.A. because I can find any-

thing in the world to eat, right here. It's such a meeting place for all sorts of people. A true celebration of an international world. It just makes me sick to hear people speak so cynically about something so positive and to make assumptions about people based on their color (129)

Emi asks the waiter for two forks, then asks her neighbor, holding the forks out, "Would you consider using these in your hair? Or would you consider that... unsanitary?" (ibid.)

Tropic of Orange is full of little gems like the passage above. Collectively, these episodes reflect the author's critique of feel-good multiculturalism and ethnic nostalgia.[12] This is a part of Yamashita's larger overarching project of critiquing the dominant assumptions and discourses of border studies via the genre of fiction. Rather than presenting a summary or tracing the development of border theory over the last two decades, I would like to comment on the current state of affairs, which I see as a neoconservative return, especially in the light of 9/11, to rethinking and redefining the notion of the "border" in border studies. Or, as Johnson and Michaelson put it in the introduction to their anthology, *Border Theory*, "the 'border' in border studies remains the problem" (15). The problem, as I see it, is that the critic has to take into account not only the geographical and political borders that map or demarcate the end of one particular territory and the beginning of another, but also the "soft borders" that are nowadays "produced within broadly liberal discourse: benevolent nationalisms, cultural essentialisms, multiculturalisms, and the like – in short, [by] the state of 'border studies' [itself]" (ibid., 1).

Tropic of Orange avoids the trap of these "soft borders" by producing not a feel-good multiculturalism, but by critiquing it through the voices and thoughts of Emi, as illustrated in the passage above, and also through two other characters in the novel who are represented as mentally insane and excluded from the society in which they live – Manzanar Murakami and Arcangel. The latter, a figure based on real-life author and activist Guillermo Gomez-Pena, is a vaga-

---

[12] The depiction of the transcultural nuclear family in Lee's and Yamashita's novels warrants comparison. Interestingly, both families (Henry-Lelia-Mitt and Bobby-Rafael-Sol) are dysfunctional, and it takes a series of reconciliatory gestures on the part of husband and wife before the family can be restored, albeit sans son in Native Speaker. In both novels, the estrangement of the women from their male spouses, and their departures in order to stay in another country for a period of time also signal, in my opinion, a literal act of emancipatory border-crossing which represents the problems that cross-cultural relationships can have too, and hence the undermining of feel-good multiculturalism within the private sphere of the home.

bond with supernatural physical strength and who doubles up as El Gran Mojado, a shaman-like wrestler who performs as a transborder messiah during his final apocalyptic wrestling match against SUPERNAFTA. The reference to NAFTA (North American Free Trade Agreement), a trilateral trade bloc created by the governments of the United States, Canada, and Mexico in 1992, and one of the largest trade blocs in the world according to nominal Gross Domestic Product (GDP), is, of course, intentional. When SUPERNAFTA, who wears a titanium body suit, finally shoots a missile into El Gran Mojado's human heart before he implodes, the performance is over. Yamashita writes, "[t]he audience, like life, would go on." (263)

The characters of Manzanar and Arcangel/El Gran Mojado problematize the notions of "agency" and "structure," to borrow two terms from the realm of the social sciences, whereby the former refers to the capacity of individuals to act independently and make free choices, and the latter to factors like social class, gender, ethnicity and religion which limit or influence the opportunities that individuals have. Modern social theory (particularly that posited by Anthony Giddens, Pierre Bourdieu, and Thomas Luckmann, among others) sees structure and agency as complementary forces instead of two forces that are dialectically opposed – i.e. that structure influences human behavior, and humans are capable of changing the social structures they inhabit. However, the characters of Manzanar and Arcangel demonstate that they will always continue to exist on the fringes of society because they will not, and cannot, assimilate to the rest of society. A displaced person, disenfranchised resident, illegal alien or person without "status," and even more so, one of color, cannot be part of the feel-good multiculturalism that Yamashita clearly wants no part of.

By drawing upon the traditional trickster figure in her creation of the character of Arcangel, who resists and challenges social conventions, Yamashita is also urging her readers to examine social constructions of racial and ethnic identity politics. In comparison to Lee's *Native Speaker*, which, as I argued, represents the difficult, yet necessary process of articulating a viable transnational identity politics because the latter is an act of empowerment for the Asian American immigrant, Yamashita playfully and irreverently subverts the ubiquitous phenomenon of feel-good multiculturalism in a transcultural present, hence forcing the reader to rethink existing discourses on identity politics. In challenging the reader to make sense of the fragmented, yet strangely gridlocked, text, Yamashita's novel also confronts the reader with the question of where s/he would draw the boundaries in the era of a new world order, where the "soft" borders of benevolent nationalisms, cultural essentialisms and neo-liberal multiculturalisms need to be eliminated altogether.

Conclusion

In a world of near instant communication, Kenichi Ohmae proclaims, the nation state is irrelevant (2005, 91). Ensuingly, he states, "[t]he global economy acts to discipline governments and to streamline regions. Borders are nothing but a burden for old nationstates" (93). In this chapter, I have tried to demonstrate that critics like Ohmae who argue that the last decade has witnessed the demise of the nation-state and the opening up of global channels of communication and interaction may be slightly short-sighted in their outlook. Borders might be "nothing but a burden," but they certainly continue to be just that – a burden. In an effort to illustrate what it means to pose a challenge to traditional assumptions of identity politics within literature, I have chosen two novels that use two different approaches in their attempts to do so.

While Chang-Rae Lee's *Native Speaker* destabilizes the conventional Asian American immigrant narrative by situating Henry Park's quest for identity within the overarching framework of a detective story, Karen Tei Yamashita's *Tropic of Orange* conflates elements of magical realism, popular and media culture, in order to unsettle existing definitions of the border narrative, hence complicating notions of border identities. Reading the two novels comparatively illustrates that there is never merely one way of critiquing and rethinking established forms of identity politics in a globalized era. Rather than trying to offer a unanimous solution to the problem or posit one way of going forward, perhaps what we should do is simply let go and enjoy that space of (to cite Lionnet and Shih once again) "exchange and participation […] without necessary mediation by the center" (5). But perhaps I should let the conclusion of *Tropic of Orange* speak for itself:

> But then he sees it too. He sees the line where it gets cut through the orange. So he grabs the two ends. Is he some kind of fool? Maybe so. But he's hanging on. […] Little by little the slack on the line's gone. Thing's stretching tight. Just Bobby grabbing the two sides. Making the connection. Pretty soon he's sweating it. Lines ripping through the palms. How long can he hold on? Dude's skinny, but he's an Atlas. Hold on 'til his body gets split in two. Hold on 'til he dies, famous-like. […] What's he gonna do? Tied fast to these lines. Family out there. Still stuck on the other side. He's gritting his teeth and crying like a fool. What are these goddamn lines anyway? What do they connect? What do they divide? What's he holding on to? What's he holding on to?

He gropes forward, inching nearer. Anybody looking sees his arms open wide like he's flying. Like he's flying forward to embrace.

Don't nobody know he's hanging on to these invisible bungy cords. That's when he lets go. Lets the lines slither around his wrists, past his palms, through his fingers. Lets go. Go figure. Embrace.

That's it. (267-68)

Works Cited

Balasubramanyam, Rajeev. "The Rhetoric of Multiculturalism." *Multi-Ethnic Britain 2000+:New Perspectives in Literature, Film and the Arts*. Ed. Lars Eckstein, Barbara Korte, Eva Ulrike Pirker and Christoph Reinfandt. Amsterdam: Rodopi, 2008. 45-63.

Bauböck, Rainer, "Cultural Citizenship, Minority Rights, and Self-Government." *Citizenship Today: Global Perspectives and Practices*. Ed. T. Alexander Aleinikoff and Douglas Klusmeyer. Washington, D.C.: Brookings Institution Press, 2001. 319-48.

Bhabha, Homi. *Nation and Narration*. London: Routledge, 1990.

Bourdieu, Pierre. *Outline of a Theory of Practice*. Trans. Richard Nice. Cambridge: Cambridge University Press, 1977.

Deleuze, Gilles and Félix Guattari. *A Thousand Plateaus*. Trans. Brian Massumi. London and New York: Continuum, 2004.

Dengel-Janic and Lars Eckstein. "Bridehood Revisited: Disarming Concepts of Gender and Culture in Recent Asian British Film." *Multi-Ethnic Britain 2000+: New Perspectives in Literature, Film and the Arts*. Ed. Lars Eckstein, Barbara Korte, Eva Ulrike Pirker and Christoph Reinfandt. Amsterdam: Rodopi, 2008. 45-63.

Engles, Tim. "'Visions of me in the whitest raw light': Assimilation and Doxic Whiteness in Chang-rae Lee's *Native Speaker*." *Hitting Critical Mass* 4.2 (Summer 1997): 27-48.

Friedman, Susan Stanford. "Migrations, Diasporas, and Borders." *Introduction to Scholarship in Modern Languages and Literatures*. Ed. David Nicholls. New York: Modern Language Association, 2006. 899–941.

Glissant, Édouard. *Poetics of Relation*. Trans. Betsy Wing. Ann Arbor: University of Michigan Press, 1997

Glixman, Elizabetth P. "An Interview with Karen Tei Yamashita." *Eclectica Magazine* 11.4 (October/November 2007) http://www.eclectica.org/v11n4/glixman_yamashita.html.

Last accessed 15.02.09.

Hall, Edward T. *Beyond Culture*. New York: Anchor Books, 1976.

Hasegawa, Linnea Marie. Articulating Identities: Rhetorical Readings of Asian American Literacy Narratives. Unpublished dissertation (2004). University of Maryland, College Park.

Hauser, Johannes. "Structuring the Apocalypse: Chaos and Order in Karen Tei Yamashita's *Tropic of Orange*." PhiN (Philologie im Netz) 37 (2006). http://web.fuberlin. de/phin/phin37/p37t1.htm. Last accessed: 15.02.09.

Kim, Sue-Yon. "Chang-rae Lee's *Native Speaker*: Acknowledging, Contradicting, Transcending the White and Yellow." *Journal of English and American Studies* 4 (2005). http://jeas.co.kr/sub/cnt.asp?num=36&volnum=4. Last accessed: 13.02.09.

Johnson, David E. and Scott Michaelsen, eds. *Border Theory*. Minneapolis: University of Minnesota Press, 1995.

Lee, Chang-Rae. *Native Speaker*. New York: Riverhead Books, 1995.

Li, Florence Hsiao-Ching. "Imagining the Mother/Motherland: Karen Tei Yamashita's *Tropic of Orange* and Theresa Hak Kyung Cha's *Dictee*." *Concentric: Literary and Cultural Studies* 30.1 (January 2004): 149-67.

Lionnet, Francoise and Shu-mei Shih, eds. *Minor Transnationalism*. Durham: Duke University Press, 2005.

Ohmae, Kenichi. *The Next Global Stage: Challenges and Opportunities in Our Borderless World*. Philadelphia: Wharton School Publishing, 2005.

Robertson, Roland. "Glocalization: time-space and homogeneity-heterogeneity." *Global Modernities*. Ed. Mike Featherstone, Scott Lasth and Roland Robertson. London: Sage Publications, 1995. 25-44.

Schuurman, Frans. "The Nation-state, Emancipatory Spaces and Development Studies in the Global Era." *Globalization and Development Studies: Challenges for the 21st Century*. Ed. Frans Schuurman. London: Sage, 2001. 61-78.

Yamashita, Karen Tei. *Tropic of Orange*. Minneapolis: Coffee House Press, 1997.

TWO: POLITICS OF LONGING

CHAPTER SEVEN

Diasporic Hereafters in Jhumpa Lahiri's "Once in a Lifetime"

Delphine Munos

In the recent literature of the Indian-American diaspora, the accelerated time/space of late capitalism, the far-reaching influence of an electronic media culture and the paradoxes of a new global interaction are generally associated with a transnational turn in the diasporic subjectivity which, as Vijay Mishra remarks in *The Literature of the Indian Diaspora* (2007), distinguishes "new" diasporas from "old" ones and calls for more flexible notions of "homeland" and "arrival" (3). This "transnational turn" indeed complicates the space of migrant identity construction and makes it inadequate to now represent immigrant self-fashioning in terms of a prefabricated opposition between "India" and "America" or in terms of a one-directional movement from the homeland to the New World.

Perhaps because it is coupled with zigzagging paths to new states of belonging, the contemporary diasporic subjectivity is frequently perceived as emblematic of concepts such as "fluidity," "multiple affiliations," and "national non-attachment." Hybridity theorists such as Homi K. Bhabha and James Clifford, to name but the two most influential ones, tend to celebrate today's diasporic experience as the quintessence of cosmopolitan freedom and postnational modes of belonging. To other critics versed in postcolonial theory, such as Peter Childs and Patrick Williams, transnationalism signals the emergence of a "new ethic" according to which "an increased celebration of heterogeneity and plurality" may gradually come to replace "a regressive and resistant insistence on a lost homeland" (210). However, contrary to theoretical expectations, the return of India on the stage of migrant identity construction constitutes one of the most recurrent features of the post-90s literature of the Indian-American diaspora. In that sense, this literature can be seen to problematize what "transnationalism" and "diaspora" stand for by showing that the steady discarding of grand narratives such as the American Dream, the immigrant success story and the melting-pot ideal by no means coincides with what could be called a post-national refiguring of the homeland. In popular texts such as *Desirable Daughters* (2002) by Bharati Mukherkjee or *The Vine of Desire* (2002) by Chitra Banerjee Divakaruni for instance, the re-metaphorization of diasporic subjectivity against multiple and simultaneous time zones undermines the narrative of U.S. exceptionalism by exposing the fault-lines of an assimilationist approach to cultural identity. Interestingly, it also reveals the blind spots and constructed nature of an ideal transnationalism, thus forcing us to step out of an increasingly institutionalized post-colonial discourse and to revise the narrow set of prefabricated paradigms by which the Indian diaspora in the United States is generally investigated.

At the start of the 21st century, it seems indeed that "India" is being re-positioned at the crossroads of conflicting representations within the contemporary diasporic subjectivity, straddling both categories of the old and the new. Unsurprisingly in this context, the "un-transnational" ideology of the return is depicted as still running deep in the first and second generation migrant imaginary. This transgenerational trend is aptly captured by Vijay Mishra, who argues that one's "homeland" is always already conceptualized "as very real spaces from which alone a certain level of redemption is possible" (2). Even more compellingly in this respect, in Jhumpa Lahiri's recent collection of short stories, *Unaccustomed Earth* (2008), the notion of homeland and the trope of the return are not unavoidably and exclusively tied up with a nostalgic, backward-looking stance but can also be associated, albeit in a circuitous way, with the advent of new becomings for a second generation that, in the author's own words, must come to terms with an "intense pressure to be two things: loyal to the old world and fluent in the new" ("Change and Loss" 3).

The ambiguous moral rehabilitation of Mishra's idea of "homeland as redemptive space" along with Lahiri's opening up of the notion of return to a seemingly paradoxical promise of futurity constitute joint sources of inspiration for this study. In Lahiri's second collection of short stories and more particularly, in the concluding section of the book that comprises three linked but distinct texts grouped under the heading of "Hema and Kaushik," the finding of one's place in the world is indeed depicted as being achieved at least as much through cultural transmogrification, hypermobility and cosmopolitan freedom as by addressing the memory traces of the past and the compulsion to return, either in a physical or in a psychological way. Mishra's attempt to explore the idea of "writing diaspora"in analogy with writing trauma or writing mourning, is illuminating in this context, because it constitutes a theoretical framework able to bear witness to the maintenance of a diasporic imaginary structured by the loss of the Motherland, whether this loss involves firsthand experience of migration or originates from a "phantom loss" imagined and refigured by the second generation.

Drawing on Mishra's theorizing of the diasporic imaginary and on a close reading of the short story opening *Unaccustomed Earth*'s trilogy, "Once in a Lifetime," this essay explores Lahiri's representation of the second generation as consisting of disconnected, directionless, precarious individuals who, though burdened by broken filiations and transgenerational memories of loss, remain insistently attached to a lost and yet "un-dead" world, long after their parents have themselves managed to disengage from it. Throughout "Once in a Lifetime," Hema's and Kaushik's destinies interconnect, diverge and meet again, as if the two characters' life courses were drawn to one another by the necessity of returning to a world of shared origins and re-engage with the past in order to lose themselves in a vortex of infinite regress or alternatively, to better negotiate a sense of future. By narrating Hema's and Kaushik's parallel journeys from childhood to adolescence, Lahiri rewrites the notion of return as melancholic attachments through which the unsymbolizable gap left by the absence of the Motherland can be represented, renegotiated and perhaps then, put to rest. Thus, I wish to show that not only does Lahiri use melancholy as a means of representing second-generation subjectivities haunted by impossible mourning and unclaimed legacies, but also that she rehabilitates the notion of return as a way of accommodating the spectral presences inherent in diasporic hereafters. Showing that melancholy and returning also bear the seeds of new becomings, "Once in a Lifetime" participates in the rethinking of a politics of (melancholic) memory in relation to diaspora.

Imagining Entangled Genealogies

As the first of the three texts that are grouped under the same heading, "Once in a Lifetime" deals with Hema's and Kaushik's first encounters as children and then as teenagers while introducing, both in a structural and in a thematic way, the motifs of return, loss and death that will recur throughout the short-story cycle. Although it constitutes a structural link uniting all of the three narratives under study, the use of apostrophe is particularly prominent in the first text of the trilogy. The dismantling of identity and the dislocation of time are inherent in this apostrophic form, in which a "narrating I" keeps addressing a voiceless yet all-pervading "you" from an indeterminate time and space. In "Once in a Lifetime," this narrative mode further reinforces a sense of doubleness and confusion in relation to time and identity. Indeed, not only is Hema as narrator split into a "narrated I" and a "narrating I," but Kaushik as addressee and character is also divided into a "narrated you" that is firmly rooted in the past time of the story and a phantasmal, intangible "addressed you" that only exists as a projection of the narrator's voice and thus extends its ethereal existence beyond the margins of diegetic time. In fact, the first lines of the text suggest that the implications of Kaushik's presence in Hema's life somehow exceed the confines of her own conscience since, from the outset, his presence already expands beyond the traces he left within her memory: "I had seen you before, too many times to count, but a farewell party that my family threw for yours, at our house in Inman Square, is when I began to recall your presence in my life" (Lahiri 223).

Here, ironically enough, the first inscription of Kaushik's *presence* within the narrator's memory almost coincides with his physical *absence*, since the move of Kaushik's family "all the way back to India" also marks the commencement of Hema's recollection of him. More generally, Lahiri's text makes it clear that Kaushik's and Hema's relationship is characterized from the very beginning by a blurring of the boundaries between absence and presence, return and arrival, but also between Self and Other. Hema's recollection of the farewell party during which she first registered Kaushik's existence is indeed associated with the memory of an unbecoming traditional outfit that she has to wear for the occasion, an outsized kurta that was sent by her grandmother from Calcutta and whose waist is eloquently "wide enough to gird two of [her] side by side" (223). What the narrative suggests here is that Hema's first conscious memory of Kaushik is coupled with, and thus somehow related to, the imagining of a phantom alter-ego whose addition to her own self would be necessary to literally fill in an identity gap both opened and outlined by a costume that embodies the Indian world of origins. The long-lasting influence and ambiguous positioning of Kaushik's absent presence at the frontier of Hema's self is represented by the winter clothes that she indirectly takes over from him and that she has to make her own, years after Kaushik's departure for India. Forced indeed by her mother to "incorporate" Kaushik's clothes in her wardrobe as she "grows into them" (226), Hema is symbolically made to inhabit the very old skin that Kaushik shed after he left the New World; or rather, she is compelled to project herself into the same layers of self that once shaped Kaushik's own identity. Hema's inability to literally tailor her identity to her own measurements arouses in her a feeling of profound revulsion for Kaushik's clothes, which come to be positioned at the centre of an anxiety of identity:

> I found these clothes ugly and tried to avoid them, but my mother refused to replace them. And so I was forced to wear your sweaters, your rubber boots on rainy days. One winter I had to wear your coat, which I hated so much that it caused me to hate you as a result. [...] I never got used to having to hook

the zipper on the right side, to looking so different from the
other girls in my class with their puffy pink and purple jackets.
[...] I wanted desperately to get rid of [the coat]. I wanted it to
be lost. (226)

In this excerpt, Hema displaces onto Kaushik her rage at being forced to wear a coat that marks her as different and that does not suit the gendered codes of her American peers, as if Kaushik was crystallizing the impossibility for Hema to escape the grip of both a parental and a communal way of life and to fully identify with an American mainstream. Therefore, not only do clothes embody the porous boundary between exterior and interior, between Self and Other, but they also signify the ill-fitting and unaccommodating nature of the diasporic legacy for Hema as a child. In this context, the label that Hema's mother irons inside Kaushik's coat with her daughter's name on it not so much cancels out the garment's alien genealogy as it throws into sharper relief the interlocking of its familiar and unfamiliar origin. Faced up to the "Unheimliche" nature of her heritage by the forced appropriation of Kaushik's coat and the apposition of a name tag that nevertheless marks it as her own, Hema experiences a crisis of the proper that culminates in her attempt to abandon the coat in the school bus. Rather perversely, however, it is the name tag that eventually brings Kaushik's coat back to her, suggesting that it is her name that binds her to an inescapable yet unfamiliar legacy, fastening her to an identity that is literally knit in the very fabric of Kaushik's old self.

The impossibility to fully disentangle Kaushik's and Hema's genealogies from one another constitutes a recurrent feature of "Once in a Lifetime," as when Hema retraces her early childhood and seems to remember a time when Kaushik's mother became inseparable friends with her own, to the point where the two women ended up pooling resources and sharing every single chore in their respective households:

They shopped together for groceries and complained about
their husbands and cooked together at either our stove or yours,
dividing up the dishes for our respective families when they
were done. They knitted together, switching projects when one
of them got bored. When I was born, your parents were the
only friends to visit the hospital. I was fed in your old high
chair, pushed along the streets in your old pram. (225)

While this quotation makes it clear that the intertwining of Hema's and Kaushik's life-courses goes back a very long way, it also emphasizes the pivotal role the two mothers played in creating a tightly-knit community that would unite both of their families. Besides, by revealing that Kaushik's parents, the Choudhuris, are the only ones to visit the hospital on the occasion of

Hema's birth, the above passage presents the sisterhood initiated by the two women as a form of substitute for far-off filiations, thus suggesting the large extent to which lack and absence underpin the compensatory kinship both mothers seek to recreate. Interestingly, although the narrative indicates that it is the visual recognition of Hema's mother's Bengaliness that first draws Kaushik's mother to her, it later on implies that, much more than their shared origins, it is their presence in the U.S. and their joint experience of loneliness that both triggers and enables their friendship:

> In Calcutta they would probably have had little occasion to meet. Your mother went to a convent school and was the daughter of one of Calcutta's most prominent lawyers [...]. My mother's father was a clerk in the General Post Office, and she had neither eaten at a table nor sat on a commode before coming to America. Those differences were irrelevant in Cambridge, where they were both equally alone. (225)

By indicating that "India" only constitutes a trigger of sorts while "America" somehow represents the "great leveller" and the "great enabler" in the two mothers' relationship, Lahiri introduces an alien presence at the center of the fiction of common Bengaliness that bonds the two mothers together and repositions the fracture provoked by their relocation in the U.S. as invisible core of their sense of kinship. In this context, the script of cultural sameness that serves to unify and rationalize away the family-like structure surrounding the two women can be seen as a means to displace and obscure a sense of loss and isolation which paradoxically constitutes an underlying yet powerful identificatory drive, and consequently, a mainspring of affiliation. Through the genealogy of their mothers' sister-like friendship, Lahiri therefore intimates that Hema's and Kaushik's connection as much originates in the reconstituted sense of kinship that bonded them together when they were children as it derives from an urge, passed down through the generations, to cling to a fantasized narrative of common origins. The latter serves to cover up their inheritance of loss[1] even as it invisibly feeds on it, thus positioning their relationship as an allegorical – yet spurious – means to bridge, across the generations, the fissures initiated by their mothers' migration to the New World. It is therefore no wonder that Kaushik embodies for Hema a "fantasy of origin" which finds itself embedded in the narrative retracing the encounter of their mothers. Of key interest in this respect is the way in which the text bears witness to the precise moment when Kaushik's and Hema's mothers met for the first time, a period when Hema was yet to come out of her mother's womb:

---

[1] I have borrowed this phrase from the title of one of Kiran Desai's books, *The Inheritance of Loss* (2006).

Our mothers met when mine was pregnant. She didn't know it yet; she was feeling dizzy and sat down on a bench in a small park. Your mother was perched on a swing, gently swaying back and forth as you soared above her, when she noticed a young Bengali woman in a sari, wearing vermillion in her hair. [...] She told you to get off the swing, and then she and you escorted my mother back home. It was during that walk that your mother suggested that perhaps mine was expecting. (224–25)

What is most striking here is that the narrator paradoxically gains access to a "time of origins" prior to her own birth, as if the first-person narration exploded its own structural boundaries in terms of focalization and could now expand its scope to times and recollections beyond the narrator's conscious reach. In this excerpt, the subtle, nearly imperceptible switch to first-person omniscience reflects in a structural way the high permeability of Hema's consciousness to trans-generational "memories" and perceptions that cannot, strictly speaking, be her own. Through this narrative shift, Lahiri suggests a causal link between Hema's effort to trace the genealogy of her connection with Kaushik back to its very beginning and the progressive dissolving of her identity in the memory traces of her own mother. In other words, the narrative implies here that there is no returning to the originating moment of the bond between the two protagonists without a collapse of identities between the generations and a dismantling of the polarities between inner and outer, between fantasy and reality, as well as between the past and the present.

The thematic aspect of this excerpt both echoes and complements its structural implications since, in many ways, Hema's recollections from beyond the womb, so to speak, can be seen to accommodate whilst also displacing the primal fantasy of being there "at the very beginning." As Karl Figlio points out in his essay "Getting to the Beginning," although the most classic originating scenario centres on the primal scene of parental intercourse, primitive moments of origination can take on a variety of forms. What underpins the different versions of this classic narrative, however, is the omnipotent totalizing fantasy of witnessing, or even taking part in, one's own conception (Figlio 154). Hema's transgenerational "memories" take on renewed meaning in the light of Figlio's remarks, mostly because they can be seen to conflate two originating moments into one. The originating moment of encounter between Kaushik's mother and her own – and thus, by extension, the beginning of Kaushik's and Hema's relationship – is indeed juxtaposed with the news of Hema's coming into the world, as if the narrator was refiguring the past in order to rebirth herself under the auspices of the two mothers' budding sisterhood. Moreover, by recasting Kaushik's mother as "instructress in pregnancy" and "breaker of the good news," Hema indirectly refashions Kaushik as witness to her symbolic coming into the world, and consequently she fuses their selves together by inserting *him* inside the primitive moment of *her* own origination. In this respect, not only can Hema's "fantasy of origins" be seen to position Kaushik as a recovery agent of sorts, indeed as a means to reengage with her ancestry, but it also captures the way in which the narrator unconsciously transforms and reproduces across the generations an imaginary narrative of common origins that once bonded Kaushik's mother and her own together.

Reaching out Beyond Transnationalism and Diaspora

Although the return of Kaushik's family back to the United States after a seven-year absence opens a new phase in the relationship between the two families, Hema's perception of Kaushik remains underpinned by the same desire to restore an illusionary sense of essential wholeness, thus providing the narrative with a sense of continuity, even of repetition, across time. In fact, much as clothing metaphors suggest that Kaushik crystallizes an anxiety of identity for the protagonist as a child, it is the reallocation of space between the two adolescents during the Choudhuris' residence at Hema's place that now reveals how deeply her relationship to Kaushik affects her sense of self. More precisely, Hema's forced relinquishing of her room to Kaushik for an unspecified amount of time triggers in her the feeling of literally not being at home in her own house and thus reopens the crisis of the proper that she experienced when having to appropriate her guest's winter coat. While the giving up of her room positions Kaushik as an irritating alien presence that Hema needs to accommodate in more ways than just one, it also associates him with the menace of being thrust back in infancy. On her guest's arrival, Hema is indeed meant to abandon the self-imposed "American" challenge of sleeping alone in a room of her own and revert to the Indian practice, which has been encouraged by her mother all along, to sleep on a cot in her parents' room. In this respect, not only does Kaushik come to represent the impossibility for Hema to let go of the unassimilable Indian part of her identity in spite of her American birth, but, in a much similar way to what happens in her "fantasy of origins," her guest also embodies a threat of regression, a menace that her second-generation Indian-American identity may be dissolved in her parents' more monolithic version of Indianness. Significantly in this context, Hema compares the process of having to empty her room and pack up her things before Kaushik's arrival with the preparations she would make before departing to her parents' country of origins:

> It was like deciding which of my possessions I wanted to take on a long trip to India, only this time I was going nowhere. Still, I put my things into a suitcase covered with peeling tags and stickers that had travelled various times back and forth across the world and dragged it into my parents' room. (230)

Here, although her journey to her parents' room proves almost motionless in terms of physical distance, Hema's decision to use a suitcase that had travelled many times between India and the United States somehow indicates that her microscopic trip within the confines of her own house may nonetheless result in opening new vistas on her parents' country of origin. For one thing, Hema's move to her parents' private space provides her with a unique perspective on the fault-lines characterizing the relationship between transnational and diasporic Indians and more particularly, on the socio-cultural "Indian gap" that comes to separate the two families, by allowing her to overhear disapproving comments her mother only makes at night on the extent to which Bombay changed Kaushik's parents and made the Choudhuris, uncannily enough, "more American" than the United States ever did (235). Clearly, Lahiri's text shows that the arrival of Kaushik's family straight from Bombay introduces Hema to another model of Indianness which, unlike her parents and the diasporic community surrounding them, overtly revels in so-called "Western" treats such as stylish clothes, first-class transcontinental plane tickets and whisky-drinking. As the protagonist soon realizes, this upper-class, contemporary version of "Bombayite Indianness" increasingly unsettles her parents' own middle-class standards. On a more subterranean level, it also disrupts their archetypal diasporic representation of India as a place of origins frozen in time and immune to corrupting Western influences. The exchanges Hema overhears in the privacy of her parents' bedroom can be seen to throw into even sharper relief what the resurfacing of Kaushik's parents has inadvertently started to reveal, that is, the excessively traditional, "more-Indian-than-Indian" character of the U.S.-based form of Indianness the protagonist was born and raised into. Far from inhibiting the "immediate schoolgirl attraction" (234) Hema feels for Kaushik on the day of his arrival, her mother's complaints about her guests seem to intensify it instead. Yet, this is not to suggest that Hema's infatuation is exclusively fuelled by a typically adolescent urge to oppose and challenge parental authority. In fact, while Lahiri implies that, through her crush, the protagonist somehow subverts the type of Indianness she was reared to observe, on the other hand the narrative emphasizes the suggestion that

Kaushik is paradoxically perceived by Hema as more relating to her parents than to herself.

Hema's infatuation with someone who, she feels, "belong[s] to the world of [her] parents" (234), and who nevertheless embodies a "Bombayite Indianness" that shatters the very foundations of her parents' cultural identity, is not as contradictory as it may seem. Lahiri indeed intimates that Hema's "teenage crush" on Kaushik represents less a way to challenge her parents' ossified form of Indianness than an imaginary means to reach out beyond it, that is, a way to overstep her parents by retrieving and carrying out an ahistorical mythology of single-root Indian identity that would iron out difference and reconcile the two families. Rather symbolically in this context, Hema fantasizes that she can infiltrate the partition of her parents' bedroom and reach out through it to Kaushik, who sleeps in her own room, "just on the other side of the wall" (235). Not only does Hema's daydreaming about Kaushik express a longing for immaterial forms of being that would render walls and separations between them powerless, it also centres on fantasies of full incorporation and speechless recognition, as if once their identities had been connected with one another, they could effortlessly merge and dissolve in a core of sameness: "After dreading it all this time, now I was secretly thrilled that you would be sleeping [in my room]. You would absorb my presence, I thought. Without me having to do a thing, you would come to know me and like me" (234).

Here, Hema's daydreaming is clearly reminiscent of the script of instant recognition and "unity-in-sameness" that once helped to unify and rationalize away the community-like structure binding the two families together across major class differences. In this respect, it is rather ironic that the protagonist's fantasy of "unity in absorption" is counterpoised with her mother's ever-inflating complaints about having "unwittingly opened [her] home to strangers" (245), as if Hema's romantic fantasies represented a means to redeem the growing resentment and sense of estrangement her mother experiences in relation to the Choudhuris, especially as regards her old friend. In fact, Lahiri suggests that Hema's infatuation partakes in a self-appointed mission of redressing the "Indian gap" between the two families and, more generally, of building a phantasmal bridge of continuity between two conflicting versions of Indianness: on the one hand, a strongly traditional diasporic Indianness in keeping with what Monisha Das Gupta would call the first-generation invention of the "authentic Indian immigrant family" (574), and on the other a Westernized "Bombayite Indianness" that bears witness to the early stages of "Shining India," as Pankaj Mishra mockingly labels the New India in a recent article[2]. Unsurprisingly in this context, the "unrequited crush" Hema nurtures on Kaushik proves somehow transmutable into a growing fondness for his parents. Indeed, it is partially alleviated by the affection the Choudhuris lavish on her, as when the narrative indicates that the attention Hema gets from the mother "almost makes up" for what she does not get from the son (246). In what follows, the interlocked substitutive and supplementary character of the protagonist's feelings for her guest will be emphasized, so that it will become even clearer that Kaushik represents for Hema a surrogate for what is thought to be missing at the origin, or rather, a liminal entity which, while embodying a central void, simultaneously verges on the border between absence and presence because it also potentially carries within itself the means of replenishing it.

Performing the Phantom Loss of the Motherland

In many ways, the arrival of the snow Kaushik has been craving for ever since his return to the United States both signals a loosening-up of the invisible line that is drawn in the house between Hema's parents and her guests and a sense of release in the "forced intimacy" that pervades all interactions between the two families. By triggering happy recollections of the last winter the Choudhuris spent in Cambridge, snow revives fond memories of the farewell party that was thrown by their hosts on the eve of their departure for India, and these nostalgic reminiscences result in uniting Kaushik's and Hema's parents in a common sense of sadness about the passing of time and the gilded era of their friendship. As if to signify the resurfacing of a sense of community between the two families, Hema's father indulges in a "small taste of whisky" while Kaushik's mother suddenly regains an interest in cooking, which she had lost, significantly enough, when the "Cambridge days" were over. Even if they constitute a mutual, belated acknowledgment of two different ways of living, or rather of two different interpretations of Indianness, these symbolic incursions on the others' territory more seal the separateness of the two families than they gesture towards their final reconciliation. Nostalgia is in fact a great leveller, albeit a fairly artificial one. Like snow which gives a semblance of unity by covering up the landscape and enrobing it with an all-white surface, nostalgia indeed unites the Choudhouris with their hosts only because it conceals traces of dissent beneath the veneer of idealized memories.

---

[2] Pankaj Mishra appropriates this metaphor from the 2004 central government political campaign in India. See his article, "The Myth of the New India."

Very symbolically in this context, the outing that Hema and Kaushik undertake in woods deemed "off-limits" by Hema's parents culminates in the uncovering of tombstones coated with snow, as if both characters were literally digging up what remained of their joint inheritance underneath the varnish of the nostalgic togetherness their parents temporarily managed to recreate. Cemeteries as places of second-generation epiphanies and encounters with destiny constitute a recurrent motif in Lahiri's work, as exemplified in the author's previous book. Notably, it is while exploring an East Coast cemetery during a field trip that Gogol, the U.S. born "desi" protagonist of *The Namesake* (2003), realizes that most of the Founding Fathers' tombstones bear first names as "odd" and "unthinkable" as his own. Although Gogol keeps on perceiving, throughout the novel, his incongruous name as an embarrassing testimony to his estrangement from culturally-exclusive scenarios of total and direct filiations, his fleeting positive identification with the Founding Fathers and their "flamboyant" names nevertheless inscribes him in a collateral myth of origin that prefigures a strong, yet circuitous, affiliation, with "these very ancient Puritan spirits, these very first immigrants to America" (Lahiri 2003, 71).

In "Once in a Lifetime," cemeteries also come to signify the way in which partial filiations can be transformed through time and generations into solid rerouted hybridized affiliations. However, Lahiri's short story refrains from presenting hybrid destinies as a given that might, in due course, automatically and benignly befall all second-generation members of the Indian-American migrant community. Kaushik's and Hema's joint endeavour of "unburying the buried" (249) ends up emphasizing the extent to which the moorings of their interconnected genealogies anchor them, in fact, to quite divergent destinies and personal histories. In a similar way to what happens in *The Namesake* as Gogol explores some of the Founding Fathers' sepulchres, Hema's and Kaushik's uncovering of the last of the tombstones belonging to the Simonds, a family of six, initially results in the resurfacing of a name, Emma, whose uncanny resemblance with that of the protagonist suggests that, in spite of her Indian origin, she is, like Gogol, inscribed in a collateral lineage that takes its roots in the American earth. The specific narrative twist of "Once in a Lifetime," however, lies in Kaushik's revelations, which further problematize the interlocking of Hema's unearthing of her hybrid destiny with the imagining of her death via the concrete evidence of a tombstone bearing a (translated) version of her name. It is indeed significant that Hema's sense of disturbance at the similarity of Emma Simonds' name and her own *only* turns to shock and devastation as Kaushik unveils the hidden agenda behind his family's circular migration to the United States, by referring to his mother's breast cancer and her desire to flee not only the "suffocating attention" her family in India had started lavishing on her but also the reflection of her impending decline through the eyes of her own parents.

Hema's reaction indicates that Kaushik forces her to confront a diasporic truth that is far more unthinkable, therefore far more traumatic, than the imagining of her own "rooted" death in American soil. Through these confidences that he asks Hema not to divulge, Kaushik indeed signifies his difference with the protagonist in terms of personal history, which obliges her in turn to let go of the transgenerational fantasy of cultural unity she had projected onto him and thus to face up to her own singular hybrid destiny without the protective shield of any totalizing myth of origin. Even more compellingly, by disclosing the causal link between the onset of his mother's disease and his family's flight from India, Kaushik evokes the unsettling possibility that India, the Motherland, should constitute a place of origins only, where no beginnings and endings can ever converge, whence no embodiment of finitude, therefore no meaning, can ever arise. Kaushik's mother's refusal to be buried in American soil or cremated in India makes it clear, moreover, that she can conceive of no final destination at either end, no solid form to both encapsulate and signify her death. Her desire that her diasporic body should be reunified not with the Earth, but with the Sea, a domain evocative of immortality and the unlimited, adds up a further disturbing edge to the family secret surrounding her disease, since it serves to signal a suspension of symbolic language as regards the agony of embodiment, that is, decay and Death, but also, at the other end of the spectrum, ontological consistency and Meaning. In this respect, Kaushik's wish that, instead of having to "scatter [his mother's] ashes into the Atlantic," as she instructed, she should be buried "somewhere" (249), hints at his sense of burden that he has to forge a coherent sense of self in a world in which no concrete sanctuary can ever trigger the memory of his originator and thus bring her back to him into (symbolic) existence.

Undoubtedly, Kaushik's anticipated inability to accept that his mother's remains should dissolve into the water destines him to a history of endless drifting in the face of death and portends a sense of disorientation and disconnectedness no country or affiliation might be able to alleviate. Kaushik's ordeal resonates with particular poignancy in a migrant context, because his inability to objectify the loss of his mother both duplicates and encapsulates what Vijay Mishra sees as the open wound at work in the diasporic imaginary, that is, the absence of the Motherland – an absence engendering so incommensurable a sense of loss that it often remains unrepresentable and transforms the mourning for the land of origins into endless melancholia.[3] Mishra's attempt to investi-

---

[3] See Mishra's *The Literature of the Indian Diaspora*, especially its introduction and third chapter.

gate the notion of writing diaspora in analogy with writing trauma or writing mourning is illuminating in the context of "Once in a Lifetime," mostly because it constitutes a theoretical framework susceptible to bearing witness to the maintenance of a specifically "diasporic" imaginary structured by the loss of the Motherland, whether this loss actually involves firsthand experience of migration or derives, more abstractly, from a "phantom loss," that is, from the imagining and refiguring of the first-generation experience by the second-generation – what Marianne Hirsch conceptualizes as "postmemories."[4] Building upon Cathy Caruth's belief that trauma can be transmitted to those who have no direct experience of its source, Mishra indeed suggests that the trauma of migration, which he compares to the "primal wound" one experiences as an infant, is somehow always already inscribed in second-generation migrant subjectivities, but as a gap emptied of meaning, an unsymbolizable absence. More generally, Slavoj Žižek likens trauma to "a point of failure of symbolization, but at the same time never given in its positivity" (qtd. in Mishra 118). Mishra's examining of the numerous ways in which diasporic and traumatic subjectivities intersect makes it clear, moreover, that processes of transference *among* generations often come to repeat, and are thus highly likely to further complicate, the transmission of an interlocked diasporic and traumatic imaginary *between* the generations. Quoting Caruth, Mishra more generally wonders whether "history, like trauma, is never simply one's own [...] history is precisely the way in which we are implicated in each other's traumas" (116). With the caveat that the "sanctity of memory" should not be disoriented because of this paradox in any case, Mishra indeed underlines that the transmission of trauma often invalidates the very idea of rigid boundaries between inner and outer, between victim and perpetrator or – what will be of key interest for the purposes of this study – between onlooker and partaker. "The transmission of trauma to another," Mishra continues in this sense, "is not via identification (the classical Freudian position) but by the witnessing of the fracture in language and by being haunted or possessed by what it hides" (116).

Mishra's theorizing of the diasporic imaginary opens new vistas for interpreting Hema's reaction in the wake of Kaushik's revelations. For in between the lines of Kaushik's reluctance to accept the programmed unearthiness of his mother, so to speak, Hema can only glimpse a horror far greater than the

---

[4] It is worth mentioning here that Marianne Hirsch's concept of "postmemory" originates from the need to conceptualize the kind of "memoried" imaginings of place children of Holocaust survivors engage in so as to be able to imaginarily "locate" in space and time their parents' life *before* the Holocaust. Interestingly for the purposes of this chapter, Hirsch believes that the notion of "postmemory" is also useful to describe "the second-generation memory of other cultural or collective traumatic events and experiences" (662).

"rooted" projection of her own finitude, as if the phantom of the Motherland was indeed beckoning through Kaushik's virtually bereaved "pre-memory" of his mother's departure. Linking endless exile to disembodied death on the one hand and loss to impossible mourning on the other, Kaushik's confidences indeed rewrite his mother as an "un-dead" presence which, like the Motherland, can be imagined as disowning finitude through her everlasting impact on her offspring. To use Mishra's words, Hema can only be "haunted or possessed" by what Kaushik's revelations "hide": the unacknowledged fantasy that diasporic bodies shall be capable of perpetually haunting the living by being thought of as still existing "on the other shore" – a potentiality arousing as much dread as desire, which uncannily resurrects the haunting void left by the absence of the Motherland, able to extend its clutch through time and generations. Consequently, what is traumatically *repeated* through the interstices of Kaushik's confidences is the "postmemory" of the Motherland, in other words, the unsymbolizable void at the (invisible) heart of Hema and Kaushik's second-generation destiny. That Kaushik's and Hema's joint encounters with destiny should be sealed in a cemetery located within ill-fated woods where, the narrator mentions twice, a boy was lost, never to be found again, casts an even more tragic light on the characters' experience by signifying that diasporic legacies, like black holes, are powerful enough to swallow up their heirs.

What thus comes to unite the two characters towards the end of "Once in a Lifetime" is less a myth of common descent and single-root Indianness than the resurrection of the "phantom loss" of the Motherland and a shared secret that propels Hema into adulthood by endowing her with a knowledge her own parents are denied. Perhaps because they exacerbate the threat of being perpetually caught in the frozen temporality of an undying diasporic hereafter, postmemories of loss, however, prove no fertile ground for the emergence of a sense of generational empathy between Hema and Kaushik. The narrative indeed emphasizes Kaushik's aloofness as he waits for Hema to finish crying and recover from the blow his confidences inflicted upon her, significantly "looking down at the tombstone of Emma Simonds" (250) in the meanwhile, as if he were taking the measure of his own tragic isolation by contemplating the marker of Hema's rerouted "American" fate. Likewise, Hema and Kaushik's final parting and the physical distance maintained between them as she follows him back home seem to indicate that the symbolic unearthing of the Simonds' graveyard precipitates a form of mental separation between the two characters which is somehow complicated by an underlying sense of resentment:

> I followed you along the path you had discovered, and then we parted, neither of us a comfort to the other, you shovelling the driveway, I going inside for a hot shower [...]. Perhaps you be-

lieved that I was crying for you, or for your mother, but I was not. I was too young that day, to feel sorrow or sympathy. I felt only the enormous fear of having a dying woman in our house. I remembered standing beside your mother, both of us topless in the fitting room where I tried on my first bra, disturbed that I had been in such close proximity to her disease. I was furious that you had told me, and that you had not told me, feeling at once burdened and betrayed, hating you all over again. (250–51)

This excerpt makes it clear that Kaushik's mother's disease triggers so powerful an anxiety of death in Hema that she proves incapable of reaching out and commiserating over her guest's predicament, as if she were indeed transfixed by the "enormous fear of having a dying woman in [her] house." The memory of standing half-naked beside Kaushik's mother in a fitting room and being offered her first bras reaches paroxysmal intensity as she now realizes that the woman she has been looking up to ever since as a role-model of refined yet liberal Indian womanhood was in fact undermined by breast cancer all along. The present given by this precursor in female hybridized cultural identity takes on a rather ominous meaning in this context. First presented as a means to initiate the young girl to her budding womanhood and as a token of affection symbolizing the passing down of a version of Westernized Indianness the U.S.-born protagonist can easily emulate, perversely enough the bras that Hema receives as a gift come to be tainted in retrospect by the shadow of disease and death. In other words, Lahiri suggests that the symbolic legacy Kaushik's mother bequeaths to Hema not so much promises the future as it blocks the way to new becomings.

Perhaps because they result in curdling a positive identification into an impossible one, Kaushik's revelations arouse profound anger in Hema, as if she held him responsible for the demise of a model she is keen to embrace. In this respect, the resurgence of Hema's feelings of rage and resentment towards Kaushik signals her desire to distance herself from him, as their final parting towards the end of the story intimates, whilst also indicating a compulsive urge to create a form of melancholic ties which, through hatred, enables Hema to take revenge on, and thus indirectly to preserve, the absence of an ideal she proves incapable of relinquishing completely. Again, the narrative emphasizes the substitutive and supplementary nature of Hema's feelings for Kaushik who, for Hema, keeps representing a placeholder for what is missing in the present, whether the narrative identifies this lack as a narrative of common origin, as the phantom gap left by the "un-dead" absence of the Motherland or, eventually, as an ideal hybridity that could sustain the forging of a coherent Indian-American sense of self.

Therefore, although the uncovering of the Simond's graveyard first prefigures the differences between Kaushik's and Hema's fates, it also positions loss and the burden of facing up to it as major components uniting the two characters' destinies, suggesting moreover that melancholy and impossible mourning can in fact cement their attachment across time and beyond physical presence. In many ways, "Once in a Lifetime" emphasizes Hema's and Kaushik's common isolation towards the close of the narrative, as Hema comes to understand that neither the diasporic Indianness her parents embody nor the more glamorous form of hybrid identity Kaushik's mother incarnates can provide her with adequate role-models and help her envision a sense of future. Clearly, the ending of "Once in a Lifetime" shows that Hema's ambivalence towards Kaushik ties her up more closely not only with his own fate of impossible mourning but also with the diasporic imaginary and its melancholy inflections, as theorized by Mishra. This is not to say that Lahiri's text solely reduces Kaushik to a transitionary figure and ends up simplifying a relationship that, to the protagonist, proves in fact as alienating as it is enabling. In this respect, the renewed sense of loyalty Hema experiences in relation to her guest's secret long after his family moves out exacerbates all the ambiguity of their relationship, since the protagonist's indefectible allegiance can be seen as an implicit tribute to the generational isolation she shares with Kaushik or, conversely, as a compulsion to endorse Kaushik's melancholic assumption that his mother's desire to leave no traces on Earth testifies to the unrepresentable character of her finitude. Either way, the last lines of "Once in a Lifetime" reveal that Hema's attachment to Kaushik enables her to gain a significant measure of independence from her parents. Keeping the secret about Kaushik's mother's disease even as her parents feel they are "being snubbed" now that the Choudhuris have a house of their own, Hema divorces herself from her parents' brand of class-obsessed and narrow-minded Indianness by reasserting the memory of Kaushik's symbolic passage through her room: "I was back in my room by then, on the other side of the wall, in the bed where you had slept, *no longer hearing them*" (251, emphasis added).

This "no longer hearing them" initiated by Kaushik's passage in Hema's life crystallizes a rupture between "you" and "them" and marks the passing of a "narrated I" whose ear is still tuned to the voice of her parents, whose identity is still undifferentiated from that of the first generation. Therefore, the end of "Once in a Lifetime" can be seen as hinging on a self-reflexive point of emergence able to look back, if such a thing can be imagined, on the coming-into-being of the narrator's voice – a voice that can only materialize, or so it seems, at the end of the "circuit of communication" (Culler 59) with a textual Other engendered by the apostrophic form. Finally, Hema-as-narrator seems to acquire her own voice not only by turning away from that of her parents but through a "detour via the Other" (Castro 118) or rather, through the inscription of the Other's absence in the repository of the text. To put it differently, the hybridization of the traces of the Other's absence that are structurally embedded in Lahiri's text and the "piece of otherness" that Jonathan Culler sees to be inherent in apostrophe give voice, give life. In this sense, although Hema and Kaushik remain insistently attached to a lost and yet "un-dead" world through the melancholic bond they end up sharing, the last line of "Once in a Lifetime" performs a (hybrid) promise: the promise of alchemizing the encounter with Otherness into the possibility of mourning.

Works Cited

Castro, Brian. "Auto/Biography." *Looking for Estrellita*. Queensland: University of Queensland Press, 1999. 98–123.
Childs, Peter, and Patrick Williams. *An Introduction to Post-Colonial Theory*. New York: Prentice Hall, 1997.
Culler, Jonathan. "Apostrophe." *Diacritics* 7.4 (Winter 1977): 59–69.
Das Gupta, Monisha. "What is Indian About You? A Gendered, Transnational Approach to Ethnicity." *Gender and Society* 11.5 (Oct. 1997): 572–96.
Desia, Kiran. *The Inheritance of Loss*. New York: Grove Press, 2006.
Divakaruni, Chitra Banerjee. *The Vine of Desire*. New York: Doubleday, 2002.
Figlio, Karl. "Getting to the Beginning: Identification and Concrete Thinking in Historical Consciousness." *Regimes of Memory*. Ed. Susannah Radstone and Katherine Hodgkin. New York: Routledge, 2003. 152–66.
Hirsch, Marianne. "Past Lives: Postmemories in Exile." *Poetics Today* 17.4, Creativity and Exile: European / American Perspectives II (Winter 1996): 662–86.
Lahiri, Jhumpa. *The Namesake*. London: Flamingo, 2003. London: Harper Perennial, 2004.
-----. *Unaccustomed Earth*, New York: Knopf, 2008.
-----. Interview with Christopher Taylor. "Change and Loss." *Guardian*. 2008. 21 June 2008. Web. 18 Feb. 2009.
Mishra, Prakaj. "The Myth of the New India." *New York Times*. 2006. 6 July 2006. Web. 18 Feb. 2009.
Mishra, Vijay. *The Literature of the Indian Diaspora: Theorizing the Diasporic Imaginary*. New York: Routledge, 2007.

Mukherjee, Bharati. *Desirable Daughters*. New York: Hyperion, 2002.

CHAPTER EIGHT

Gendered Transnational Spaces: Arab 'Safari'[1] Situated in Hanan Al-Shaykh's *Only in London*

Şebnem Toplu

Migration, diaspora, hybridity, multiculturalism and transnationalism have been going on for centuries, yet why we are increasingly concerned with what Bruce Robbins calls "different modalities of situatedness-in-displacement" (250) may be for the reason that globalization subjects people to a variety of accelerated cultural movements while the focus on identity has been increasing, even for the statically situated persons. As a result, these circumstances shift the question of the relationship between culture and identity to a more complicated conception of an in-between, hybrid identity; that is, a self fluctuating between two or more homes, added to the ongoing fluidity of identity through time and space. Taking into consideration this highly complex phenomenon, Kwame Anthony Appiah states that "identity may not be the best word for bringing together the roles gender, class, race, nationality and so on play in our lives, but it is the one we use" (15). Similarly, María Martínez González maintains that identity must not be understood as an essence, a fixed identity, but as "a process of constant building" and adds that the process of identity construction is similar to a journey, which is not fixed before it starts (26). Thereby, the discussion on transnational identities becomes significant with the constructive forces of displacement from home and cultural hybridity, in the efforts concerning the trajectory of space.

The conception of 'home' has become significant in Britain especially since the postcolonial era with the flow of migration from the old colonies to the 'mother country' or 'motherland.' Thus, with accelerated movement of expatriates, space itself has become the core of identity. In the prologue of her book *Home Truths*, Susheila Nasta states that "[h]ome, it has been said, is not necessarily where one *belongs* but the place where one *starts* from" (1, original

---

[1] Arabic word for travellers

emphasis). Yet, when people are relocated in various places and feel that they belong to some of these, the multiplicity of homes creates distinct identities.

Such is also Avtar Brah's assertion in her book *Cartographies of Diaspora Contesting Identities* (1996). Brah was born in India, raised in Uganda, educated in the United States and lives in England; she points out that she belongs both to India and Uganda, claiming a dual identity, rather than a transnational one, in fact, disregarding the influences of her American education and British location on her hybrid identity. Brah claims that the fragmentation of transnational identities is only a fragmentation to the Western perception and reveals her own life experience to illustrate her contention. During the last year of her high school she applies for a scholarship in the United States. After the selection process she is called for an interview by an "all-male" panel that included representatives from various universities in the United States. A member of the panel asks "Do you see yourself as African or Indian?" (2). Brah points out that the interviewer uses the term 'Indian' "in the general sense that it was often used in East Africa to refer too all people of South Asian descent" (2). Moreover, the question is "absurd" for Brah who thinks: "Could he not see that I was *both*?" (2, original emphasis). Not wholly rejecting the conception of a unique identity in constant construction, Brah argues that one can contain multiple identities. To illustrate her point she maintains that Uganda is where she had spent all but the first five years of her life, and that she also remembers her childhood, the first five years in Panjab, India, and concludes that her identity is formed of those two cultures. However, she replies as the interviewer expects her to: "I am an Ugandan of Indian descent" (3). Years later, after completing her education in the United States, she writes in *Cartographies of Diaspora Contesting Identities*:

> [b]ut, of course, he could not *see* that I could be both. The body in front of him was already inscribed within the gendered social relations of the colonial sandwich. I could not just 'be'. I had to *name an identity*, no matter that this naming rendered invisible all the other identities- of gender, caste, religion, linguistic group, generation. (3, original emphasis)

One can state that there is a paradox in Brah's assertion of a unique dual identity. Although she carries both national identities as her unique self, she also points out that naming an identity is hard because of a "range of cultural variables," yet these cultural aspects are supposed to form the dual identity she claims to have. In fact, I believe that not labeling it as such, she implies a transnational identity, formed by her Indian and Ugandan selves. Therefore, she holds a transnational self, containing both identities. Moreover, significantly, for transnational people, it is possible to utilize any cultural identity accordingly, as Al-Shaykh's novel discussed in this essay likewise discerns.

Furthermore, Brah's elaborating on the question of home is quite exclusive, since she states that there are qualitatively two signifiers for home. One is 'home' in the form of a "simultaneously floating and rooted signifier" (3); it is an

> invocation of narratives of "*the* nation". In racialised or nationalist discourses, this signifier can become the basis of claims- in the proverbial Powellian[2] sense- that a group settled "in" a place is not necessarily "of" it. Idi Amin asserted that people of Asian descent could not be "of" Uganda, irrespective of how long they had lived there. (3, original emphasis)

On the other hand, the second signifier of 'home' for Brah is "the site of everyday lived experience. It is a discourse of locality, the place where feelings of rootedness ensue from the mundane and the unexpected of daily practice" (4). Thereby, home as the latter signifier "connotes our networks of family, kin, friends, colleagues and various other 'significant others'. It signifies the social and psychic geography of space that is experienced in terms of a neighborhood or a hometown. That is, a community 'imagined' in most part through daily encounter" (4). Brah's latter signifier of home then is revealed as a space "with which we remain intimate even in moments of intense alienation from it" (4). In the same vein, this chapter explores the conception of transnationality in the Lebanese writer Hanan Al-Shaykh's fiction *Only in London* (trans. 2001). I will map the gendered transnational spaces of the novel's Arab expatriate protagonists and the English protagonist Nicholas in London by examining Al-Shaykh's treatment of home in a multicultural England.

Transcultural Relationship Between London and Dubai

From sociological points of view, multiculturalism and transnationalism reveal particularities according to history and culture. Streamlining the focus to women and multiculturalism in Britain thus discloses some generalities and particularities. In this sense, multiculturalism denotes a very heterogeneous category of people who can be differentiated according to gender, religion, linguistic group, class and the wide range of diasporic experiences in their local and global specificity which foregrounds the politics of transnationality. Moreover, as John Lie highlights in his essay "Diasporic Nationalism," "the very possibility of transnationalism denies the irriversibility of the migration

---

[2] Enoch Powell (1912-1998), British politician, Conservative Party Member of Parliament between 1950-1974.

process" (356). As do numerous British women writers, so, too do Hanan Al-Shaykh's novels explicitly challenge the roles of women in the traditional social structures of the Arab Middle East. However, in *Only in London*, Al-Shaykh takes a different stance by placing her characters in the multicultural metropolis. Arriving on the same plane from Dubai, the lives of the Iraqi Lamis, the Moroccan Amira and the Lebanese transvestite Samir are restructured while fluctuating between belonging and unbelonging to the space they are relocated in.

It is also important to note here that Al-Shaykh's choice of Dubai for departure is significant in the way that her choosing London as a destination focuses on the transcultural realtionship between London and the enigmatic Arab world far beyond. To the group of expatriates who form an Arab diaspora in London, Al-Shaykh also appends the Englishman Nicholas, an expert at Sotheby's on Islamic daggers who also experiences a culture clash after having been located in Oman for a significant period of time. As a result, covering the underlying drama with comedy, Al-Shaykh's novel teems with memory, exile, ambivalence, and dislocation of the four people thrown together as the turbulance that the airplane hits, a turbulence which literally and ironically hurls them up and down, to meet each other in flight.

Already during this flight, identity becomes a key issue in Al-Shaykh's novel. The word "identity" derives from the Latin "identidem," an adverb meaning "repeatedly, again and again" (Craft 149). In recent years, however, the question of 'identity' has become central to various social sciences and it has taken on different connotations depending upon the context. Consequently, identity is "regarded in some sense as being more contingent, fragile and incomplete and thus more amenable to reconstitution than was previously thought possible" (du Gay 2). In this vein, the reconstitution of identity becomes more complex in diasporic and hybrid transnational spaces, where it is hard to construct a static stance. Two of Al-Shaykh's women protagonists, Lamis and Amira, have diverse backgrounds and occupations, yet their drama unfolds similarities in their efforts to survive and to retain their freedom in London, while fighting against both patriarchy and matriarchy, their haunting traditional backgrounds. Lamis divorced her wealthy Iraqi husband a month ago and comes back from a trip to Dubai visiting her parents and sister. Amira, on the other hand, left home at a young age and lives off immoral earnings.

Lamis' parents had run away from their home in Najaf, Iraq, from Saddam's threat to Beirut, Lebanon, when Lamis was twelve years old. At the prospect of a rich Iraqi suitor, it was her mother who first pleaded, then threatened and forced her to marry him, to pull the family out of poverty. Lamis marries him, moves to London, lives with her husband and mother-in-law, has a son and thirteen years later she divorces her husband, leaving the custody of her son to him and comes back from Dubai to lead her solitary life. Al-Shaykh mainly focuses on Lamis' dilemma as a young divorcee in London: torn between her parents' opposition to her divorce and her obligations as a mother to her son, Khalid, while trying to assess the emerging love affair with Nicholas in her new found freedom. On learning that Lamis was asking for a divorce, it is initially her mother who wails over the phone from Dubai, basically for a mercenary motive: "'You've ruined yourself and us, just like your father did'" (12). She is convinced that Lamis cannot survive as a woman without her husband's money:

> 'What about your son? Have you no heart? Did you forget you gave birth to Khalid? If you wanted a divorce you should have made his life hell so that he'd have been the one to ask for it, not you!' she screamed in a deranged voice. 'Or ... or... made him fall in love with another woman, even if you had to find her for him. Why don't you learn to play these tricks? By asking him for a divorce, you idiot, you aren't even entitled to a loaf of bread, let alone your child. Oh God. Everything will be lost- two buildings in Beirut, two flats in London- all that wealth will be down the drain. But now, listen, you have a British passport, you can sue him and get half of everything ...' (12).

A few months later, her father tries to dissuade Lamis from her decision, utilizing a patriarchal discourse, primarily stressing her obligation as a mother:

> 'Now you've tasted freedom, is it the paradise you expected? Of course it's not! How can it be when you left your son, a jewel bestowed on you by the Almighty to treasure? You're living in your ex-husband's flat and you haven't organized a job for yourself [...]. Why don't you go back to your husband? A friend of his called me. I think he was trying to act as a go-between.' Fear seized Lamis, and she shouted at the top of her voice, 'No, no, no. I don't want to go back to him.' She began to sob uncontrollably. (186-87)

Both parents stress Lamis' responsibility as a mother and threaten her with financial difficulties. Meanwhile, Lamis' feelings keep oscillating between guilt that emerges from her haunting traditional background, past memories of familial oppression, and elevation by the freedom she could not yet get adjusted to. Although she has lived in London, she had been confined to her Iraqi husband and her mother-in-law's will for long years. Lamis "did not dare even to think about what she wanted, still less how it might be expressed. She always let her husband decide for her, and her mother-in-law decided for him" (10). Here, the significance of hierarchy among women is disclosed explicitly; although a woman herself, the mother-in-law is quite oppressive over the daughter-in-law and Al-Shaykh reveals the fact that, while living free in London, Lamis is haunted by her mother-in-law's, more than by her husband's, domination.[3] There is no mention of a father-in-law, which invites speculations about whether in the absence of a father, the mother-in-law is in a stronger position as the mother of a son and hence oppresses both the son and the daughter-in-law as a possible revenge of matriarchy against patriarchy.

However, in relocating herself, Lamis' primacy is in assimilating and belonging to England in her efforts to eradicate her oppressive past. Living in the Arabic closed circle of her in-laws and their friends for thirteen years, the first thing that strikes Lamis in her emancipation is that she does not know any English person. Consequently, she makes a list of resolutions in which she puts forward her determination that England is going to be her country. Her list consists of the following points: "[l]earn English properly, look for a job, make friends with some English people and stop eating Arab food" (19). Thus, Lamis' resolutions reveal that her trajectory is towards eradicating her Arab self and relocating her space as a British person in England. In this vein, her priorities for Britishness are language, community and food. Lamis adds "not because the garlic and coriander make my breath smell, but because this kind of food makes me feel safe and secure and reminds me of childhood and home" (19), hence Al-Shaykh signifies the poignancy of memories for diasporic identities. Nevertheless, in order to belong to their new home, the diasporic identities have to unshed the secure covers of childhood and home, challenging their new, insecure, but independent lives. Intended for deconstructing her ethnic identity, Lamis primarily starts taking private English classes. The initial dialogue is poignant in illustrating the concept of an adopted home. Lamis states: "'I need to look for work. I think having an English accent could be the key.' 'In other words, you've taken England as your second home.' 'No, as my first home'" (53). Her teacher also confirms what Lamis has found out by instinct, namely that "altering the way you speak affects your personality inside ... You should stop eating Arab dishes, because subconsciously you'll be saying their names" (53-54). Again food triggers language and as a result, memory of home, which in Lamis' case is paradoxically both Iraq and her husband and mother-in-law in London. With her son, Khalid, on the other hand, she keeps a special relationship; firstly as a single mother, then as a couple with Nicholas.

---

[3] It is quite significant that neither the mother-in-law nor the husband is named; this suggests that Al-Shaykh focuses on their institutional functions rather than their identities.

Nonetheless, the mother and son's psychological relationship is not elaborated on by the writer, which certainly would divert the topic and would create a different novel.

Al-Shaykh's narration, on the other hand, reveals that the ambivalence of transnational identity is quite complicated as is also specified in Lamis' love affair with Nicholas, an Englishman she met on the plane from Dubai. They meet accidentally when Lamis drops her British passport during the turbulence, and Nicholas finally finds and delivers it back to her. Amira invites them both to her home for dinner, but quite early in her independent stance, Lamis refuses to attend.

Since Lamis decides to stretch her boundaries after a while, she goes to Leighton House to watch a performance and visit an exhibition. The only friend she has of her former life before her divorce is her Iraqi friend Belquis. Yet, their relationship is also disclosed as problematic. On her return from Dubai, she dials Belquis' number but stops before she reaches the end, doubting whether Belquis is still her friend: "Didn't friends of newly divorced couples become like footballs, not knowing which team's net they were going to land in?" (11). Nevertheless, Belquis calls her a few days later, reproaching her for not being in touch. Lamis tries to act "naturally," although she thinks of explaining to Belquis that she had taken a decision not to see anyone from her "past, that her friendship with Belquis was mainly due to her marriage" (57). Lamis cannot bring herself to say anything and, "with a tearful sense of defeat" (57) she agrees when Belquis suggests they meet at Leighton House where there is a performance and an exhibition. Lamis decides to dress "differently" for the occasion since she wants Belquis to "see her as someone who was happy to be divorced, free: neither repressed of reckless, but balanced and composed" (58).

Yet, catching sight of Belquis at Leighton House illustrates to Al-Shaykh's protagonist the past that she ran away from. Belquis embodies "the cult of the single brand; the Chanel bag, the Chanel buttons: the intertwined 'c's like a pair of forceps" (59). Lamis recalls the numerous charitable functions where the Arab women "vied with each other over their clothes and social status" (59). Belquis signifies the rich Arab women in London who take classes at Sotheby's or Christie's in table decoration, the history of chocolate, bridge, flower arranging and so forth and who afterwards meet in a restaurant, "feeling that they'd earned it, confident that they could say they hadn't wasted their time in this country" (59). Their social life signifies the superficiality of the vain rich Arab women who try to delude their oppressed selves by spending money recklessly, ironically showing off to each other, rather than uniting in solidarity. Thereby, Belquis represents the stereotypical Arab women who obey their husbands' orders. Representing the other oppressed women, she strongly objects to Lamis' divorce although she says "I get nausea and feel faint, sick. I'm not happy" (59). Since Belquis' friendship is limited and bound with patriarchy, her rejection of Lamis mental situation about her marriage and her mindless effort of enticement is pathethic: "'perhaps you've got an inner-ear infection or a tapeworm, or you've been eating too much chocolate'" (59). Hence, Belquis sums up everything Lamis hates; women who are the show off embodiment of their husbands. Consequently, Lamis runs away and hides from her, revealing: "When I look at Belquis it'll be her husband's face I see. He'll be hiding behind her hair, telling her off for still talking to me" (60). The narrator also reinforces this idea adding that "[m]any of the women she [Lamis] knew during her marriage had the strange habit of metamorphosing into their husbands on certain occasions, especially at charity balls, and taking not only their names but their physical appearance" (60). Therefore the comment signifies Al-Shaykh's criticism of patriarchy's strength in enforcing women not only to invisibility, but also on an appalling mimicry of themselves on public occasions, which may have the purpose of forging their duplicates in their wives. The author voices the illustration of the situation in the following terms:

> they probably saw Lamis herself in the guise of her ex-husband, smoking a fat cigar and receiving people, holding forth on his political views: "I've tried everything. I've made my fortune. I'm in my fifties. I've achieved what I set out to, and now I want to go into politics." (60)

Explicitly put, it is always the 'I' for the husband for whose narcissistic self the wife does not exist except for serving the purpose of reinforcing his being in duplication. Hence, Lamis never meets Belquis again in her new life since Belquis is both the personification of all the oppressed women and their dominating husbands of Lamis' former life.

Keeping away from Belquis at the Leighton House, Lamis sees Nicholas again and is able to make the first move, introducing herself as the woman whose lost passport he has handed back on the Dubai plane. Although Lamis could not dare to join Nicholas and Amira's dinner because of her lack of courage in her new, independent life, Nicholas remembers her and they start seeing each other. In a short time they fall in love, yet, knowing each other better does not improve their relationship since Lamis' identity is fluid and "will always be contingent" (Craft 155). Doris Sommer underpins that "transculturation" or "creativity derived from antagonism" results in "double consciousness" (305). Following Brah, Linda J. Craft also maintains that diasporic identities "no longer have to be diluted by assimilation, but rather can be strengthened and, at the same time, nuanced through an ongoing process of negotiation, adaptation, and remembering. In short, one need not lose oneself to find oneself" (Craft 155). Nevertheless, the arguments on identity are quite complex. In the same vein, yet slightly different, Connie D. Griffin, in her article entitled "Excentricities: Perspectives on Gender and Multi-Cultural Self-Representation in Contemporary American Women's Autobiographies," points out that the politics of location that arises in contemporary women's self-representational narratives:

> articulates a paradoxical position; it is not merely one of location or dislocation, but, rather, the co-existence of the two as the marginalized subject shuttles back and forth between them to weave a sense of self within a perceived position of absence. Out of this weaving comes a reconstruction of a past perceived by the hegemonics of centricity as having no history at all. It is from this position, a third place of paradoxical being, one that I describe as ex-centric, that some female subjects seek to express themselves. Such subjects are in the process of mapping new cultural spaces (321).

In this vein, Al-Shaykh enables Lamis' attaining the co-existence of location and dislocation through a more complex position because Lamis has to relocate herself more than once: she moves from oppression in Iraq to Lebanon, then from London to her husband's Arab community and finally she manages to relocate herself in London as an independent woman. Thus the 'weaving' a sense of self between location and dislocation that Griffin notes is possible although the 'ex-centric' position moves its center to a transnational position balanced towards the English. Hence, for Al-Shaykh's protagonist Lamis, losing the part of her oppressed self and reconstituting her identity as wholly liberated and confident is not possible since Griffin's 'third place' attained by having no history at all cannot easily be discerned since eradicating the past from identity is an intricate process and the presence of Lamis' son Khalid, who lives with his father and grandmother, adds to the complexity of situation.

At the beginning of her freedom, Lamis is quite timid and keeps her private life from Nicholas. Lamis' meeting with Nicholas' friends reinforces her timidity since she can neither build nor reveal self-confidence like the Europeans. She also perceives that 'everybody,' which signifies Nicholas' English friends, sees in her an Arab-Iraqi rather than a 'person.' When she specifies to Nicholas that "[i]t made me wonder about you and me" (160), Nicholas confesses:

> 'I thought about it, too, when I found myself so attracted to you. Was I drawn to you because I was involved in the Arab world? I agree, it happens sometimes ... but only at the be-

ginning ... It's like having a beautiful Arab dagger in your hand. After a while you cease to think about where it came from. You marvel at the wonderful craftsmanship but otherwise its origin is neither here or there. You appreciate it and love its beauty for itself.' (160)

On the other hand, Al-Shaykh unveils that their relationship is fragmented and finally disrupted because of Lamis' traditional Arab background and her feeling of guilt. Lamis cannot wholly leave her flat and move to Nicholas' house, cannot dare to introduce him to her son Khalid, and cannot go to Oman with Nicholas for a few months, fearing that the information on her British passport about her birth place will cause her trouble. Finally, Nicholas abandons her without a word and goes to Oman alone. This causes Lamis to suffer for a long time until she attains enough courage to join him. While Lamis is convinced that being European equals being confident (158), Nicholas, who works in Oman for considerably long periods of time, contrarily reveals that:

[t]he more contact I have with other cultures, the more I find us naïve. We really don't understand the political situation in your country. And the more I travel, the more I discover ways in which we English are odd. In my childhood, I thought we were quite normal; yet now I think of the English as being introverted, shy, clumsy. We lack self-assurance. We have so many taboos [...] (161).

Thus, Nicholas also somewhat reconstitutes his identity through his own transcultural experience in reverse. A "certain nomadism," Stuart Hall maintains, characterizes the contemporary immigrant subject who must always negotiate both center and periphery (119). Hall also underpins that the experience of diaspora is defined "not by essence or purity, but by recognition of a necessary heterogeneity and diversity, by a conception of 'identity' which lives with and through, not despite, difference by hybridity" (119). As a result, diasporic identities are those which are constantly "producing and reproducing themselves anew, through transformation and difference" (Hall 120).

Amira's and Samir's Dissidence in London

Al-Shaykh's narration carries equal weight for Amira as much as Lamis, nonetheless, Amira's feelings and self-evaluation are not elaborated on in the novel as much as Lamis'. Although Amira is dissident against both the class and gender structure of Morocco and the Arab world in general, her engaging in prostitution as a tool of avenging both patriarchy and poverty defies all moralistic conceptions. Her location in London supplies her with a better positionality since she can easily detect the type of men with whom she would like to connect. Amira comes from a very poor, low-class family in Morocco, as one of many children. The function of class structure also affects Amira's gendered transnational discourse. Determined to have a better life, she gets engaged with a student at a young age, but when her mother refuses to present the promised dowry, her lover deserts her and Amira runs away from home, either to commit suicide or fight to get rich. Amira reconstitutes her identity on the conviction that the world goes around in money and that she would gain it through men, by using her skill, beauty and intelligence. As the third person narration unravels, at the Hyde Park Speaker's corner she would have liked to say: "It is so simple- in this world there are the rich and the poor. The occupation of the poor is to milk the rich, to save the rich from being bewildered and confused about how to spend their fortunes" (217). Having witnessed an Arab princess in a luxurious hotel, Amira compares her own pitiful childhood in poverty to that of the Princess and refashions herself, impersonating an Arab princess and becomes quite successful at it, until she is found out and beaten by an Arab Prince. Her dissidence against her own culture's gender role is revealed in her choosing Arab men as her clients, stating that they need their own 'kind,' "in their own surroundings and their own language" (167) in London, signifying Arab men's insecurity in dislocation.

However, compared to what Lamis immediately realizes after her divorce, Amira never mentions the fact that she does not have any English friends. Her closest friend is the Egyptian Nahid whom she met ten years ago in a hospital in Richmond, where they were both having abortions: Amira, pregnant by a client and Nahid by the owner of a cabaret where she danced. They become good friends confiding everything to each other to such an extent that when the Englishman Stanley asked Nahid to marry him, her first concern had been "whether it would threaten her friendship" (108) with Amira. They divorce a few months later, straight after their return from Cairo ironically because of Stanley's cultural misunderstanding, dislocated in the Arab world. He insults her and her compatriots prompted by the sight of the overworked donkeys, calling her people "savages" (220). Nahid gradually stops her communication with Amira by never returning her calls. When finally Amira goes to visit Nahid she is shocked to find her friend as a woman whose "head muffled, wearing a long djellabah" and after a short talk with Amira, not really explaining why she has changed, she opens the door to several women wearing headscarves and introduces them as "My sisters in Islam" (207). Disbelieving the situation, Amira tries to visit her friend after some time and Nahid reveals that she has cancer. They become close friends again until she dies. Al-Shaykh briefly evokes the notion that the religious shelter for transnational personae forms in distress: Nahid's turning to religion by redemption from their immoral occupation and learning about her fatal illness is almost simultaneous, so Amira keeps wondering which came first, Nahid's covering her head or learning about her fatal illness. Al-Shaykh also criticizes the function of religious superstition as hypocrisy in two instances. When Amira visits her mother in Morocco, she does not let Amira sleep with her sisters in the same room so that she would not contaminate them because of her occupation. Likewise, although the mother welcomes the financial help she receives from her daughter, she does not literarily touch her daughter's 'polluted' money until a pious neighbor comes and cleanses the money by prayer. The second instance is that at Nahid's deathbed, a woman whom Nahid met "recently at the mosque" (219) does not let Nahid's ex-husband Stanley see her for the last time because they are divorced, standing guard at the bedroom door and saying "No, no, no." (219) until Stanley starts crying, "sobbing like a child" saying "I want to talk to her, say goodbye, and give her this bunch of flowers" (219). Amira intervenes screaming at the woman: "'Are you saying that quack faith healer who took the Dupont lighter and said he'd have her back on her feet in a couple of days has more right to be in her room than the man she lived with? What kind of nonsense is that?'" (219-20) and allows Stanley to enter Nahid's room. The so-called traditions implied by Al-Shaykh are significant in the way that they reveal religious tokenism, focusing mainly on the oppression of women. Certainly, Al-Shaykh's humorous and ironic tone creates a shrewd stance for her to critique the Arab community.

Characterizing Amira as a prostitute, Al-Shaykh focuses on hierarchy in gender relations. Amira voices that women of 'her kind' are considered as lesser humans:

> she refused to sleep with Iraqis after they invaded Kuwait, then stopped sleeping with Kuwaitis because they drove other Arab nationals out of Kuwait. But she'd stopped getting involved in politics- prostitutes, whores were not a part of society. They weren't born of a mother's womb: they grew on trees, without fathers or brothers or sisters or relatives of any sort. One punter was shocked when she told him she was an experienced chef, as if she wasn't entitled to any other job. (255)

Moreover, it is not only men, but also women who look down upon Amira; especially her best friend Nahid, after she started covering her head. Despite her sorrow over Nahid's death, Amira does not give up her profession and goes on living with the Lebanese homosexual Samir, calling him Nahid, with affection. In their article "Who's agenda Is It? [sic]," Moira Dustin and Anne

Phillips hold that developments in Britain reflect a shift from a shallow but widely endorsed multiculturalism to a growing preoccupation with abuses of women in minority cultural groups. Dustin and Phillips point out that "[f]our main issues have been debated in the media and have become the basis of either public policy or legal judgment: forced marriage, honour killing, female genital cutting and women's Islamic dress" (405). For Dustin and Phillips the treatment of these issues has often been problematic, due to discourses that tend to misrepresent cultural minority groups as monolithic entities, and initiatives to protect women becoming entangled with anti-immigration agendas. It has therefore proved hard to address abuses of women without simultaneously promoting stereotypes of culture. In other words, the dilemma is centered around whether the host country should interfere with communal life or not, since the questions of culture are merged with questions of religion with complicated and sometimes with contradictory results. It may also be the reason why Al-Shaykh only includes Nicholas as an English persona in her fiction and excludes English society in general while concentrating on highly extremist individuals from the Arab society as illustrated by a divorcee, a prostitute and a transvestite. This may signify that Al-Shaykh discloses Arab society with variables; the rich and the poor, the honest and the dishonest, and the religious and the non-religious, in an attempt to obliterate stereotyping. Thereby, although hierarchically regarded at the lowest level, transnationality provides a luxurious life for Amira.

Parallel to Amira, Samir finally has a chance to reveal his homosexuality in London and creates his own means of freedom. Smuggling a cappuccino monkey to London, he earns some money, but more importantly and ironically, their mutual affection enables Samir to realize that he likes his monkey more than his enforced family of a wife and five children. The narrator notes, "Samir had been in London two months. It was strange, he felt he belonged there and nowhere else, and he missed nobody. If he dared to tell the truth, he would say that he didn't even miss his children" (149). The writer also adds that the sole reason for that is not Samir's performing his transvestite identity but also his other civil liberties:

> he was doing what he always wanted to do: make people laugh [...] London was freedom. It was your right to do anything, any time. You didn't need to undergo a devastating war in order to be freed to do what you wanted, and when you did do what you wanted, you didn't have to feel guilty or embarrassed, and start leading a double life and ultimately end up frustrated. (149)

Thereby, despite all the disputes on identity Al-Shaykh's protagonist claims that duplicity of self also arises from the oppression of the community, the location where one is supposed to belong, but does not.

However, it is also significant that Al-Shaykh keeps Samir within the boundaries of the Arab community in London, ironically revealing that the dislocated Arabs on the margins are more inclusive of sexual marginalities. As the narrator unravels, it was Samir's mother who sent him to a psychiatric hospital when she had found out that he was "singing and dancing on the roof terrace wearing her blue nylon nightie, her lipstick and high heels" (150) at the age of eleven. The doctor advises them to show him plenty of affection, but three years later, Samir attempts suicide and is sent back to the same hospital. Amira takes care of Samir in London and allows him to live with her, on condition that he does the cooking and the cleaning for her. Amira, the monkey and Nahid construct Samir's family in London. After a series of comic episodes that disclose Samir's affection for English men, Samir's wife and her five children who live in Sharjah, come to London unannounced to live with him. Since she is too naïve to realize that Samir is a transvestite, she displays fits of jealousy after finding women's clothing in the wardrobe. She first believes that Samir has an affair with Amira; when she is reassured that Amira is only a friend, she insists that the women's clothes in her husband's apartment belong to his mistress. In the end, the wife goes back taking her children and Samir is liberated to live his life as he desires. The monkey which symbolizes Samir's bond to his previous home also runs away and liberates Samir to construct his new self. Gay sexualities and transnational migration is a complex topic. As Denise A. Segura and Patricia Zavella hold in their article "Gendered Borderlands," a feminist borderland project interrogates multiple meanings of borders and borderlands while a nuanced analysis of the intertwined processes of gay sexualities and transnational migration reveal that "[d]espite their marginality within heteronormative discourses and practices on both sides of the U.S.-Mexico border [...] gay subjects negotiate location and materiality so as to express their complex identities and support one another" (539).

Conclusion

As stated at the beginning of this paper, Samir and Amira regard London as home, a space where they can perform their marginalities, which is in line with the second sense of what Brah coins as "a psychic geography of space" where they are allowed the freedom of the country they are 'in' but not 'of.' They regard their transnational situatedness as a space where they can belong to their own Arab community, yet perform their genuine selves, not attempting to assimilate as in the instance of Lamis. Whether Lamis can transform from her transnational space and become 'of' England is doubtful. As Brah contends:

> I know now and I knew then that "looks" mattered a great deal within the colonial regimes of power. Looks mattered because of the history of the racialisation of "looks"; they mattered because discourses about the body were crucial to the constitution of racisms. And racialised power operated in and through bodies. (3)

Transnationalism is the conception of diasporic experiences through Eastern and Western dissimilarities that cause poignant waves in the fluidity of identity constructions. Nevertheless, arguing through Brah's contention, home is where there is a sense of "feeling at home" (4). Thus, despite their looks and the underlying drama, Al-Shaykh's characters choose to go on contented, because despite the feelings of guilt enforced by their traditional backgrounds, they are able to reconstitute their identities "only in London."

Works Cited

Appiah, Kwame Anthony. "The Politics of Identity." *Daedalus* 135.4 (Fall 2006): 15-22.

Brah, Avtar. *Cartographies of Diaspora Contesting Identities*. New York: Routledge, 2003.

Craft, Linda J. "Mario Bencastro's Diaspora: Salvadorans and Transnational Identity" *MELUS* 30.1 (Spring 2005): 149-168.

Du Gay, Paul, Jessica Evans and Peter Redman, eds. *Identity: A Reader*. London: SAGE, 2000.

Dustin Moira and Anne Phillips. "Whose Agenda Is It: Abuses of Women and Abuses of 'Culture' in Britain." *Ethnicities* 8.3 (2008): 405-424.

González, María Martínez. "Feminist Praxis Challenges the Identity Question: Toward New Collective Identity Metaphors." *Hypatia* 23.3 (July–September 2008): 22-38.

Griffin, Connie D. "Ex-centricities: Perspectives on Gender and Multi-Cultural Self-Representation in Contemporary American Women's Autobiographies." *Style* 35.2 (Summer 2001): 321-23.

Hall, Stuart. "Cultural Identity and Diaspora." *Contemporary Postcolonial Theory: A Reader*. Ed. Padmini Mongia. New York: St. Martin's Press, 1996. 110-21

Lie, John. "Diasporic Nationalism." *Cultural Studies Critical Methodologies* 1.3 (August 2001): 355-362.

Nasta, Susheila. *Home Truths Fictions of Diaspora in Britain*. Basingstoke, Hampshire: Palgrave, 2002.

Robbins, Bruce. "Comparative Cosmopolitanisms." *Cosmopolitics: Thinking and Feeling Beyond the Nation*. Ed. Pheng Cheah and Bruce Robbins. Minneapolis: University of Minnesota Press, 1998. 246-64.

Segura, Denise A. and Patricia Zavella. "Gendered Borderlands." *Gender & Society* 22.5 (October 2008): 537-544

Sommer, Doris. "Choose and Lose." *Multilingual America: Transnationalism, Ethnicity, and the Languages of American Literature*. Ed. Werner Sollors. New York and London: New York University Press, 1998. 297-309.

CHAPTER NINE

"Merely a Trick of Moonlight": The Accidental Triangulation of Love, Power, and Narrative in Zadie Smith's *White Teeth*

Jessica Weintraub

only connect –E.M. Forster

In "Leda and the Swan," W.B. Yeats ruminates whether Leda, while coupling with Zeus, "put on his knowledge with his power" (line 14). How power is exchanged, shared, partitioned or transferred in the ongoing relationship between colonizer and colonized has been examined by theorists, poets, and novelists, many of whom describe the transfer of knowledge/power achieved through love, either the love that comes through understanding and fellowship, or through the transformative power of Eros. By depicting a rape, Yeats' sonnet conflates the erotic with violence; here, Eros at its most dangerous pitch, is an entry point into investigations of power dynamics. As Michel Foucault so famously decried: "pleasure and power do not cancel or turn back against one another; they seek out, overlap, and reinforce one another" (48). If "complex mechanisms and devices of excitation and incitement" (48) linking pleasure and power are narrative in nature, and if History is an abstraction comprised of a constellation of biographies and autobiographies – the stories people tell themselves and the stories people tell each other (i.e. personal histories) – then pleasure-power codes are found most tellingly in fictional narratives themselves, rather than other genres of depiction or reportage. Looking closely at tangential points of this transmission helps us grapple with the dynamics and interstices of love, power and a historically-driven narrative in Zadie Smith's novel *White Teeth*. Didier Coste in *Story and Situation: Narrative Seduction and the Power of Fiction* states that "an act" of communication becomes narrative "when imparting a transitive view of the world is the effect of the message produced" (4). Characters declare and silence their feelings for each other throughout the novel and each choice, however accidental, to reveal and/or to conceal emotionality accumulates within and under political-cultural themes. Since both love relationships and historical relationships shadow each other, and underscore the umbrella thematic concerns of the novel – the friction inherent in what Laura Moss calls "everyday hybridity" in contemporary London – love relationships mimic, subvert, inform and at times redeem the "bloody" history that the novel more overtly exposes, and indeed shape the narrative itself.

White Teeth is primarily set in late twentieth-century London and traces several generations of two families, the Joneses and the Iqbals. The book begins with Archie Jones, a working-class Englishman, attempting to gas himself to death in his car. He is saved by Mo, a halal butcher (Archie's car is blocking the butcher's delivery driveway). Later that same day, Archie meets and marries Clara, a Jamaican woman who immigrated to London with her mother, Hortense. Archie's best friend is Samad Iqbal, a Muslim from Bangladesh. The men both fought for the British in World War II. While the middle-aged men, equally baffled by change they cannot imagine, symbolize postwar England, Magid and Millat, twin sons of Samad and his wife, Alsana, and Clara and Archie's daughter, Irie, all born in England, form a contemporary trifecta of English culture and, much like nineteenth-century surveyors in the Himalayas, triangulate previously under-mapped areas of transnational "realms of truth" (as Foucault phrases it in *Madness and Civilization*) in order to trace the evolution of Englishness.

The novel is nominally divided into four sections headlined by one or more main characters, but the divisions are, to use the novel's trope, overlapping and crowded rather than gapped. The narrative voice is intimate, wry, consistent, and almost all-knowing. Rather than individual portraits, even characters' deepest, most inner thoughts are often relayed within the context of other people's thoughts and actions. The telescopic narrative style creates an interlocking, interconnected landscape, much like the physical and cultural topography of late twentieth-century London. Each section title also includes two dates, banner years around which much of the narrative is corralled, and/or years important to the headline main character in terms of his/her/their development. The first three sections depict scenes of what Ann Laura Stoler calls "tense and tender ties" (829) separated by a generation ("Archie 1974, 1945"), 130 years ("Samad 1984, 1857"), or nearly a century ("Irie 1990, 1907"). Each of the first three sections begins in the present or near present and then glances back in the form of a chapter called "The Root Canals of [...]" (71, 203, 295). The result of this form is an almost xylophone effect through time, zigzagging across and back national boundaries that mimic migration patterns – and re-migration iterations. Magid, tricked by Samad and dropped off at Heathrow without any warning or goodbyes, is sent to Bangladesh as a sacrifice for his father's adulterous relationship with his sons' teacher, Poppy Burt-Jones. After eight years, Magid returns to England "more English than the English [...]

sporting a "stiff upper lip [...]brushing [his teeth] six times a day, [and] ironing [his underwear]" (350). In spite of even these examples of enculturation, and in the midst of a burgeoning London multiculturalism Sander L. Gilman, in "'We're Not Jews': Imagining Jewish History and Jewish Bodies in Contemporary Multicultural Literature," insists that "because of their visibility and in spite of their seeming hybridity [...] all the children were foreigners" (128). The narrator first appears to disagree with this assessment; however, at the end of the list of multicultural names, there is an abandoned bed, a restless lover, and a knife:

> This has been the century of strangers, brown, yellow, and white. This has been the century of the great immigrant experiment. It is only this late in the day that you can walk into a playground and find Isaac Leung by the fish pond, Danny Rahman in the football cage, Quang O'Rourke bouncing a basketball, and Irie Jones humming a tune. Children with first and last names on a direct collision course. Names that secrete within them mass exodus, cramped boats and planes, cold arrivals, medical checkups. It is only this late in the day, and possibly only in Willesden, that you can find best friends Sita and Sharon, constantly mistaken for each other because Sita is white (her mother liked the name) and Sharon is Pakistani (her mother thought it best—less trouble). Yet, despite all the mixing up, despite the fact that we have finally slipped into each other's lives with reasonable comfort (like a man returning to his lover's bed after a midnight walk), despite all this, it is still hard to admit that there is no one more English than the Indian, no one more Indian than the English. There are still young white men who are *angry* about that; who will roll out at closing time into the poorly lit streets with a kitchen knife wrapped in a tight fist. (271–72, original emphasis)

Smith's conflation of violent desire within its objective correlative – heaving, "cleaving" (359) land – delineate the fraught relationships between the older (in terms of generational time spent on English soil), possibly whiter English and the newer, possibly browner English men and women. After the double event of the 1907 Jamaican earthquake (during which Hortense was born) the inside-outside histories of happening, a description of race relations described as "a man returning to his lover's bed after a midnight walk" (271-72), the "reasonable comfort" with which "we" have "slipped into each other's lives" (271) seems sketchy, slippery, uncomfortable, and bleak. Why has the man been out of bed walking at midnight except if he was feeling somewhat anxious? And yet, he does return to the bed, the site of erotic love, the mysterious variable, an escaped FutureMouse (a genetic experiment that Marcus – who is connected to Magid, Millat, and Irie – conducts, only to have it elide into the crowd, a "small, brown rebel mouse" (448) in the last line of the novel.

Love is a mediating and motivating force in a novel more overtly about ethnic identities. *White Teeth* asks a series of questions that appear to be outside of multi-ethnicity, but in fact are central to its definition: Is a deliberately historically-informed narrative merely a tool to frame emotion – the "unspeakable"? How does love work within contemporary racial discourses – can it even exist within these loaded and mutually dependent relationships? Is love a strategic tool within unbalanced power relationships, or are any genuine gestures of positive affirmation impossible within the climate of the dominant power discourse? How does love affect the trajectories of history, and what occurs to the triangulation of speaker, auditor and subject, when love is the subject? How is this different than desire intermingled and colluded by ownership?

Relo or Subprime: Location, Location, Location

Smith chooses to locate her story, her history, in a mouthscape (white teeth), the focus of desire, hunger, kisses, language, oral storytelling, lies, and/or promises. Both a pure and a profane place. Teeth are a source and symbol of violence. They clench in anger and pain, rip and tear out of ferocity or hunger, protect us, feed us, clack against each other, gnash in pain or pleasure. They are also a tool of eroticism. At their most prosaic, they are intricately involved in eating, a sometimes-social activity. When we "break bread" together, we are really ripping it apart into swallowable bites with our teeth. Teeth then, with their myriad uses and Janus-like function of simultaneously performing two opposite *metiers*, are a bodily representation of the word "cleave" – "the double meaning of *cleave*" (359, original emphasis) – the word that Magid starts to explain to Irie on her errand to bring the warring twin brothers together in "a neutral place." Irie asks herself: "Did he know which was worse, which was more traumatic: pulling together or tearing apart?" (ibid.). The mouth, a polarized, twinned space, capable of feeling and causing both sides of hybridity: a space of *jouissance* and "extreme pain and agonizing dislocations" (Radhakrishnan 753) is Smith's candidate for a "third space," a place of loss, of memory, and unrelenting hope for connection, put most effectively by Irie:

> She got a twinge—as happens with a sensitive tooth, or in a "phantom tooth," when the nerve is exposed—[...] She felt an ache (like a severe malocclusion, the pressure of one tooth upon another) [...] where he had kissed her once in the

middle of a storm. Irie wished she could give herself over to these past-present fictions: wallow in them, make them sweeter, longer, particularly the kiss. (379)

By choosing to locate her narrative in the mouth, it seems as if Smith herself is forcing us to acknowledge, explore, and even judiciously "celebrate" (Moss 11) the crevices of human relationships as the makers and movers of history, however "bloody" that history may be. In her own words, her novel is "what should be, can be and maybe will be" (Lyall), a hope that relies on a unique humanistic pedagogy and the lucky accidents resulting from art-making: tools that work in tandem to activate readers' pathos and logos merging to alter perception. Her novel, although it is many things, is especially an argument for the coincidental and accidental embedded in everyday existence, both of which are signifiers for romantic love and its trajectories or far-reaching consequences: a version of history, as opposed to the grand events enumerated in history books and newspapers, which resembles "the decision to not do, to un-do; a kiss blown at oblivion" (9). And yet, the novel is attempting to delineate "oblivion" by ruthlessly remembering and intermingling two centuries of colonial ties, ties that have from the beginning been an admixture of conflict and desire.

Although Smith's text appears to give predominance to cultural, ideological, and religious "fundamentalism," love colors each of those conflicts, and, as Catherine Belsey writes in "Postmodern Love: Questioning the Metaphysics of Desire," love "is itself another kind of fundamentalism," which renders it "at once endlessly pursued and ceaselessly suspected" (685). *White Teeth* uses a variety of love relationships to explore and explode power dynamics engendered by love plots, the so-called "kiss[es] blown at oblivion." The most powerful incident illustrating the conflation of love, history, and power is the story of Ambrosia – Clara's grandmother Irie's great-grandmother – and Captain Durham, Hortense's parents. The tale is revealed near the end of the novel, but the shadow of it casts back and colors the contemporary love affairs of Archie and Clara, Samad and Poppy Burke-Jones, and most devastingly, Irie and the Iqbal twins. The first female Bowden we meet is Clara. Like Hans Christian Anderson's *The Little Mermaid*, who trades her fishtail and her tongue – and with that the ability to speak – for a pair of women's legs for a chance of love with a human Prince, Clara's toothlessness seems to stand for generations of "education" and silencing by generations of English colonial powers, beginning with Hortense's mother, Ambrosia, who is seduced by English officer, Captain Charles Durham, under the auspices of teaching the young Jamaican girl Latin and to read from the Bible. "If this were a fairy tale," the disembodied narrator remarks in "The Root Canals of Hortense Bowden" chapter, Captain Durham would have "saved" Ambrosia and their crowning child, Hortense. Durham

> does not seem to lack the necessary credentials [...] It is not that [...] he doesn't want to help her, or that he doesn't love her (oh, he *loves* her; just as the English loved India and Africa and Ireland; it is the love that is the problem, people treat their lovers badly). (299, original emphasis)

During the "terrible Jamaican earthquake [on January 14, 1907]" (298), the church literally falls around Ambrosia, crushing her rapist so thoroughly that his false teeth skitter across the floor. By telling the story of Hortense's birth and Ambrosia's rape in the midst of a Historical Event reported on in newspapers and known to all, Smith reminds us that "every moment happens twice: inside and outside, and they are two different histories" (299). At the same time that another Englishman, Sir Edmund Flecker Glenard, is groping the abandoned and pregnant Ambrosia, "inside there was [Hortense's] galloping heartbeat" (ibid.).

The correlation between Hortense "kicking at [the fat hand of Glenard hot against her mother] with all of her might" (298), the "crush of a million muscles that wanted desperately to repel Glenard's attempts at an education" and the crushing geological Act of God are difficult to discount. What happens inside can trigger what happens outside; the personal morphs into the political by this route. Seismic emotionality reverberates in political and historical topographies, causing inner and "outer" histories to shatter. In the fragmentation that ensues during the internal and geological earthquakes, the earth's subjective "turbulence of its "[Lacanian]'fragmented' body [..., what] precedes Eros and which will come to inhabit desire" (Belsey 695). Every entity is rent simultaneously, each wrenching collapses into one another, until it is impossible to discern the starting point that might have set the other "cleaving" in motion. Bodies, landscape, infrastructure, as well as tidy notions of divine intervention divide and fall with equal abandon. The most enduring powers are the ones based on rules that historically and by necessity "ignore exceptions" (300). Under this rigid schema, it is impossible to imagine natives in general as unlucky agents of collusion in their own victimhood. This system cannot imagine or allow genuine feelings of passion or fellowship; therefore, no matter how fervent Captain Durham's love for the "'educated Negress' he wished to marry [who] was not like the others" (300), she can only be a "whore" (300). Still, if we read Ambrosia's internal earthquakes (labor and fear) and the fetus that is Hortense kicking against Glenard's "groping" (298) hands *as* Jamaica itself violently bucking in an attempt to unseat the white foreigners on its back, then we see desire splitting Empire along the very faults its European rulers have ignored: "the floor cracked, the far wall crumbled, the stained glass exploded [...] the ground split – a mighty crack! – [...] and the ground continued to vibrate" (299). Smith concludes that there are mechanizations of history that cannot be reversed by love when she writes, "But maybe it is just the scenery is wrong. Maybe nothing that happens on stolen ground can expect a happy ending" (ibid.).

Reading Jacques Derrida's *The Post Card: From Socrates to Freud and Beyond*, published in 1986, would confirm a postmodern view of "true love" as unable to transcend the confines of history and power relations, the realities of "Isaac Leung [...], Danny Rahman [...], Quang O'Rourke [...], and Irie Jones" (271) notwithstanding. The novel's narrator dampens the hopefulness implanted in the names as soon as they are incanted: "Children with first and last names on a direct collision course. Names that secret within them mass exodus, cramped boats and planes, cold arrivals, medical checks" (ibid.). The monikers are now the products of lovers and lovers treating each other badly, in which "histories [are inescapable,] embedded in their very names" (Moss 14). Irie embodies the shadow narrative of *White Teeth* and is the mobilizing force of the novel. She is most definitely the descendent of Ambrosia, the woman who is compared to a colonized country, and therefore, tracing the metaphoric transformation, both are indivisible from that slice of "stolen ground." Irie is the post-colonial version of her grandmother, "stuck between a rock and a hard place, like Ireland, like Israel, like India" (351). She has more power and choice than Ambrosia, she is still "a girl" in the world, longing for "flickable" hair, a slimmer body, and a place in the landscape of desire. She is most certainly a "girl" as she is enfolded in the pseudo-liberated, and therefore incredibly sexist Chalfen household, upstaged by the returned, dapper Magid. She is a "*secretary*, whereas Magid was a confidant, an apprentice and disciple…The golden child. The chosen one" (352, original emphasis). As Ambrosia is the personification of colonial Jamaica, Irie embodies "Ireland, Israel, India" – countries that have inherited the strife of their colonial days and play out contemporary violent scenarios among and between their own people. Irie does not pine after a blond, blue-haired, white Anglo Saxon; she is not Irish Sinead O'Conner crooning "I love you my hard Englishman" ("This Is/Is Not A Rebel Song"). She does not attempt to re-colonize the colonizer; she falls in love with her best friend, almost-brother, fellow multicultural, Millat.

Immediately after making love with Millat, and being immediately rejected by him, Irie marches over to the Chalfen's to seduce Magid.

> She grabbed him, kissed him, and made love to him without conversation or affection [...] , and when he came she was gratified to note it was with a little sigh as if something had

been taken from him. But she was wrong to think of this as a victory...As the moon became clearer than the sun [...] Magid says, "'It seems to me [...] that you have tried to love a man as if he were an island and you were shipwrecked and you could mark the land with an X. It seems to me it is too late in the day for all that. (382)

Clever, "saddened" Magid is probably deliberately invoking colonial language to describe Irie's love for Millat as well as her attempt at punishing both brothers for being *"unable to love her"* (381, original emphasis). The translation from the idiom of love to the patois of colonialization – or the colonial gaze – is eerily and troublingly seamless. Of course Irie attempts to colonize Millat – it is in her genes and her history; the post-colonial move is that she – a "blacky-white knight" (ibid.) in contemporary London, is furiously trying to mark her designated metaphysical spot with "an X." While "the touch of memory, the touch of ten years of love unreturned" (ibid.) makes Millat and Irie's passion "inevitable" (ibid.), "the touch of a long, long history" problematizes it: where can Irie place the 'flag' of her love, when even the body of lovers are described in the colonial terms? The only space available to Irie is Millat's "chest [j]ust at the point between two belts where his heart, *constricted* by the leather, beat so hard she felt it in her ear" (ibid., emphasis added). Irie tries to discover a place on Millat's body where she can stake her claim, but his body is always-already claimed by historical and religious constraints that bind it, easily misconstrued as a site of tortured love: "it was natural that Irie should mistake the palpitations that come with blood restriction with smoldering passion" (380). If we read the constraints wrapped around Millat as simulations of passion, it follows that we must interpret Captain Durham's love for Ambrosia as inspired by culturally-determined restrictions as well.

The fact that Irie and Millat's "inevitable" coupling occurs on a prayer mat bears significance in terms of the novel's conflation of love and religion, or identities formed by love relationships and those formed by quests for spiritual identities, and history. The narrative upholds Shiva's warning to "never [date] an English girl. [Because it n]ever works. Never [...] Too much bloody history" (122). Millat almost falls in love with a white Englishwoman, Karina, but his involvement with KEVIN, which is what explicitly forbids sexual contact with white woman, and therefore inhibits the creation and development of love, causes him to break up with her, cruelly: one of the many examples of religion and politics trumping and triumphing over more poetically romantic possibilities. Samad, while conducting his own experiment to re-colonize the colonizer (or the female version of it, Mem Sahib) is "accidentally" found out by his sons and Irie as he is about to embark on his adulterous affair with red-haired, freckly Poppy Burke-Jones, which forestalls the initiation of their presumed consummation. Poppy, brandishing her present for Samad, a red toothbrush, transfers the shame to Samad and brands him with a more contemporary example of a Scarlet Letter.

The "situation" (to use Chandra Talpade Mohanty's definition in her seminal article "Under Western Eyes: Feminist Scholarship and Colonial Discourses") of a narrative and narrative events are often what mediates human relationships. However, this "situation" is not static, detached from the history that creates it and those who people it, or solid. It is not, nor can ever be a "neutral place" (366), it is besmirched by historical power struggles that now play out on Millat's prayer mat and by ripping off Magid's "shrink to fit" (353) Levis. Even – or especially – between the children of immigrants, what is most evident is "Mr. Death, your new lover" (317), not a topography conducive to love and connection, but a dredging up of the old, "the sheer *quantity* of shit that must be wiped off the slate if we are to start again as new. Race. Land. Ownership. Faith. Theft. Blood. And more blood" (378). Love might have possible redemptive qualities, but it is too dangerous and volatile to be "neutral." Belsey writes: "Love is a Victorian value. The nineteenth century supposed that the problem was repression: desire released was therefore desire fulfilled. At the end of the twentieth century we know better – or worse" (702).

"Neotraditionals": Postcolonialism/Postmodernism's Infinite Elasticity

Kwame Anthony Appiah's insightful, incisive article, "Is the Post- in Postmodernism the Post- in Postcolonialism?" reminds us that, like the "neotraditional" (337) art exhibit that frames his piece, while postcolonialism, like postmodernism, might provide a "space-clearing" (348) in the aftermath of nineteenth century colonialism, the practice of the two "post-" words do not imply an actual "transcendence" (348) of colonial attitudes. Rather, in Appiah's argument, postcolonialism implies a "passing through" (ibid.), an absorption, and an appropriation of (still the Other's) goods, art, services – and even more troublingly – people and relationships. In Appiah's powerful rendering, the result is late twentieth-century capitalism superimposed over the tenants of nineteenth-century colonialism. The colonial relationship is similar to the love relationship in that the Other is desired; it is conceivable that love is a legitimating discourse for power, especially within colonial and post-colonial relationships, which, I argue, encompass the range of relationships in a post-colonial world. Most theorists concentrate on the negative outcomes of desire and love in a post-colonial context. Sabine Broeck goes so far as to inquire, "Has post-colonial love – as one scenario for relations – in Europe been possible? Or are all transcultural, transracial relationships doomed to be framed as rape and/or exploitation [sic]" (17)? R. Radhakrishnan quotes Ella Shohat's essay "Notes on the Post-colonial," to underscore the metaphoric connotations in the word "post" in post-colonial that "conflates politics with epistemology, history with theory, and operates as a master code of *transcendence*" (751), which is in effect what Smith is doing "creatively." Shohat translates the idea of transcendence as a "going beyond [...] in bad faith," however transcendence has an equally valid metaphysical meaning deserving of scrutiny. Radhakrishnan differentiates between "necessary" and "mere gestures" of transcendence (752). We inherently desire to connect to others, and are naturally compelled and intrigued by the Other. Therefore it follows that love and friendship serve as transporting mechanisms from an alienated, truncated identity towards what Turner calls *communitas* which can be a community of two, or *furrawn*, the Gaelic word that means the kind of talk that brings strangers to intimacy. Love can be read into, and indeed can be used to incite Dipesh Chakrebarty's "historical transitions" (4) of individual narratives which in turn create historically validated hybridized identities.

Roy Sommer, in "'Simple Survival' in 'Happy Multicultural Land'? Diaspora Identities and Cultural Hybridity in the Contemporary British Novel," argues that it is the "multicultural novel in Britain" which legitimizes the "diasporic experience [...and the] notion of hybrid identities" (165). He further asserts that "authors such as [...] Zadie Smith who are less concerned with politically correct...representations of ethnic diasporas than with the collective perception and construction of cultural alterity and fictions of [...] ethnic purity"(ibid.) are more effective than "the first type of multicultural literature [...] the tradition of migrant narratives [...] of the 1950's whose gloomy titles signal what the first generation of hopeful immigrants encountered in the streets of racist London: loneliness, second class citizenship and unbelonging" (166). It is true that one of the many reasons *White Teeth* is so effective is Smith's use of a contemporary setting which lends itself to her "cosmopolitan, often ironic approach to culture and tradition [which] questions the very notion of stable identities" (ibid.). The setting is familiar to most of her readers, and since we are able to imagine ourselves within it, we are not capable of distancing ourselves from our own location within a postcolonial space, a space that can and must be interpolated as "the project of positive unoriginality" (Morris 10). The novel acts as a sort of "known history, something that has already happened elsewhere, and which is to be reproduced, mechanically or otherwise, with local content" (Morris 10), the London of *White Teeth* is a setting in which all urban readers are locals. However, Sommer is off-point when he deems Smith less "authentic" solely because she eschews political correctness in her illustration of multi-ethnicity; the "truth" or "authenticity" of an entire culture can *only* reside in the prismatic and often contradictory nature of its individual parts, not in a portrayal of "collective" culture with all of its abstractions, generalities, and obscurities.

As Laura Moss in "The Politics of Everyday Hybridity" argues, *White Teeth* is too invested in ethnic, cultural, linguistic, and racial conflicts to truly be a "post-post colonial narrative" (11). If it were then clashing definitions of events would not repeatedly spark or literally burst into flames like the multiple bonfires in the novel; history would be removed from or obscured in the novel, not "rampant" (Moss 11) throughout it. *White Teeth* places us firmly in a world where characters "cannot escape their history anymore than [we ourselves] can lose [our] shadow[s]" (Smith 399). The Neverneverland of "lost shadows" is not even acknowledged as an illusion by any of the characters, even Millat and Magid, the brothers in the novel, "race towards the future only to find they more and more eloquently express their past, that place where they had *just been*" (Smith 385, original emphasis). That "place" (or, "spaces times time" as R. Radhakrishnan defines it in "Post-coloniality and the Boundaries of Identity" (752) is precariously rooted in the London of the last quarter of the twentieth century *and* Bangladesh (the same can be said for Irie's colonial Jamaica and prewar England, although she is not a twin). It is itself a twinned entity, like the brotherhood that is Millat/Magid, "tied together like a cat's cradle, connected like a seesaw, push one end, other goes up" (Smith 183), altered but not extinguished by Millat's attempt to perform as "Mark Smith" (126), Irie's attempt to achieve "flickable" (228) hair, or Magid's return from India as "more English than the English" (348). It is the characters' experiences, not solely their "determined" ethnic identities, which causes and aids them in "(re)inventing themselves" (Sommer 174). The characters' searches for identity do not eclipse their searches for love; in fact, specifically for Samad, Irie and Millat, desire enhances and informs reinvention: for what better way to reinvent than through love? The contemporary locations of love and desire (that is, England) while certainly too fraught to be deemed "neutral ground" are at the very least not "stolen" – and perhaps might be the only place where a microcosm of "the utopia of race relations" (Lyall) can possibly exist. Although she concedes the very real threat of racist violence against non-white Britons, Laura Moss posits that Smith's characters have more power to "choose" hybridity in contemporary London, in a way that the "educated" Ambrosia does not (Moss 13).

Irie, Millat, and Magid have more choice and expression in terms of their sexuality, but they are still enmeshed in alienation, and durable romantic connections elude them throughout most of the novel. Irie has potentially more "options" than Alsana, who is assigned to a marriage partner before she is even born, and black, toothless Clara; Irie is neither dazed nor wide-eyed as the victimized Ambrosia at the hands of Durham. She is savvy and aware of the capitalist manipulations of emotion: "[love] is a four-letter word that sells life insurance and hair conditioner" (378), and yet is still able to genuinely feel love. However, Irie knows that she does not fit the 1980's and 90's ideal for female sexuality and beauty, or perhaps any century's ideal. She attempts to insert her curvy black self into the famous Shakespearean sonnet "My Mistress' eyes are nothing like the sun" by using close reading skills and a viable argument: "Is [the dark lady] black? [...] I just thought [...] like when he says here: *Then will I swear, beauty herself is black*...And the curly hair thing, black wires—" (227). Her teacher, Mrs. Roody, who is the color of "strawberry mousse" and yet calls herself "dark," disallows the interpretation; she has no sense of history or knowledge of the creative process, how it speaks in code to veil its less overt meanings:

> [The dark lady]'s not black in the modern sense. There weren't any Afro-Carri-bee-yans in England at that time...I mean I can't be sure, but it does seem terribly unlikely, unless she was a slave [...] and he's unlikely to have written a series of sonnets to [...] a slave, is he? (227)

Captain Durham, had he the inclination, would have written love poems to Ambrosia. For all we know, he did write them. However, Irie is shut out of the romantic tradition symbolized by Shakespearean sonnets, and in the next scene visits a hair salon to try to achieve "flickable" (228) hair, an instance of "everyday hybridity": a choice to attempt inclusion in a more modern romantic ideal.

It is nearly impossible to separate pure choices with their accidental counterparts – the whims, coincidences, hunches, coin-tosses, and illusions that contribute to choices. Smith seems to be aware and interested in the complex molecular make up of choice, and begins the first section of her book with an E.M. Forster quote that illuminates the accidental rather than the teleological, or rather, the teleological embedded or inherent in the accidental:

> Every little trifle, for some reason, does seem incalculably important today and when you say of a thing that "nothing hangs on it" it sounds like blasphemy. There's never any knowing...which of our actions, which of our idlenesses won't have things hanging on it forever. (Forster 73)

Forster, one of Smith's forebears as a incisive novelist of the heyday of British colonialism (especially renowned for his keen interpretations of Anglo-Indian relations in his 1924 novel *A Passage to India)*, is brought up later to exemplify the genteel Anglo invasion of India internalized by Magid when he returns from his "education" in India. In the novel, *Where Angels Fear to Tread*, Forster dramatizes the abandonment of social conformities by juxtaposing a once-proper-no-longer-young English lady's denouncement of middle-class values and the reticence and the fear of those who go to Italy to rescue her from her sexual abandon and reckless marriage to a young Italian man. The would-be rescuer Philip Herriton is, in his own words, afraid of "colliding" with others in intimacy, with its inherent violence – a deeper interaction than "involvement," which, under Alsana's definition is "neither good nor bad [, but] simply a consequence of [existing]" (363). In this new landscape of contemporary Britain, where everyone lives in each other's pockets as a matter of course (ibid.), a fear of collision is impossibly out-dated; the necessary and unavoidable collisions between races, cultures, and desires are what comprise Homi Bhabha's "third space." I argue, along with Moss, that the space is not a lacuna or a nebulous "in-between" (Bhabha 39), but a vibrant, crowded, shared space, where incessant jostling is bound to cause mishaps, clashes, and unlikely parings.

The "trifles" and "idlenesses" that Forster correctly points to as having larger, unknowable significance both beautifully connected to Archie's life – saved because he was gassing himself in the path of a meat truck "accidentally" rescued by Mo Hussein, a recent immigrant, mindful of profits which derive from the satisfaction of others' hunger (in his case, for meat), the most fundamental and necessary desire of all. It is impossible to determine which collisions or arrested collisions will fall through the cracks of narrative and memory, and which ones might become fundamentals – the keystones of our constructed selves. Now that many of us have so many choices about who and what to be, now that the socio-cultural gears that shape us have been partially revealed, do we have more control over the fundamentals? In the novel, it appears that the fundamentals, if more fluid than in the past, remain a powerful force. By exploring the crevices between dictum and desire, Smith intimates that the powerful fundamentals of romantic urges into a *mostly* socially-determined multicultural, multiethnic, multi-religious world cannot be left out of the equation. After quoting the Oxford English dictionary entries for "fundamental" and "Fundamentalism" in her third-to-last chapter heading, she adds a snippet from the 1931 ditty "As Time Goes By" ("You must remember this, a kiss is still a kiss,/a sigh is still a sigh;/The fundamental things apply,/As time goes by"). When Magid returns from India, Alsana bestows a reprieve, an almost forgiveness of Samad that takes shape in the form of definite answers: "Yes, yes, yes. No, no, no. The fundamentals" (351). But Smith does not let us – or Samad – rest in the absolutes. If James Joyce ends *Ulysses* on the word "yes," Smith makes the postmodern move and smudges it with a caveat. After Samad unilaterally decides to send Magid back to Bangladesh without consulting his wife, Alsana spends the next eight years of Magid's exile only answering her husband with the words "maybe" and "possibly" (178). Upon Magid's return to London, she starts answering in the affirmatively definitive again. Still, Samad realizes that this "change in Alsana...was a blessed relief, but it wasn't enough" (351). Not only have both his sons "failed him" but, in a postmodern context, the affirmative is more elusive and, counter-intuitively, less satisfying, even less truthful-seeming. "The fundamentals" (351) – challenge the questions that are posed, rather than answering them.

One avenue we have to determine the shape of our journey is the choice of our marriage or romantic partner. Smith quotes Corinthians I, chapter seven, verse nine: "It is better to marry than to burn" (39). Marriage is one of the key fundamentals, as dictated by religion, social mores, and perhaps individual aspiration. And yet, poets throughout the ages trace and revel in the myriad of "chance-iful" versus pre-determined nature of romantic "collisions" and attachments. Irie does not marry, although at the end of the novel she and Josh are "lovers" which is perhaps the postmodern version of marriage, and Ambrosia does not marry the father of her child: Ambrosia is not allowed to marry her white lover as dictated by English colonial law; Irie is "allowed" not to marry her white lover, Josh, but chooses, for the moment, not to, nor does she reveal which twin is the father of her unnamed "fatherless" (448) daughter. Clara is caught in the generation of having the "privilege" of interracial marriage – which is lucky for her as she has no other options to eat, except in the confines of her mother's household, where Jesus is stuffed down her throat along with food. On Clara and Archie's wedding day (Valentine's Day), Archie receives one of the many "curiously" apt letters from his fellow cyclist, Horst Ibelgaufts: "I feel not an inconsiderable warmth at the thought of the union of one man and one woman in lifelong cohabitation. It is truly remarkable that we undertake such an impossible feat" (43). It is a feat. Archie and Clara are the roads they have – unwittingly – traveled to each other; they meet after a string of coincidental events, punctuated by his narrowly-avoided death, fueled by the betrayals of one of the fundaments – that is, marriage, and Clara's reckless fleeing from one of the other fundaments, that is the suffocating religion practiced by Hortense and Ryan Topps. The house where they both stumble into is the most concrete example of a "third" or "in-between" space, functioning as it does as a sort of halfway house for the displaced: a place where accidental collisions are bound and determined to happen: "something happened by accident. That accident was Clara Bowden" (19):

> Clara saw Archie through the gray-green eyes of loss; her world had just disappeared, the faith she lived by had receded like a low tide, and Archie, quite by accident, had become the bloke in the joke: the last man on earth. (38)

It seems essential to know where Archie and Clara were coming from, how the accident of their meeting was engineered. First we are enlightened as to Archie's misogyny: "[Ophelia] was not to know that women never stayed as daylight in Archie's life; that *somewhere* in him he didn't like them, he didn't trust them, and he was able to love them only if they wore haloes" (7, emphasis added). Smith chooses to have Archie married before, and this fact, combined with attempted suicide that starts the novel, sets up her argument about love and history as shadow narratives of each other. We are told that Archie "had not spent New Year's morning gagging on the tube of the vacuum cleaner because he loved [his first wife, Ophelia]. It was rather because he had lived with her so long and had *not* loved her" (7, original emphasis). Archie and Ophelia met in Italy just after the end of World War II, a time of fragmentation and loss of identity. They meet by chance, propelled by events that have little or nothing to do with their own inclinations or desires. It seems obvious that people fleeing shattered ideologies and carrying with them (as Archie does) vast amounts of shame would have a difficult time connecting to other war-torn people and forming genuine bonds with them. Only an unreasonable accident shimmers with positive abstractions such as love and truth. For her part, "Clara might never have run into the arms of Archie Jones if she hadn't been running, quite as fast as she could, away from Ryan Topps" (23). Both the inception of love and the "in-between" space of the immigrant are fueled by loss, an emptied out devotion and/or identity. Archie knows "that's what divorce is: taking things you no longer want from people you no longer love...All broken things were coming with him" (8), which includes Clara.

For Archie, the affirmation of life is simple: "a beautiful woman in a doorway with a come-hither look" (15). When Archie sees Clara, he sees "that come-hither look...tinged with a kind of sadness, disappointment, like she didn't have a great deal of other options" (21). Hope for a better life enfolds into love tended through marriage. We are never aware of a great love or grand passion in Archie and Clara's relationship as a married couple with their own constellation of desires and disappointments, as Clara drops out of the narrative soon after the birth of Irie. Archie may not be brave (appropriately brave anyway) or bright, but he understands that love and commitment renew us, that the introduction and inclusion of the Other will rejuvenate us – provide comfort, excitement, (new markets, new possible converts, new land) when all else fails. If it accomplishes nothing else, love is expansionist. It is the most powerful colonizer that exists. Archie might be a hollowed-out Englishman, a signifier and "mirror of the end of Empire" (Lowe 177), devoid of wit and moxie – those preciously-guarded English axioms, but he does have the fortitude to fall in love again, and to create a remarkable person such as Irie. Archie uses the last dregs of his ancestral colonial heritage to spirit Clara away (they are married six weeks after they meet), but he performs this colonial urge with much more life-affirming bravery and an almost passionate kindness than, say, Captain Durham, and this unwarranted benevolence shows up in the thoughtfulness and awareness and large capacity for love in Irie. Soon after the birth of Irie, Clara and Archie's relationship – something that changes, undergoes conversion, causes conversion, expands and contracts over time, exits the narrative. It is as if Irie picks up the thread of their union, and hooks it over herself, Millat, and Magid. Archie and Clara do create a "blacky-white knight" (381), the most courageously loving character in the narrative.

In *White Teeth*, as in *Where Angels Fear to Tread*, love – the unrequited love of, say, Irie for Millat, and the institutionalized versions of Archie and Clara, Samad and Alsana, even Joyce and Marcus' Chaflinism which smacks of smug middle class co-dependence – is propelled by accident and coincidence. That Smith would pepper her protagonists' search for identity in an increasingly hybridized world with such a romantic trope as 'love is fate' is surprising. However, as Virginia Woolf writes in *The Voyage Out*, "It can't only be an accident. For it was an accident-- it need never have happened" (417). Although their moniker belies it, Joely and Crispin, the FATE activists, are unaccidental; everything about their relationship seems pre-meditated and packaged. Like Marcus and Joyce, they are smug colonizers. They are described as "indivisible" (396), unlike atoms or genes, and therefore unaccidental. They are calculating and overly earnest, full of naïve fervor about the wrong causes, and pathologically clueless. One cannot read the metaphysical concept of "fate" into the moniker FATE. Although Crispin and Joely stage violent collisions in the name of animal rights, Josh, infatuated with Joely (who teases him relentlessly), bemoans:

> And the double-cunt of it was, theirs was a marriage of true love, total spiritual bonding, and dedicated political union…among the members of FATE, Joely and Crispin's marriage served as a kind of cosmogony, an originating myth that explained succinctly what people could and should be […] they were *worshiped*. (395-96, original emphasis)

Again, the conflation of religion and love, as expressed in the dual meaning of the word "worshipped," is seen as suspect.

Smith chooses to invoke fate when she sums up Irie and Josh's coming together at the end of the novel. Smith copies Woolf's move to place essential character information in parentheses such as in "(Mrs. Ramsey was dead)" and "(for Irie and Josh become lovers in the end; you can only avoid your fate for so long)" (448). Does this bode good or ill for the lovers, as they bathe in the waters embracing a reclaimed island, where we can imagine a braver Josh "doing all the things he wanted and all the things he never dared" (411) before? Although Smith provides a "happy-ever-after ending" for Irie and Josh, she does not let us simply revel in the "rightness" of their edenic consummation, but continues, in one of her most unbridled narrative intrusions, to admonish us and teach us that love is accidental, not assumed, in any circumstance. Thus illustrates the following passage:

> What was it about this unlovable century that convinced us that we were, despite everything, eminently lovable as people, as a species? What made us think that anyone who fails to love us is damaged, lacking, *malfunctioning* in some way? [...] We are so convinced of the goodness of ourselves, and the goodness of our love, we cannot bear to believe that there might be something more worthy of love than us. Greeting cards routinely tell us everybody deserves love. No. Everybody deserves clean water. Not everybody deserves love all the time. (382, original emphasis)

So what can we hold on to in this novel, if love is too volatile, too historically-dictated and determined? In Smith's novel, friendship functions as a redemptive force. Less problematically and more healingly than passion, friendship can more easily cross class and color lines to negotiate "third spaces." History is invoked, when speaking of amity, as a less problematic, and in fact, dynamic force in the creation and maintenance of friendships: "'But you're different,' Millat Iqbal would say to the martyr Irie Jones, 'you're *different*. We go way back. We've got history. You're a *real* friend. They [that is, Millat's constrant stream of sexual conquests] don't really *mean* anything to me'" (224, original emphasis). And yet, as earnest as Millat is in his view of friendship based on shared history (and as heartbreaking as Irie feels being categorized as a friend), is it simply their shared version of Englishness, their plural identities, that makes their relationship enjoyable and beneficial? Sommer writes that "[a]lthough it has been argued that, considering the multicultural transformation of British, one should speak of British cultural identities or 'Englishnesses' in the plural form rather than of one national identity to which the cultural status of a master-narrative can be ascribed" (Sommer 158). In that vein, Archie and Samad both order Mickey's fry-ups every night at O'Connell's Poolroom to the tune of "three eggs, beans, two rounds of toast, and mushrooms" (Smith 204). Although Samad routinely berates himself for having a nonbeliever as his best friend, the relationship that he and Archie share is essential to Smith's vision of cacophonous cultural amiability. "Me and Sam? We go way back" (41), Archie says with pride. The two men met during wartime, which seems particularly fitting. War is often a time when boundaries are blurred and redrawn according to necessity and urgency, and often those makeshift borders prove to be more durable than the previous ones. Charles Taylor's *Multiculturalism: Examining the Politics of Recognition* (1994), presents a dialectical model of multicultural identity. Brian Milstein both problemitizes and clarifies this model. Milstein's unpublished paper, "On Reading Charles Taylor's Politics of Recognition," postulates that "Taylor's theory is a dialectical model of personal identity which assumes that the behaviour of one's 'significant others' such as parents and friends towards the 'self' is of vital importance to the constitution of individual identity." Under this rubric, the most successful relationships in the novel might not be the most successful relationship romantically speaking, but the ones that recognize the other as who they are, a "good man" – Archie, "a real friend" Irie, and not the whitewashed, rationalized infatuation of Joyce for Millat or even Irie's more complex but unanswered love for Millat. Because Taylor is mainly interested in "cultural or collective identities of diasporic minorities" and not interested in the individual migrant" and his/her relationship with other individuals, he quickly translates his principle "from the private to the public sphere" (152). In order to be successful in her inquiry, Smith, as a novelist, must, stay rooted in the private lives of her characters, and hope that the magic of good fiction will happen – that these specific characters can lend themselves to make broad statements about the multicultural as a whole.

White Teeth is a narrative location where the fundamentals of love and power coalesce. What Smith illustrates so well is that love, like history, is open to interpretation. If love and history are somehow conflated to form a "third space" that is informed by but not dictated by the past, then perhaps love can help heal bloody wounds. Love as a form of salvation is a weary poetic trope, and yet, it is within the complexities and hope – the blissful unknown – where multicultural communities might find the only possible peace, because, as Smith writes, history is inextricable from identity. Although it remains true that "immigrants cannot escape their own history anymore than [anyone] can lose [their] own shadow" (Smith 385), it is equally valid that "you go back and back and back and it's still easier to find the correct Hoover bag than to find one pure person, one pure faith, on the globe. Do you think anybody is English? Really English? It's a fairytale!" (196). There is no unallocated place left, if there ever was. Even "the land they call 'India' goes by a thousand names and is populated by millions, and if you think you have found two men the same among that multitude, then you are mistaken. It is merely a trick of moonlight" (85). Radhakrishnan states that the "post-colonial search for identity in the Third World is beset primarily with the problem of location" (755). I would argue that this search is just as location-bound in the so-called First World, and not just for immigrants: we are all postcolonists now[1], and therefore our "dilemma then is not between two pure identities..., but between two different narratives and their intended teleologies" (758).

Our two different (one inside, one outside) narratives or "histories" (to use Smith's word) touch, and these collisions both become and propel narrative aims. After all, as Dan Punday suggests in *Narrative Bodies: Toward a Corporeal Narratology*, "narrative characters become meaningful when they touch and interact" (81). Although narratological tradition has sometimes

> neglected those [...] textual indices of contractual and transactional understandings – that themselves realize the narratives as communicational acts and open them, as verbal structures, onto a world of events and change. Not the actual historicity of texts, but the markers, within them, of historical situation—these are what a renewed narratology, concerned [...] might take as its object" (82).

Smith has accomplished just that: detailing the inner histories of narrative while at the same time entwining them with more historically prominent concerns, gathering them into the "politics and poetics" of colonial and postcolonial love relationships. Irie's name chosen by Clara as one of Clara's final important acts in the novel "If it's a girl, I tink I like *Irie*. It patois. Means everything *OK, cool, peaceful*" (64, original emphasis), which could sum up the relationships at the end of the novel, up to and including the escape of FUTUREMOUSE, the twice-saved life of the French doctor, the twins wrenched apart, and all of the problems between people living together in a

---

[1] I do not mean to imply that we are all – regardless of nationality, race, and country of origin – postcolonialists in terms of our actual power relationships or postcolonial experiences. Susan Sontag's assertion that we all have AIDS was a call to assume social responsibility that frames the AIDS pandemic, not as a falsely-equalizing metaphor. In a similar vein, I am indicating that we are all, regardless of circumstance, living in the shadow of postcolonialism and require vigilant awareness not to fall into its suffocating embrace. To quote Shari Stone-Mediatore's "Chandra Mohanty and the Revaluing of 'Experience,'" Mohanty discusses experience as "a strategically chosen location from which to envision alternate futures" (132, Note 14) born of the inherent tensions between language and intra- and inter-encounters.

small space. Archie and Clara and Samad and Alsana have their first of what seems like many drinks at O'Connell's, Irie absconds to Jamaica with Josh, and the world keeps turning ... all expressed in terms of love:

> True lovers row, then fall the next second back into each other's arms; more seasoned lovers will walk up the stairs or into the next room before they relent and retrace their steps. A relationship on the brink of collapse will find one partner two blocks down the road or two countries to the east before something tugs, some responsibility, some memory, a pull of a child's hand or a heartstring, which induces them to make longer journeys back to their other half. (45)

The characters are now "more seasoned lovers," up to the tasks, burdens, altercations, and possible *jouissance* – all caused by what Yeats called "the mythic stupidity of the blood" – of the hybridized, fractious, alchemical twenty-first century. We, like the characters in *White Teeth* reach – strainingly – towards our "other hal[ves]." As the offspring of thousands of minds moving upon silence, we, like Smith's characters, begin to heal our postcolonial histories through the unlikeliest of accidents of love and connection. Through a language as free as possible from the politics of feeling, even amidst the frissons of teeming historical enactments, that makes stories out of the decay, root canals, bridges, and the moonlit glow of our white teeth.

Works Cited

Appiah, Kwame Anthony. "Is the Post- in Postmodernism the Post- in Postcolonial?" *Critical Inquiry* 17. 2 (Winter 1991): 336-57.

Belsey, Catherine. "Postmodern Love: Questioning the Metaphysics of Desire." *New Literary History* 25, 3. (Summer 1994): 683-705.

Chakrabarty, Dipesh. "Post-coloniality and the Artifice of History: Who Speaks for 'Indian' Pasts?" *Representations* 37 (Winter 1992): 4.

Coste, Didier. *Story and Situation: Narrative Seduction and the Power of Fiction*. Minneapolis: University of Minnesota Press, 1989.

Derrida, Jacques. *The Post Card: From Socrates to Freud and Beyond*. Translated. Alan Bass. Chicago: University of Chicago Press,1987.

Foucault, Michel. *The History of Sexuality Volume One*: An Introduction London, Penguin, 1981.

Gilman, Sander L. "'We're Not Jews': Imagining Jewish History and Jewish Bodies in Contemporary Multicultural Literature." *Modern Judaism* 23. 2 (May 2003): 126-55.

Forster, E.M. *Where Angels Fear to Tread*. Dover: New York, 1905.

Lowe, Jan. "No More Lonely Londoners." *Small Axe* 9 (March 2001): 166-80.
Lyall, Sarah. "A Good Start." Interview with Zadie Smith. *The New York Times Book Review* 105:18
Lyotard, Jean-Francois, and Georges Van Den Abbeele. "The Different, the Referent, and the Proper Name." *Diacritics* 24.3 (Fall 1984): 3-14.
McClintock, Anne. "The Angel of Progress: Pitfalls of the Term "Post-Colonialism." *Social Text* 31/32, (1992): 84-98.
Mediatore, Shari Stone. "Chandra Mohanty and the Revaluing of 'Experience.'" *Hypatia*. 13.2. (Spring 1998): 116-20.
Milstein, Brian. "On Charles Taylor's 'Politics of Recognition.'"
Unpublished paper. New School for Social Research, New York.
Mohanty, Chandra Talpade. "Under Western Eyes: Feminist Scholarship and Colonial Discourses." *Boundary 2* 12.3 (Spring-Fall 1984): 333-58.
Morris, Meaghan. "Metamorphoses at Sydney Tower." *New Formations* 11 (Summer 1990): 10.
Moss, Laura. "The Politics of Everyday Hybridity: Zadie Smith's *White Teeth*. *Wasafiri* 39 (Summer 2003): 11-18.
Punday, Dan. *Narrative Bodies: Toward a Corporeal Narratology*. New York: Palgrave Macmillan, 2003.
Radhakrishnan, R. "Post-coloniality and the Boundaries of Identity." *Callaloo* 16.4 (Fall 1993): 750-71.
Smith, Zadie. *White Teeth*. Vintage: New York, 2000.
Sommer, Roy. "'Simple Survival' in 'Happy Multicultural Land'? Diaspora Identities and Cultural Hybridity in the Contemporary British Novel." *Diaspora and Multiculturalism: Common Traditions and New Developments*. Ed. Monika Fludernik. Rodopi: New York and Amsterdam, 2003. 159-79.
Stoler, Ann Laura. "Tense and Tender Ties: The Politics of Comparison in North American History and (Post) Colonial Studies." *The Journal of American History* 88.3 (Dec. 2001): 829-65.
Taylor, Charles, et al., eds. *Multiculturalism: Examining the Politics of Recognition*. Princeton: Princeton University Press, 1994.
Woolf, Virginia. *The Voyage Out*. Oxford: Oxford University Press, 2009.

CHAPTER TEN

Borderland Strangers in Caryl Phillips's *A Distant Shore*

Josiane Ranguin

Born on the Caribbean island of St. Kitts, raised in Yorkshire and now living in New York, Caryl Phillips considers the issues of nationality, belonging and identity of central importance: "Britain remains a country for whom a sense of continuity with an imagined past continues to be a major determinant of national identity" (Phillips 2002, 296). Phillips goes on to recognize that this "failure of national imagination," the inability to acknowledge the presence of non-European influences within the British culture and psyche, generated literary answers from authors who "experiment with discontinuities of time, and revel in the disruption of conventional narrative order" to become "disrupters of national continuity" (Phillips 2001, 292). Stephen Clingman, in his essay "'England has changed': Questions of National Form in A *Distant Shore*" perceptively attests to Phillips's masterly control of formal disruption:

> There are spaces and times within the space and time of the national, in which versions of migrancy and internal exile co-exist but do not fully align, in which nation and narration are far from cohesive, horizontally unified, or identical. The sheer complexity of the novel's variations on this formal embodiment are hard to capture without a moment-by-moment sequencing of its account [...]. (51)

A Distant Shore (2004) focuses on two characters: Gabriel, an African refugee who chooses Solomon as a second name when he starts a new life in the north of England, and Dorothy, a retired music teacher who feels estranged in her own country, and progressively develops a psychotic behavior after a series of traumatic events. Both characters, the British national and the asylum seeker, share the same feeling of disconnection with their environment, but their friendship is cut short by the racist assassination of Solomon. Disruption of space and time is the narrative echo of their fractured lives. The first chapter focuses on Dorothy's arrival to Stoneleigh, a 'new development'(1), her encounter with Solomon and their relationship until his death. The second chapter narrates Gabriel's odyssey from an African country torn by civil war to England, while the third chapter concentrates on Dorothy's life after her divorce, her unhappy affairs with married men, her retirement, and her arrival in Stoneleigh for a new beginning. In the fourth chapter, Solomon describes his arrival in Stoneleigh, his reaction to the hate mail he receives, and his progressive interest in Dorothy. The final chapter finds Dorothy embattled in the secluded space of a psychiatric hospital, her silence being her only weapon against her feeling of isolation and homelessness. Out of the five chapters, only the second and third are not first person narratives, which underlines that this narrative mode seems to be restricted in the novel to the exploration from within of the feeling of foreignness, and the monitoring of the minute fluctuations of behavior or feelings of Dorothy and Solomon, both strangers in their new environment, and both ultimately reduced to silence, through death or psychosis.

The intention behind *A Distant Shore* is then to examine the way various characters, be they British nationals, or economic and political refugees immigrating to Britain, envision national identity. Immigrants are allured by idealized images of England, while Britons are depicted as facing a new image of Britain they are finding difficult to apprehend. The irony is that, in what appears as a time clash, the outdated beliefs about British identity that have been nurtured by asylum seekers are returned in prime condition to the mother country. Phillips compares the immigrants to pilgrims, using Benedict Anderson's image, since the members of the former empire are travelling from the periphery to the centre of power: "one by one they have made their way through the gap in the hedge and into the muddy field, and like a band of pilgrims they are strung out, one behind the other, with Gabriel at their head" (122).

The ideals of Britishness are brought back to a country whose social construct of national identity has shifted and appears, when confronted to its former image, all the more in mutation or under attack. A British character, Dorothy, analyzes identity as having no real link to nationality, since she feels estranged in her own country. "This is not my home" (312), she admits, while undocumented immigrants like Bright, who stows away with Gabriel to cross the British channel, espouse their adopted country with eagerness and determination. The sense of belonging is shown as a fragile feeling that is created and nurtured by the individual himself, but can be destroyed by a hostile environment. National identity as monolithic is then exposed as a fallacy since all the characters evoked in the text come to express their own idiosyncratic vision of identity.

As we follow Dorothy and Solomon in their haphazard quest of love, Phillips establishes a cartography of migration that I will explore, starting from his taxonomy or, to borrow from Walkowitz, a "collation" (539) of the lives of several migrants from the world over, to then explore the village as an allegory of the nation, home as microcosm of the nation, and finally conclude on the final frontier of identity, the human body.

Identity Politics in Strange Territories

In a discussion of identity politics in *A Distant Shore*, Phillips stresses that "race" is only one among the many traits that may come to define identity:
> I'm more concerned with "identity" than with "race." The latter is just one component in the former, along with religion, gender, nationality, class, etc. This is obviously a novel about the challenged identity of two individuals, but it's also a novel about English - or national - identity. (Turner 2007, 1)

The disruption inscribed in Phillips's work is echoed in his own claim as a migrant writer. Displacement and migration inform both his life and work as though displacement and writing across borders were a way to escape pigeonholing in any national literature, shifting perspectives offering new vistas. In "Border Crossings," Phillips expressed his feelings about the United States:
> I have never really felt myself to be at home in the United States. [...] But the United States does not punish me, or laugh at me, or belittle me for being who I am. I have been able to cross the Atlantic and enter into the society, and my sense of displacement is, in the context of my parents' experience, deeply designer in character. (218)

Movements, fluidity, reinvention of oneself as part of a strategy of representation, become the strategy itself. This is a political stance, as Stuart Hall points out:
> How things are represented and the "machineries" and regimes of representation in a culture do play a *constitutive* and not merely a reflexive, after-the-event role. This gives questions of culture and ideology, and the scenario of representation - subjectivity, identity, politics - a formative, not only an expressive place in the constitution of social and political life. (91)

Phillips consciously takes this disruption of national continuity further by working not only on the conditions of production but also on the conditions of reception of his work. Walkowitz understands this production as "comparison literature" which is "an emerging genre of world literature for which global comparison is a formal as well as a thematic preoccupation" and which is "asking us to understand comparison as the work of scholars, to be sure, but also as the work of books that analyze - as Phillips's do - the transnational contexts of their own production, circulation, and study." (536)

"A forced or eager flight into strange territory" is, in Toni Morrison's terms, the common lot of the world refugees. What is underlined in the sentence is the migrants' perception of the European environment as foreign and what is communicated is a vision of the search for asylum as a process of colonization in reverse, members of the former Empire exploring mother countries as foreign territories. Yet, fleeing poverty or abuses of human rights, asylum seekers do not emerge unscarred from a "deeply felt and painful experience" (Phillips 2006, 219) and *A Distant Shore*, where no migrant wishes to or can return home, charters world migration to include Africa, Asia, as well as Ireland and more surprisingly Scotland. The refugees choose England for its language, and the promise of a decent treatment:

> What draws the immigrants to England? Language (since Solomon is an English speaking West African). The second thing is the sense of historical fair-play of Britain. The idea that somehow, Britain is country of decency and good manners, civility, and that one will be able to participate because this notion of kind, of paternal benevolence that Britain gives out towards colonial, or former colonial subjects, I think lives on.
> (Phillips 2004, radio interview)

The illegal crossing of boundaries when there is no turning back is a traumatic experience engaging body and soul. The narration of Gabriel's flight from his country ravaged by civil war allows Phillips to give a vivid account of the harrowing process of exile. Gabriel, the only boy in the family, has no other choice than leaving, since his father and his family died in order to protect his life as he was hunted down for having allowed the massacre of villagers by the bloodthirsty soldiers he was supposed to lead. In order to survive and leave, he kills his friend, a shopkeeper, and steals his money to pay for being smuggled out of the country by his uncle.

> In the past few days his uncle has aged many years and Gabriel feels as though he too has added considerably to his thirty years. Despite his uncle's assurances, Gabriel knows that in many ways their journey is only now beginning. And only the strongest among them will survive. (119)

Migration is an endurance test that encourages the survival of the fittest. Premature aging signals that migration, as a traumatic experience, is deeply disruptive, as though global displacement were another type of world scale holocaust. The same stigmata are described on concentration camp inmates in *The Nature of Blood,* another novel by Phillips: "Young bodies rusted like old taps" (168). The Chinese man who shows them how to cross the Channel is clearly marked out as a man who will not survive: "The Chinese man told me that for those with no money the only way to England is the boats. If we do not try, then we are defeated" (134). He "appears to be suffering badly with a cold" (133) and "begins to cough loudly into his chapped hands" (133). Unable to cling on to a metal chain on the side of the ship crossing the Channel, he dies swallowed by the sea, another casualty of the global flight from the dangers of political oppression or utter destitution. Various migrants such as these draw a map of the world within the British space: thus, as Clingman perceptively observes, "*A Distant Shore* shows transnational faultlines within national space" (94).

In the course of the novel, Phillips charters a map of immigration within Britain with asylum seekers coming from Africa, Asia and Europe. Gabriel, who belongs to an unnamed minority ethnic group in a West-African country comes to realize that to start a new life, he will have to erase his past. Even though the welcome in England is somewhat strained, he keeps hope alive:

> Gabriel knows that if he is going to live again, then he will have to learn to banish all thoughts of his past existence. There can be no sentiment. Hurtling blindly down this highway, he knows that with every gasp of the acrid air beneath the heavy tarpaulin, life is taking him beyond this nightmare and to a new place and a new beginning (94).

A foray in a bar elicits a comment which reveals that migrants are now enacting an exploration of the Old World, a discovery in reverse. They have the drive and energy of modern-day explorers. Gabriel remarks: "This is not the England he thought he was travelling to and these shipwrecked people are not the people he thought he would discover. Under this sad roof, life is stripped of ambition and it is broken" (176). All the same, to migrate is to grow, as he tells his unfortunate companion about to die in the detention centre they have been sent to: "Said, you must continue to allow hope to grow" (80). This new beginning is literally stated: "'I am a one-year old man who walks with heavy steps. I am a man burdened with hidden history" (300). The poignant image reflects the conflation of past trauma and new expectations within the same subject and suggests the extensive internal readjustment at work when experiencing displacement.

Falsely accused of rape, Gabriel is befriended by the Andersons after his release from the detention center and becomes caretaker-cum-watchman in a new development in the north of England. But to his dismay, Solomon keeps receiving hate mails: "This is England. What kind of place did I come to?" (40). The only answer Dorothy can give is: "It's where I'm from" (41), as though she were unable to criticize her home country or question its mores. She then realizes that race might be an aggravating factor. "I haven't given it much thought, and perhaps this is my failing, but Solomon is the only colored person in the village. In the town, there are plenty of dark faces, but in this village he is alone" (45).

Unfortunately, Solomon does not have the keys to properly fight what is ahead of him "At home it was relatively simple to distinguish a man of a different tribe or region, but among these people I was lost" (273). Not knowing the local cultural code causes him to overlook his initial fear of England: "but my lack of knowledge of the ways of the English caused me to be fearful" (273). He stays in the village, instead of fleeing it like the Epsteins who left because the mother, a doctor, was both a woman and Jewish. Dubbing "hate mail" "communication" (292), the repetition of his absence of fear shows both courage and blindness to the forces of hatred at work in the village: "I am not afraid of this communication, but it is difficult for me to know what to do. To discard the offending article would probably be the wise decision, but I wish to keep it although I am not sure why. Perhaps to show that I am not afraid" (293). Racism is a rampant disease made apparent when dog mess is shoveled into his letter-box: "These people are unwell, for decent people do not conduct themselves in this way. Writing to me with their filth is one thing but this is savage" (300). Through the shift of perspective occasioned by this outrageous act, the modern-day explorer discovers the savagery in the heart of Europe.

Still, Solomon, being the son of a chief, an elder, "a man who decided disputes and punished crimes" (282), sees his new job as a watchman invested with a meaning it does not have in this new surrounding as can be understood from these reflections: "I am familiar with this village, and this area, but now it is to be my home. I am to be the night-watchman, and my job will be to watch over these people" (280). He fails to realize that his status of watchman is not synonymous with power and universal respect: "but when I travel at night with a torch it is a different matter, for I imagine that I command respect. I am official" (295). Survival means adaptation to new living conditions, but the word "imagine" underlines Solomon's delusion. Services rendered to the community no longer entail gratitude or respect. His status as a foreigner remains his prominent feature in the eyes of the skinheads who eventually ambush him, and his function of guardian of the community is subsumed by his status of black African refugee.

This comes as a reminder that skin color acts as a portable boundary, a signifier allowing for all manners of trespassing the black person's personal space, and entitling one, if so minded, to consider that nothing black is off-limits. Such warnings appeared in *The European Tribe* (1987) when, as a homodiegetic narrator, Phillips evoked Othello, the Shakespearian character:

> His attempts to secure himself worked, but only as long as there was a war and he was needed. Othello relaxed, like the black man in the middle-class suburb who is suddenly surprised to see racist graffiti daubed on the side of his house. He though he had escaped all that, but he never could. (51)

Forgetting about one's origins becomes a flaw revealing the character's blindness to an ingrained and deep seated racism. Phillips returns to this idea in *The Nature of Blood* (1997): "Brother, you are weak. A figment of a Venetian imagination. While you still have time, jump from your bed and fly away home. Peel your rusty body from hers and go home. No good can come from your foreign adventure" (183). The undercurrent of Solomon's adventure seems to be utmost pessimism since the possibility for black persons to be allowed to forget the tension about race seems remote.

Far from being aware of the potential toxicity of his environment, Solomon appears then as a "black Uncle Tom" (Phillips 1997, 181) collaborating with the system. His lack of knowledge of the social structure of his new world will cost him his life because his trust in an idealized England is stronger than the realities he faces. When Solomon, attacked by right-wing youngsters, realizes that his life is at stake, he is pushed to the limits by despair and rage and his valiant fight before he dies may be seen as a way for Phillips to establish a continuity between the experience of slavery and the experience of being a refugee. His death reads like the restaging of the African slaves' return to their homeland through death: Gabriel, a fallen angel, had "Hawk" as a war name, and his last words, 'talking about how he was a bird that could fly' (54), evoke the final lines of Toni Morrison's *Song of Solomon*, where death and myth join: "it did not matter which one of them would give up his ghost in the arms of his brother. For he knew what Shalimar knew: If you surrendered to the air, you could ride it" (341). By using this image of the bird in flight, Phillips artfully manages to conflate through Solomon's death the traumatic experiences that genocide, slavery, forced migration and racism are, showing the toxicity of a world that seeks to negate the personal boundaries of the black individual.

Gabriel meets Bright while they are both facing the Channel and seeking to enter England. Bright was a political prisoner in Africa and has become an illegal alien in England. He is pursuing the dream of an ideal England, utterly rejecting his native country:

> But I am an Englishman. Only the white man respects us, for we do not respect ourselves. If you cut my heart open you will

> find it stamped with the word "England". [...] I speak the language, therefore I am going to England to claim my house and my stipend. (134)

He refuses to admit that equating the mastery of a given language and national membership is a fallacy. If it is true that language has a "capacity for generating imagined communities, building in effect *particular solidarities*" (Anderson 133), it does so in circumstances dictated by politics alone and, in Bright's case, we can feel that his claim to a British passport on these grounds is quite flimsy. Englishness as a last refuge, the last opportunity to find a home is an obsession but also the very ground on which Bright wants to build a new identity in a self-designed space he is determined to call home. "I am an Englishman now. I am English and nobody will stop me from going home. Not you, not these people, nobody" (134).

Salman Rushdie sees migrants as metaphors of a former self, as "people who had been translated, who had, so to speak, entered the condition of metaphor" (Rushdie, quoted in Clingman 12). Said, an Iraqi teacher, has been forced out of his country for talking to "some English people" (77). His dearest wish is to be 'translated' in England into a political refugee:

> I am no longer a teacher. I am here to begin my life again and I have the appetite to do this so they can help me, yes? I told them I have a case to present, but they do not listen to me. I tell them: please, do not send me back to my country. Not there. (79)

He shares with Bright the belief in the English language as a key to nationality and still believes in the currency of the traditional image of the Englishman as a gentleman. His belief in democracy and English decency verges on idolatry, as shown by the following question: "Is it true that in England you can smell freedom in the air? That it is a different air?" (79). But it is becoming increasingly difficult to be a Muslim refugee, particularly after the 2001 terrorist attacks: "Everybody wants to keep out the Muslim but in England, freedom is everything. [...] British people are good. I have friends who tell me the truth. I do not hate Americans, but they are not gentlemen" (78).

Said is subsequently left to die in a retention centre in the UK, abused by warders and inmates alike. Phillips shows how migration is not only unwelcome but criminalized: "England is not my country. I have done nothing. I am not a criminal man" (79). Understatement is used to show that what the inmates experience in the retention centre verges on mental torture: 'Is this true? You left this man in a cell with a dead man?" (117). We are not told that Gabriel experiences a nervous breakdown after witnessing Said die without medical attention, but only presented with the warder's comments after Gabriel's fit :

"Well, sonny, what's with all the shouting? You losing it up here?' The day warder taps the side of his head" (82) or when Gabriel is administered a tranquilizing shot: "This should hold the bugger in place" (ibid.). Refugees are shown as the ultimate destitute, leaderless guerrillas who have to fight to protect the boundaries of their only capital: their sanity and body's integrity.

Another Asian character is introduced through Dorothy, the second main protagonist of the novel, since she has an affair with a migrant from the Indian subcontinent. Mahmood is a Punjabi newsagent, married at twelve, who has left India to escape cultural traditions he no longer adheres to. His dream of further education and success have run aground, but he is unable to stomach "the disrespectful confusion of running a restaurant" (202), that is to say blatant racism and uncivilities:

> The sight of fat-bellied Englishmen and their slatterns rolling into the Khyber Pass after the pubs had closed, calling him Ranjit or Baboo or Swamp Boy, and using poppadoms as Frisbees, and demanding lager, and vomiting in his sinks, and threatening him with his own knives and their beery breath, and bellowing for mini-cabs and food that they were too drunk to see had already arrived on the table in front of them, was causing Mahmood to turn prematurely grey. (202)

He then moves with his wife to "a small English town with decent schools and among people who still had some manners" (203), only to be greeted by "the hospitable gloating of those who lived in this town" (203). Prejudice, racism and outright rejection of the foreigner are seen as prevalent and at odds with the benevolent image of England cherished by refugees.

Beyond the color bar, Mike's story is there to remind us of the wars between Ireland and England and of the fact that colonization and exile do not only concern non-European countries. In *The European Tribe*, Phillips "had the temerity to consider Europe as tribal" (xi). Using the example of ETA, the IRA or Yugoslavia, Phillips describes Europe as a continent still plagued by tribal warfare triggered by nationalism. Therefore, Mike can be considered as a soldier from tribal Europe who has laid down his arms: "We could talk about Mike's experiences growing in Ireland and how his father begged him not to fight against the English and how he first came to England on the Holyhead ferry" (295). He is also "the good Samaritan" who rescues Gabriel on a highway and shows proof of benevolence. He nevertheless appears prejudiced when Indians are concerned, as he sees them as economic refugees, as "scroungers" (291). Phillips avoids Manichean characterization and points to the difficulty of welcome even on the part of people who have had a first-hand experience of discrimination.

Mike introduces Solomon to Mr. and Mrs. Anderson who offer him shelter in their "blessed home" (292). While many indications in the text point to the Andersons as modern-day Scottish abolitionists, Scotland is not depicted as part of the United Kingdom since the space of reference is no longer the British Isles, but the world: "They were both retiring to Scotland which was the part of the world where Mum had originated" (296). Ireland, England and Scotland are placed on the same level, as nations in their own rights, as though Phillips were drawing a modified world map. The homogeneity of the nation is overtly challenged and finally denied.

The English Village as Allegory of the Nation

Very early on in the novel, England is presented as being a mutating country, where it is increasingly difficult for characters such as Dorothy Jones and her father to identify fellow citizens and refer to an imagined community, Benedict Anderson's definition of the nation being "an imagined political community" (Anderson 6). Indeed, the first section of the opening chapter of the novel, a first person narrative told through the voice of Dorothy, begins and ends with "England has changed"(3, 60). The sentences are not repeated to underline permanence in Dorothy's outlook on the changing character of England, but to bracket Dorothy's evolution. The first three sentences of the novel stress the anxiety linked to identity and identification. "England has changed. These days it's difficult to tell who's from around here and who's not. Who belongs and who's a stranger. It's disturbing. It does not feel right" (3). In *A New World Order* (2001), Phillips had already stressed the unease of feeling "of and not of a place" as a black British citizen: "I am seven years old in the north of England; too late to be coloured, but too young to be British. I recognise the place, I feel at home here, but I don't belong. I am of, and not of, this place" (4).

Thus, this novel about identity and belonging, describing a world where "coloureds" still exist, astutely starts with the uneasiness of a native English citizen who is seen as a newcomer in her own country: "We are the newcomers, or posh so-and-sos, as I heard a vulgar woman in the post office call us" (5). The faultline here is not race, but class. The uneasiness generated by displacement is echoed by the defense mechanisms of the established Weston residents, which is here a consequence of sheer change, although Dorothy lucidly remarks that a new development in a village can in no way alter its past:

> After all, our houses are set on the edge of Weston, a village
> that is hardly going to give up its name and identity because
> some developer has seen a way to make a quick buck by throw-

ing up some semi-detached bungalows, slapping a carriage lamp in the front of them and calling them "Stoneleigh." (3)

The refusal to open boundaries even to fellow nationals translates itself into annoyance: "He was annoyed, and he wanted me to know that once upon a time there had been a move to change the name of Weston to Market Weston, but it never caught on" (3). Another defense mechanism shown at work here relies on history and myth: 'once upon a time' is a hint to the historicity of the town and its permanence through time. Moreover, any attempt to put into question the pre-eminence of Weston is considered as an offence: "He told me that he had been instructed by head office to scratch out the name 'Stoneleigh' if it appeared on any envelopes. Should the residents turn out to be persistent offenders, he was to remind them that they lived in Weston" (3). Such mechanisms on the level of a town aim at re-establishing priority and order based on history and class. Offenders are the ones who fail to get their priorities right, who fail to fit in. Benedicte Ledent thus stresses that Stoneleigh is an allegory of England, class barriers acting as social frontiers, explaining that "[t]he topography of Weston demands to be read figuratively, as if Stoneleigh stood for England as a whole, or even for the world in miniature" and arguing that [t]he hill on which the new development is built conveys the social superiority (real or imagined) of its new inhabitants" (157).

In his exploration of the mechanisms of integration, Phillips shows British nationals experiencing rejection and mild hostility as newcomers. Yet, experience does not generate empathy and Dorothy, who is the object of rejection in Weston, is blind to the plight of vagrants. The vagrant is thought to know neither limits nor boundaries, and the absence of the minimal border, that of home, triggers a negative response. Dorothy qualifies her unease at her own prejudiced attitude as embarrassment: "I am almost embarrassed to admit it, but these days, whenever I go into town it's the homeless people who annoy me the most, and the frightening thing is they seem to be everywhere" (12). In this sentence, Phillips has Dorothy express three terms in which racist feelings are usually expressed: embarrassment about the avowal of prejudice, annoyance, and fear. Moreover, in Dorothy's view, transgressions are made worse when gendered:

"What you looking at?" says one of them. It's a woman, which somehow makes it worse. She sounds and looks like a gypsy, with her black hair, and her black eyes, and her grimy black hands. Sheila and I have always been scared of gypsies and Mum had told us to run away if any of them ever spoke to us. They are nasty, and they like to take away people's children, everybody knows that much. (65)

Dorothy describes the rejection of the other as atavistic: "*always* been afraid" while it is shown to be socially acquired: "*Mum* had told us" (65, emphasis added). Migration as the lifestyle of nomadic nationals elicits the same rejection, compounded here with a sexist and racist slant, with no embarrassment this time since this rejection is culturally shared by "everybody." Still, Dorothy has come a long way in the span of three months: "England has changed" is uttered a second time after having referred twice to Solomon as a friend: "and I thought of my friend lying face down in the water like a dead fish" (59) and "Maybe I should visit the small stone church and say some kind of prayer for my friend?" (60) Contrary to the first utterance, the change is not seen from the vantage point of a nationalist bemoaning the altered state of her country, but as a person whose vision of the world is larger: "For the first time, I want to leave England. To see Spain or Italy. England has changed"(60).

Dorothy's first-hand witnessing of rejection makes her and the reader more aware of the difficulties experienced by others who see the anxiety of displacement compounded with racial, social, or sexual prejudice. Yet, border crossing is not limited to foreigners since the very definition of the nation seems to be put into question by nationals themselves. For his part, Dorothy's father clearly states that his nation is not the United Kingdom but England:

> He believed that the Welsh were full of sentimental stupidity, that the Scots were helplessly mean and mopish, and they should stick to their own side of the Hadrian's Wall, and that the Irish were violent, Catholic drunks. For him, being English was more important than being British and being English meant no coloureds. (42)

If Britishness refers to the United Kingdom and the British Empire, Mr. Jones shows that he refuses the very idea of it. The prejudice he displays concerning the constituent countries of the United Kingdom that came to be part of the Union as far back as 1218 for Wales, 1706 for Scotland, and 1800 for Ireland, tends to underline the fact that tribal knee-jerk reactions are to be accounted for even in a country that is a major European power. There is dramatic irony in the allusion to Hadrian's Wall, since England came to existence well after the invasion by the Roman Empire, which was an immigration of a kind. As for "coloureds" they are "a challenge to our English identity" (42). Dorothy's father imagined community is then English, white and working-class, as he resents his daughter marrying a middle-class man.

The Body as the Ultimate Frontier of Identity

After presenting a collation of migrant lives, Phillips collates the lives of several women, another part of the submerged population: Denise, a neglected child victim of her father's and boyfriend's violence, Carla, the horrified friend of Solomon's murderers, Sheila, Dorothy's sister, who was abused by her father, and Dorothy herself who is nevertheless "concerned to make sure that the dominant narrative is male" (203). They are all part of a taxonomy of women whose body, as a frontier of identity, is a battleground. Coming from fractured or dysfunctional homes, they are in search of refuge as they share a sense of alienation from a man's world. They remain nevertheless the characters that are most empathetic to the plight of migrants who, like them, are denied the right to exert their free-will. Denise, who courageously resists the call to press charges against Gabriel for alleged rape declares: "Then Barry, he started with his fists when I didn't do what he wanted. They are sick, all of them. Just sick" (187). Katherine who works for an immigration law firm and helps refugees is an independent character who is shown to be able to exert her free will and act positively in favor of the homeless. She is nevertheless shown to have to wage a battle at home as her partner disagrees with her fight: "Gabriel, I'm sorry I can't do more for you than this, but as you can see I've got things to sort out at home" (182).

Freedom and physical integrity is not a given in their lives, and this is translated by Dorothy through the images used when recalling her affair with Mahmood: she felt like "a fish trapped" in her bed (210) and also "as an object speared" (199). Dorothy refuses to accept a role of sexual object and become submerged by "the familiar entanglement of female feelings of guilt and vulnerability" (Phillips 2009, 7). She becomes a fighter of a kind on the boundaries between sexes when she awkwardly tries to get even with her lovers, but her attempt at redress is translated as being mere harassment. There seems to be no safe haven for women in an environment where they are still trapped into predetermined behavioral patterns, and which has also become "a more brutal England in terms of violence":

> and so to her way of thinking it didn't seem to matter much where you were these days, for people seemed to feel that they could pretty much do whatever they liked to you. There had even be a story in the local paper about a woman who was badly beaten up by a gang of kids in the park across the way when she tried to stop the young hooligans from mugging her six-year old daughter for her bike. (195)

Dorothy's answer to the guilt feeling she has for having failed both her sister and Solomon, her feeling of loss after her parents' death and a series of humiliating love-affairs is to retreat into silence after her collapse: "My heart remains a desert, but I tried. I had a feeling that Solomon understood me. This is not my home, and until they accept this, then I will be as purposeful silent as a bird in flight" (312). The bird imagery is another link with Solomon. It points to her exile status and her desire to escape her stifling environment. Dorothy has chosen to inhabit a fractured space: "So our village is divided into two." (4), and this division of space reflects her fractured soul. A "secondary" victim (Luckhurst 1) of the incest committed on her sister, she laments her failure to come to her help. Her sense of self-esteem has been further diminished by her husband's casual desertion, her new role as the mistress of a married immigrant: "She does not say, I used to be the fancy woman for the Asian man in the corner shop, but he dropped me" (223), and the difficulty to ignore the social prohibitions inherited from her parents. After the strain of her sister's death from cancer, her dismissal after having been accused of harassment, and the end of her affair with Mahmood, the final blow is Solomon's death which provokes the uncovering of an internalized racial taboo. In a psychotic crisis, she hears her dead mother confirm the impossibility of a meaningful relationship with a black person:

> She goes on, but she's so upset that she can hardly get the words out. Didn't I understand what people would say about me if I were to be seen with a coloured, and particularly one as dark as this Solomon? She had not brought me up to be that type of girl. (64)

Dorothy finds sanctuary, and home, within her own psychic boundaries. Toni Morrison has remarked that "we may suddenly realize that the most obvious and fundamental location of home *is* the human body, the final frontier of identity." Morrison further asserts the fundamental role of memory as a location of home, which throws a new light on Dorothy's behavior in *A Distant Shore*: "Foreign is the designation of the curious, the not us, the rupture between self and society. Home is where the memory of the self dwells, whether those memories pawn or shrivel, determines who we are, and determines what we may become." In a defiant gesture, Dorothy decides to shut herself off from the rest of the world, being thus comforted in the thought that she is safely off-limits.

The borderline personality disorders Dorothy suffers from enable Phillips to situate within the psyche and the body the unease, disquiet and anguish the crossing of barriers provoke. As Roger Luckhurst suggests, "Trauma is a piercing or breach of a border that puts inside and outside into a strange communication" (3). Far from being the "settled female body" (Machado Saez 39) with which Solomon is unable to connect, Dorothy is a deeply unsettled woman whose quaint idea of England does not match its reality, and whose aspiration to openness and generosity clash with reactionary attitudes transmitted to her by her family or evinced by fellow villagers. While her quasi-Austenian respect for manners is seen as antiquated, blatant prejudices have free reign.

Listening to a publican talking about a Jewish family in a pub where she is having a drink, Dorothy discovers that children's names remain a criterion of eligibility to belonging: "Nobody cares much in the town, but around here they don't blend in. I mean, Rachel and Jacob. They weren't even trying" (9). Identity and nationhood become concepts that are increasingly defined individually in a constant negotiation between personal history and day to day circumstances.

In the nursing home, Dorothy realizes that it is through bonding with others that the feeling of belonging can be nurtured. Home is where you feel understood. That is why waiting for "gather[ing] some strength before going back to the world" (312), she decides to shut herself within her own body, the ultimate frontier, offering to the world the performance of a refusal to belong in a world where she is both homeless and alone. The only contact zone becomes the mask she will wear every day, as if in a dumb show. "Sometimes before dawn, as light begins to bleed slowly through the night sky, I will ease myself out of this bed and proceed to put on my day face" (312). Dorothy refuses to go on operating, collaborating with and negotiating the different faultlines of an increasingly fractured world. She openly denounces communication as a fallacy, offering a mask to the world: "And then, in the morning, just like in the real world, I put on my day face" (305). She becomes unmoored, a single unit isolated within her own psychological boundaries, trying her best to survive and keep death at bay: "They just shuffle around looking miserable, as though death has tried to talk to them in the night. Well, it also tries with me sometimes, but you're not forced to listen. There's nothing that says that you have to pay attention" (305). Clingman names this experience of utter isolation "disjunctive simultaneity of the national":

> In such an account, we are light years away from Benedict Anderson's notion of national temporality - everyone experiencing everything at the same time. Rather, separately and together, Dorothy and Gabriel's lives suggest parallel universes within the nation, operating within different fields of time and space. Here we see the cavernous and disjunctive simultaneity of the national – times within times, narratives within narra-

tives – precisely because of migrant and exilic experience, whether in (in Dorothy's case) domestic or (in Gabriel's) across formal borders. (96)

In this novel, national, social, and personal borders are questioned and challenged. The fight for freedom and self-assertion turns out to be a deadly fight in unfriendly territory. Should we fail to acknowledge and celebrate the fact that in Toni Morrison's words "The world is every foreigner's home" and stubbornly refuse to listen to "the choral accompaniment of voices" (266) that constitute an integrated nation, we are headed for a world crisscrossed by a myriad of lines, where individuals isolated within their personal boundaries will be aggregated in fictions of communities, a world Phillips envisioned in 2000:

> The New World. A twenty-first century world. A world in which it is impossible to resist the claims of the migrant, the asylum seeker, or the refugee. I watch them. The old static order in which one people speaks down to another, lesser, people is dead. The colonial, or postcolonial, model has collapsed. In its place we have a new world order in which there will soon be one global conversation with limited participation open to all, and full participation available to none. In this new world order, nobody will fully feel at home. (5)

Yet, a decade later, the world is still busy resisting the claims of all manners of exiles and most election returns in African countries tend to confirm the strength of the postcolonial model that still survives even if altered. According to one's location on the globe and position in society, access to global conversation remains either a myth or a spurious luxury. For better or for worse, the global unity and uniformity envisioned once by Phillips is far from achieved, yet the quest for home, one of Phillips's recurring motifs, is a global concern, now that environmental refugees have added their numbers to the flood of immigrants and political refugees throughout the world. *A Distant Shore*'s overall pessimism only allows us to place our hope in individual resilience.

Works Cited

Anderson, Benedict. *Imagined Communities: Reflections on the Origin and Spread of Nationalism*. London, New York: Verso, 1991.

Clingman, Stephen. *The Grammar of Identity, Transnational Fiction and the Nature of the Boundary*. Oxford: Oxford University Press, 2009.

-----. "'England has changed': Questions of National Form in a *Distant Shore*." *Moving Worlds* 7.1 (2007): 46-58.

Hall, Stuart. "New Ethnicities." *Identities: Race, Class, Gender and Nationality*. Ed. Linda Martin Alcoff and Eduardo Mendieta. Oxford: Blackwell, 2003. 90-95.
Ledent, Bénedicte. "'Of, and not of, this Place': Attachment and Detachment in Caryl Phillips' *A Distant Shore*." *Kunapipi* 26.1 (2004): 152-60.
Luckhurst, Roger. *The Trauma Question*. London and New York: Routledge, 2008.
Machado Sàez, Helena. "Postcoloniality, Atlantic Orders, and the Migrant Male in the Writings of Caryl Phillips." *Small Axe* 9.1(2005): 17-39.
Morisson, Toni. "The Foreigner's Home." (Étranger chez soi) Conférence d'Introduction, Paris, Musée du Louvre, 6 November 2006.
Phillips, Caryl. *In The Falling Snow*. London: Harvil Secker, 2009.
-----. *The Nature of Blood*. 1997. London: Vintage, 2008.
-----. *Foreigners*. London: Harvil Secker, 2007.
-----. "Border Crossings." *Displacement, Asylum, Migration: The Oxford Amnesty Lectures 2004*. E. Kate E. Tunstall. Oxford: Oxford University Press, 2006. 210-25.
-----. "Caryl Phillips, *A Distant Shore*" *Rabid Reader*. NPR, Washington. 11 Feb. 2004. Radio.
-----. *A Distant Shore*. London: Vintage, 2004.
-----. "Extravagant Strangers." *A New World Order: Essays*. London: Vintage, 2002. 288-97.
-----. *A New World Order*. London: Vintage, 2001.
-----. *The European Tribe*. Winchester: Faber and Faber, 1992.
Turner, Nathaniel. "Interview with Caryl Phillips." *ChickenBones*. Last accessed 14 August 2008,http://www.nathanielturner.com/distantshore2.htm
Walkowitz, Rebecca, "The Location of Literature: The Transnational Book and the Migrant Writer." *Immigrant Fictions: Contemporary Literature in an Age of Globalization*. Ed. Rebecca Walkowitz. Madison: University of Wisconsin Press, 2007. 527-45.

CHAPTER ELEVEN

Globalizing Africa, Universalizing the Child: Towards Transnational Identity in Ishmael Beah's *A Long Way Gone: Memoirs of a Boy Soldier*

Jopi Nyman

Recent years have shown an increasing number of representations of African child soldiers in fiction and in life writing, as can be seen in such texts as Bernard Ashley's fictional *Little Soldier* (1999), China Keitetsi's *Child Soldier* (2004), and Ishmael Beah's controversial *A Long Way Gone: Memoirs of a Boy Soldier* (2007). Such narratives tend to emphasize the survival of their protagonists by re-locating them in new social and cultural settings far away from their homes embedded in violent conflicts and ethnic hatred. In so doing these texts are also narratives of exorcism and purification that seek to remold and educate the traumatized child in order to relocate it in new worlds. As one of the most prominent examples in this tradition, Ishmael Beah's memoir places its narrator in discourses of violence, trauma, and globalization in order to construct a subject ready to enter Western modernity and "America," thus transnationalizing his identifications.[1]

Beah's book charts the life and movements of its narrator, the young Ishmael, who loses his family amidst the violence of Sierra Leone and is forced to join the Sierra Leone Armed Forces to fight against the "rebels," the Revolutionary United Front (RUF), a group of soldiers half of whom are between the ages of 8-14 (Glazer 377). Following the life of Ishmael from his first awareness of civil war, at the age of 12 in 1993, to his successful escape to Guinea and subsequent life in the United States in the late 1990s, the narrative unfolds a period of social turmoil by showing violent armed conflicts, death of civilians, and a chaotic coup. During the narrative Ishmael transforms from a young school-boy to a ruthless and drugged soldier and finally becomes a sensitive and intelligent representative of his nation's youth at a UN-sponsored meeting in New York. An international success, and acclaimed by readers, the

---

[1] I should like thank Dr. Silvia Schultermandl for her insightful comments and support in preparing this essay for publication.

simply-narrated book has not only been on the top of the *New York Times* Bestseller list but it was also the book of the week on BBC Radio 4 in May 2007. The text has also generated a debate whether all the details are true and whether its author has spent such a long time in the army and experienced all that he claims (see Gare, online).[2]

In terms of genre, Beah's autobiographical text resembles some other narratives telling of a child's experiences in extreme conditions of fear, violence, and war. In an article examining narratives of what she calls "ethnic suffering," Sidonie Smith claims that by telling and making their stories available, these witnesses to terror and abuse are positioned in a contradictory situation as they hand over their stories to

> journalists, publishers, publicity agents, marketers, and rights activists whose framings of personal narratives participate in the commodification of suffering, the reification of the universalized subject position of innocent victim, and the displacement of historical complexity by the feel-good opportunities of empathetic identification. (144)

While Beah's narrative is not directly one where ethnicity plays a major role, its use of a child narrator links it to the texts examined by Smith, Zlata Filipovici's Sarajevo-based *Zlata's Diary* (1994) and the famous *Anne Frank's Diary*, both being narratives of "lost childhood" (Smith 152). In a similar vein, *A Long Way Gone* transforms its narrator's long-awaited participation in a local talent show in a nearby village into years of forced military service. The scene is set as follows:

> To save money, we decided to walk the sixteen miles to Mattru Jong. It was a beautiful summer day, the sun wasn't too hot, and the walk didn't feel long either, as we chatted about all kinds of things, mocked and chased each other. We carried slingshots that we used to stone birds and chase the monkeys that tried to cross the main dirt road. We stopped at several rivers to swim. (7-8)

Such pastoral glimpses into childhood with its days of unlimited freedom sentimentalize the narrative and package it for consumption; the contradiction between innocence and reality is emphasized in the fact that during their leisurely walk their village is attacked. To use the words of Smith:

> The commodification of stories of ethnic suffering obscures the complex politics of international events, stylizes the story to suit an educated international audience familiar with narr-

---

[2] This debate, although interesting in the larger context of the claims to "truth" and "authenticity" in personal memoirs, is not the subject of my discussion here.

> atives of individual triumph over adversity, evokes emotive responses trained on the feel-good qualities of successful resolution, and often universalizes the story of suffering so as to erase incommensurable differences and the horror of violence. The commodification of the young girl's diary gives us a version of the story of "Anne Frank" – but with a happy ending. (154)

Such passages thus fulfill a major ideological function in directing global (mainly Western) readers towards the allegedly tragic fate of a young protagonist.

There is, indeed, a similar logic at work in Beah's story of survival and individual success. It is narrated from the safety provided by the United States, which is indicated as early as in the paratext of the memoir, an unnumbered chapter entitled "New York City, 1998" (3). This section locates Ishmael amongst his new pals eager to learn more about his past. While his friends are – quite ironically – enchanted with the alleged glory associated with weapons and warfare, the passage emphasizes Ishmael's unwillingness to reveal his past. In so doing the passage draws a contrast between the naïveté of his actual audience that finds violence "cool" and the knowledge of his implied audience, the educated readers aware of the harsh realities of civil war in Africa. What is established is an emotive identification with the ordeals of its child protagonist, now aged 17 and relocated in America:

> My high school friends have begun to suspect I haven't told them the full story of my life.
> "Why did you leave Sierra Leone?"
> "Because there is a war."
> "Did you witness some of the fighting?"
> "Everyone in the country did."
> "You mean you saw people running around with guns and shooting each other?
> "Yes, all the time."
> "*Cool.*"
> I smile a little.
> "You should tell us about it sometime."
> "Yes, sometime." (3, original emphasis)

By using the trope of the child, and more specifically of the child soldier, Beah's memoir seeks to promote an affectual economy derived from the notions of purity and innocence associated in the West with the figure of the child. Not only is this revealed on the book's cover which portrays a young boy carrying a machine gun but also in the text's insistence on presenting the child soldier as transgressing the established values and activities commonly associated with childhood. In Beah's memoir, children and adolescents, "boys our age" (37), kill and are killed. The youngsters are shown to be terrorizing the region and "patrolli[ing] in special units, killing and maiming civilians" (37). Similarly, when Ishmael becomes a member of the army, he learns to kill, not only as a combatant but also for fun, as part of competitions seeking to boost a sense of group identity. Killing is an act, as Ishmael reflects, that dehumanizes human beings and reduces them to being "simply another rebel who was responsible for the death of my family" (124):

> The corporal gave the signal with a pistol shot and I grabbed the man's head and slit his throat in one fluid motion. His Adam's apple made way for the sharp knife, and I turned the bayonet on its zigzag edge as I brought it out. His eyes rolled up and they looked me straight in the eye before they suddenly stopped in a frightful glance, as if caught by surprise. [...] I dropped him on the ground and wiped my bayonet on him. Reported to the corporal, who was holding a timer. The bodies of the other prisoners fought in the arms of the other boys, and some continued to shake on the ground for a while. I was proclaimed the winner, and Kanei came second. The boys and the other soldiers who were the audience clapped as if I had just fulfilled one of life's greatest achievements. (125)

The coldness of the narration and the representation of death as a celebration add to the disappearance of the idea of a pure child. At the same time they direct the expected audience towards lamenting a childhood violated and lost amidst violence, beyond familial networks and proper moral guidance. What this means for the audience is that it is forced to abandon its sentimentalized and West-centered understanding of the innocence of childhood in an imagined third-world country. By replacing the pastoral vision of the African countryside with a landscape of terror and death, the text foregrounds the abuse and violence pertinent to the conditions of civil war and destroys naïve visions of Africa. Instead of one Ishmael there are in fact two: a music-loving footballer and a ruthless killer.

In the view of Sidonie Smith, life narratives of this kind expound a vision of the universality of childhood that both attracts and shames the international audience, calling them to act and save the children as any parent should (158). They also transform the suffering ethnic child to a representative of "the universal abstraction of the child of human rights" that is "everybody's child and thus nobody's specific child, living in a certain location" (Smith 158). In

Beah's story, the universality of childhood, boosting audience identification with the imagined innocent child, is evoked at several points in the narrator's way of referring to the boys as mere children with no evil intent. As he puts it upon meeting a cautious and uncommunicative man with a large family, "I was [...] disappointed that the war had destroyed the enjoyment of the very experience of meeting people. Even a twelve-year-old couldn't be trusted anymore" (48). This transformation of a child into a potential killer is emphasized even further when Ishmael and his friends start their escapade, but the people in several villages mistake the multi-ethnic motley group of half a dozen adolescents for dangerous rebels: "Many times during our journey we were surrounded by muscular men with machetes who almost killed us before they realized we were just children running away from the war" (57). This culminates in their being expelled from a coastal village and the recapturing by the villagers who threaten to kill them: "'You children have become little devils, but you came to the wrong village [...] Well, this is the end of the road for devils like you. Out there in the ocean, even you rascals cannot survive'" (66). Through such instances, the reader is invited to sentimentally reflect on the helpless child under abuse.

As this shows, the local discourse of demonization and the idealistic West-centred discourse promoting the sanctity of childhood are both present in the narrative. The figure of the demonized killer-child, however, is not without a basis, as shown in the above passage telling of Ishmael's first kill. In order to represent the child as a figure of possibility, making it thus acceptable to the Western audience, the narrative both positions Ishmael in the discourse of innocent childhood and represents his actions as stemming from ideological brainwashing and drugs. In this sense Ishmael's emerging transnational identity rests on his positive characteristics that promote audience identification and locate him in a morally acceptable position open to learning. This doubleness of Ishmael's identity – he is sensitive yet brutal, a killer and a victim – conforms to what has been suggested in social and anthropological studies of child soldiers. For instance, Harry G. West has criticized a stereotypical conception portraying fighting children as ruthless killers and killing machines with no sensitivity towards their own communities (180). West suggests that the two roles – "victim and perpetrator [...] are not mutually exclusive" (180); similarly, research results suggest that in particular contexts where for instance socialization into violence is not uncommon, its meaning is not universal: "experience of violence is in significant measure culturally determined" (West 181) – this also explains its *coolness* amongst Ishmael's new friends, American high school students growing up amidst rap videos and urban gangs. It may also be noted that the anthropologist David Rosen has traced the roots of the atrocities in Sierra Leone committed by RUF to the country's social history where violence, warfare, and slavery have placed a major role since pre-contact times, and youth violence was later institutionalized in the form of secret societies that participated in violent anti-colonial struggles (Glazer 377-78).

To negotiate the essentializing discourse of the killer-child – and to make it more palatable to the Western audience – Beah's narrative emphasizes the positive aspects of the universal child and constructs it as a playful creature, prone to song and dance that express its joyful character: "We chased and wrestled each other in the sand, played somersault and running games. We even bundled up Alhaji's old shirt and tied a rope around it to make a soccer ball. We then played a game, and each time one of us scored a goal, he would celebrate with a *soukous* dance. We shouted, laughed, and sang our secondary school songs" (59). This duality of being both, a boy who performs strategic killings and school-yard banter, refutes essentialist interpretations of Ishmael's persona and, by extension, of Sierra Leone male youth.

It is through music, and American rap music in particular, that Ishmael is embedded in the transnational network constructed by the global presence of American popular culture. Rap plays a major role in the memoir as early as its opening pages where Ishmael, his brother, and several friends make preparations for participating in a talent show in Mattru Jong, a town close to their home village. The narrative reveals that Ishmael is not without links to the wider world: an American company his father works for has brought music television to his home town:

> We were first introduced to rap music during one of our visits to Mobimbi, a quarter where the foreigners [...] lived. [...] One evening a music video that consisted of a bunch of young black fellows talking really fast came on the television. The four of us sat there mesmerized by the song, trying to understand what the black fellows were saying. At the end of the video, some letters came up at the bottom of the screen. They read 'Sugarhill Gang, "Rapper's Delight."' Junior quickly wrote it down on a piece of paper. After that, we came to the quarters every other weekend to study that kind of music on television. We didn't know what it was called then, but I was impressed with the fact that the black fellows knew how to speak English really fast, and to the beat. (6)

The presence of hip-hop in Sierra Leone and the significant role it plays in Ishmael's life illustrates Arjun Appadurai's concept of mediascapes, spaces that are peculiar to the contemporary global cultural economy where cultural products cross national borders and flow uninterruptedly into other territories (35-36). Transmitted usually by electronic, audio-visual media, these "strips of reality," images as well as narratives, offer scripts for imagined lives (Appadurai 35). For Ishmael, in particular, hip-hop music and music videos offer new sites of identity, where young black men may be active and perform to appreciative audiences. In this sense Ishmael's fascination with hip-hop can be seen as an example of what George Lipsitz considers as the political basis of hip-hop: as a diasporic music it addresses the different members of African diaspora and is not limited to merely U.S. (or Western concerns) (509-10). For Lipsitz, hip-hop is a sign of oppositional, counter-hegemonic identity politics:

> At a time when African people have less power and fewer resources than at almost any previous time in history, African culture has emerged as the single most important subtext within world popular culture. The popularity of hip hop reflects more than cultural compensation for political and economic domination, more than an outlet for energies and emotions repressed by social power relations. Hip hop expresses a form of politics perfectly suited to the post-colonial era. It brings a community into being through performance, and it maps out real and imagined relations between people that speak to the realities of displacement, disillusion, and despair created by the austerity economy of post-industrial capitalism. (511)

In other words, the promise that hip-hop culture gives to Ishmael is one of community, a notion that operates at two levels. First, hip-hop links Ishmael with his friends. In the manner of adolescents all over the world, Ishmael and his friends form a pop group, desiring to perform to the music in an outfit including "baggy jeans," "soccer shorts and sweatpants for dancing," and "three pairs of socks that we pulled down and folded to make our *crapes* [sneakers] look puffy" (7). Second, it is hip-hop music, observed first on television and later on from C-cassettes that follow Ishmael everywhere until an officer throws them into a fire, that locates him in the transnational flow of globalization where identity positions are made available through identification with popular cultural celebrities and performers – and who, being black, illustrate positions of prestige and embody success to a degree hitherto unknown to Ishmael as indicated in his words quoted above: "I was impressed with the fact that the black fellows knew how to speak English really fast, and to the beat" (6).

However, as a form of *American* popular culture, hip-hop music is embedded in discourses and ideologies promoting particular locations of identity and is thus not neutral in any way. Rather, as Lane Crothers asserts, American popular culture works with and reproduces allegedly central American values ranging from tolerance and equality of opportunity to individualism and democracy (75-78). Through their representation, these values offer the international audience, including Ishmael and his friends, models and positions that they may identify with. Consequently, as Crothers argues, also American hip-hop culture shares the same basis of values but chooses to present a particular version of Americanness (92-94). It is through figures such as the notorious gangsta rapper Tupac Shakur that the dark side of American values can be noticed:

> Freedom became freedom to consume, to hate, and to dominate. Liberty became the right to do whatever one wanted to do without limit or consequence. Equality results from the violent protection of whatever is one's own. Shakur's music and life reflect the values of American public culture in their darker dimensions. (Crothers 94)

While the memoir relates rap music as a way of creating community and can be seen to promote black diasporic identifications, hip-hop culture emphasizing sexism, aggression, and unlimited consumerism has also been argued to be a tool that works for "the corporate machine and U.S. imperialism" (Hobson and Bartlow 7). As Janell Hobson and R. Dianne Bartlow write in their Introduction to a special issue of the journal *Meridians: Feminism, Race, Transnationalism*, the music industry has been at least indirectly involved in international violence by

> inspiring [...] the racialized killing of civilians overseas in cross strategies that have partnered the music industry with the military, which distributes misogynistic music to soldiers fighting in Afghanistan and Iraq so that they can be appropriately pumped up on the battlefield. (7)

This transnational identification, through music and dress pivotal to hip-hop culture, links the boys with U.S.-based international popular culture and deconstructs their Africanness. It also becomes a literal lifeline when the boys face death in the hands of the furious inhabitants of a coastal village they visit. Asked to explain what sort of weird music it is that their cassettes contain, Ishmael puts on a show and dances to the tune "OPP" (a song about two-timing) by the early 1990s U.S. rap group Naughty by Nature:

> I knew the words by heart and felt the beat. I didn't feel it this time. As I hopped up and down, hunched and raising my arms and feet to the music, I thought about being thrown in

the ocean, about how difficult it would be to know that death
was inevitable. (67)

As a result of what must have been an amusing playback performance, the chief of the village comes to recognize that "I [Ishmael] was just a child" (67-68), asks for another performance ("I Need Love" by LL Cool J), and allows the boys to leave the village. American popular music is frequently present in the narrative. Mentions range from the boys' performances and a reference to a dead rebel boy wearing "a Tupac Shakur T-shirt" (119) to Run-D.M.C. whose lyrics Ishmael copies down when released to Benin Home, a rehabilitation centre (163). It also plays a significant role during his recovery at the center in Freetown, where the kids prepare a talent show to their international guests representing "the European Commission, the UN, UNICEF, and several NGOs" (168). "I read a monologue from *Julius Caesar* and performed a short hip-hop play about the redemption of a former child soldier that I had written with Esther's encouragement" (168). While this symbolically completes his journey started at the beginning of the book, it also signifies of his future: as a result of this, Ishmael is selected as a representative of the former child soldiers to participate in an international conference on children's issues in New York, where he is to move eventually to live with his new "mother."

The point must be emphasized that the representation of music in this narrative of mobility is not beyond the sphere of ideology. As popular music links Ishmael to global youth enjoying a shared culture, its role is also to de-emphasize the significance of his specific ethnic origins, i.e., his Africanness. His survival story is recast as one of Americanization, made possible through his exposure to international culture. In addition to providing points of entry into the West, hip-hop, as well as *Rambo* (6), *crapes*, and his school-level recitals of a Shakespearean soliloquy, assist the readers in understanding the narrator as a universalized child who is part of the shared international Anglophone culture. As a result Ishmael's "otherness" is dissolved and his status as a violent child soldier abandoned.

Despite the prevalence of global youth culture as an entry point into American society, Ishmael's transition into his new life in the United States is by no means an easy one. On the contrary, the narrative of reconstructing Ishmael as an American exhibits a complex paradox which can be understood best as a representation of trauma and recovery. As I have argued, *A Long Way Gone* de-emphasizes Ishmael's Africanness by focusing on his transnational identification and entry into globalized popular and youth culture. Symbolically and morally, however, his *uninnocence* remains problematic for his forging of a new identity – after all, he is a child gone wrong, a killer and murderer, and he must be purified before he is ready to take up his position as a fully-fledged

American. While the text has already paved the way for his entry into the West through his status as a universal child, it becomes a narrative of purification by adopting a discourse of trauma that reconstructs Ishmael as an agent free from the burden of the past.

The reconstruction of Ishmael's identity – his purification – is embedded in the context of trauma and involves the problem of narrating trauma. Various critics have addressed the relationship between trauma, writing, and reading in the context of such personal and cultural traumas as the Holocaust, slavery, and the Vietnam War, all events and conditions overshadowing a person's life for a long time. In this context a particularly significant phenomenon addressed by theorists of trauma is the Post-Traumatic Stress Disorder (PTSD), defined by Cathy Caruth in the following manner:

> there is a response, sometimes delayed, to an overwhelming event or events, which takes the form of repeated, intrusive hallucinations, dreams, thoughts or behaviours stemming from the vent, along with numbing that may have begun during or after the experience, and possibly also increased arousal to (and avoidance of) stimuli recalling the event. (4)

In discussing the pathological condition in detail, Caruth pays attention to the fact that the PTSD emerges later in life, not upon the moment of experiencing a traumatic event – this is indeed the case with many soldiers returning home from the battlefield. To quote Caruth:

> [it] consists, rather, solely in the structure of its experience or reception: the event is not assimilated or experienced fully at the moment, but only belatedly, in its repeated possession of the one who experiences it. To be traumatized is precisely to be possessed by an image or event. (4-5)

What is emphasized in trauma theory is the challenge involved in narrating trauma. While the view presented by Caruth has been criticized by scholars who emphasize orthodox Freudian views (see Kilby 217-18), its emphasis on the belatedness of the trauma historicizes trauma and makes the concept useful for scholars in cultural and literary studies: "a traumatic experience can only be historical if it can manifest itself at a later date" (Kilby 220). According to Kilby, to analyze trauma is difficult as it resists representation: "trauma scholars have met the demand by arguing that the failure to represent the impact of trauma testifies to the reality of its impact. There are simply no images or words with which to capture the event" (221-22). Trauma, in other words, is an example of unrepresentability; in his reading of the writings of Caruth and Paul de Man concerning the problem of language and referentiality, or representation and reality, Tom Toremans, however, pays attention to the role that literature may have here in forming an ethical attitude:

> Caruth's rhetorical reading of de Man's writing [...] allows it to redeem this promise of a truly ethical writing, a writing that theoretically transmits trauma through the insistent and non-phenomenological reference to the "other," beyond epistemology and the duality between cognition and trope. What happens, in other words, is *literature*. (339-40, original emphasis)

The presence of the traumatizing effects of the war is overwhelming in Beah's memoir. Chapter One, for instance, shows traumatized families with children who pass through Ishmael's home village and "jump at the sound of chopping wood" (5) and refers to parents "lost in their thoughts during conversations" (5). What is portrayed as being worse than the physical and physiological effects of the war is, however, the mental and affectual damages it generates: "it was evident they had seen something that plagued their minds, something that we would refuse of accept if they told us all of it" (3). The horrors and cruelty witnessed and performed by combatant children and adults alike include villages burnt and their inhabitants killed, men and women carrying their dead children, and several visually detailed descriptions of killings and dead bodies:

> One of them lay on his stomach, and his eyes were wide open and still; his insides were spilling onto the ground. I turned away, and my eyes caught the smashed head of another man. Something inside his brain was still pulsating and he was breathing. I felt nauseated. (100)

Ishmael's transition from a boy playing soccer into a child soldier follows the need of the army to recruit most of the young boys in the village of Yele, initially safe but now threatened by the RUF. Upon joining, everyone gets a pair of new *crapes* (Adidas, Nike or Reebok) with army T-shirts and shorts (110). While the military training given is minimal, the ideological work provided is effective and emotive, centering upon a repeated mantra-like phrase: "Over and over in our training he would say that same sentence: *Visualize the enemy, the rebels who killed your parents, your family, and those who are responsible for everything that has happened to you*" (112, original emphasis). What this sentence generates in Ishmael is anger and hatred, as well as images (and later also actions) of killing rebels: "I imagined capturing several rebels at once, locking them inside a house, sprinkling gasoline on it, and tossing a match. We watch it burn and I laugh" (113). Military education is completed with watching war movies, smoking marijuana joints, and sniffing cocaine (121). While learning to perform his new role, Ishmael, however, suffers to occasional migraines hinting at the traumatizing effects of war and terror (see, e.g., 109, 121).

The turning point in Ishmael's story occurs when after years in the army he becomes one of the child soldiers selected by the UNICEF to leave the fighting and enter a civilian life. As his loyalties at this stage are with the army ("My squad was my family, my gun was my provider and protector" [126]), he resists such a change into a role he finds inferior by fighting, stealing, and misbehaving at the rehabilitation centre. Yet the traumatizing effects of the war and the loss of childhood are revealed to the reader through, first, a depiction of physical withdrawal symptoms (139) and, second, through emphasizing the need to deal with the past by speaking about it:

> But even when I was finally able to fall asleep, I would start awake less than an hour later. I would dream that a faceless gunman had tied me up and begun to slit my throat with the zigzag edge of his bayonet. I would feel the pain that the knife inflicted as the man sawed my neck. I'd wake up sweating and throwing punches in the air. I would run outside to the middle of the soccer field and rock back and forth, my arms wrapped around my legs. I would try desperately to think about my childhood, but I couldn't. The war memories had formed a barrier that I had to break in order to think about any moment in my life before the war. (149)

As the passage shows, the discourse of trauma is foregrounded in a frequent use of actual memories and in nightmares based on visual flashes from the past, all symptoms of the Post-Traumatic Stress Disorder that Caruth defines. What the text emphasizes is the need to work through the past, to remember moments of happiness and joy that pre-date the violent past should a new self be formed. "'This isn't your fault, you know. It really isn't. You'll get through this'" (151), as one of the nurses puts it after a difficult night. As is characteristic of many a trauma narrative, a major part in this process is played by Ishmael's therapist, the nurse Esther, who is the first person to whom he – unwillingly though – talks about his experiences in the war (155). This begins a new stage in his life. By gradually revealing his dreams to Esther, and through copying, studying, and singing the song lyrics of Run-D.M.C and Bob Marley, Ishmael's dreams transform and he finally dreams of his family (165). The sense of guilt, "burdensome memories" (165-66), and "gruesome details" (166) give way to an inquisitive attitude that looks at the sky and the moon, as once told to do by the grandmother, and listens to the sky as it has "answers and explanations for everything; every pain, every suffering, joy, and confusion" (166).

The function of the therapeutic discourse is to reconstruct the subject and make her/him able to cope with life in a new way. Indeed, upon resolving his traumas Ishmael enters gradually a normal life, relocates a long-lost uncle, and moves in to live with his family, enjoying their company and spending cozy evenings listening to the tape recordings of the local storyteller Leleh Ghomba (188). At the age of 16, Ishmael travels to New York to represent the children of Sierra Leone at an international meeting at the UN, where he gets to know new friends and participates in workshops on storytelling conducted by Laura Simms, a white woman with a knowledge of oral stories from all over the world, who is later to become Ishmael's new "mother" (197). What the visit to the United States reveals is also the transformation of the narrator's self as can be seen in his final speech addressed to the UN Economic and Social Council: "I have been rehabilitated now, so don't be afraid of me. I am not a soldier anymore; I am a child. We are all brothers and sisters" (199). In other words, the former abject self has been left behind in Africa, and a new self speaks itself in the West.

The emerging desire to enter the West and the United States in particular is also present in the way in which Ishmael relates himself to New York. He is fascinated by New York City, its glittering lights and skyscrapers. Times Square, in particular, comes to symbolize the urban space, its titillation, glamour, and opportunities:

> We were busy looking at the buildings and all the people hurrying by when we suddenly saw lights all over the place and shows playing on huge screens. We looked each other in awe of how absolutely amazing and crowded the place was. One of the screens had a woman and a man in their underwear; I guess they were showing it off. Madoka pointed at the screen and laughed. Others had music videos or numbers going across. Everything flashed and changed very quickly. We stood at the corner for a while, mesmerized by the displays. After we were able to tear our eyes away from them, we walked up and down Broadway for hours, staring at the store windows. I didn't feel cold, as the number of people, the glittering buildings, and the sounds of cars overwhelmed and intrigued me. I thought I was dreaming. (198)

Unsurprisingly, the return to Freetown is anti-climactic as Ishmael soon finds himself amidst a new revolution and RUF rule. Subsequently, for him the place to escape to is the United States, the land of his dreams, which he sets out to do. While the autobiography suggests that the traumas and nightmares do not entirely disappear in the United States, the reconstructed self is now in control of itself, aware of its past, civilized and ready to be inserted into America. Regardless of the fact that some of the "painful memories" of the past should be "wash[ed] away," the narrator has gained an understanding: they form "an important part of what my life is; who I am now" (19). For the reconstructed unified child, America makes possible

> to rediscover the happiness I had known as a child, the joy that had stayed alive inside me even through times when being alive itself became a burden. These days I live in three worlds: my dreams, and the experiences of my new life, which trigger memories from the past. (20)

Here, in New York, with a transformed and reconstituted self, ends the narrator's journey, or, to use the title of one of favorite reggae albums, his *Exodus* (see 162). The novel is, then, a success story, as is confirmed by its book jacket showing a smiling young man, as noted by a reviewer: "Unusually, the smiling, open face of the author on the book jacket provides welcome and timely reassurance. Ishmael Beah seems to prove it can happen" (Boyd, online).

To conclude, for Ishmael, as also for his idol Bob Marley, the reconstruction of identity is a firmly transnational process involving globalized popular culture and imagined identities which allow for identification as one of "us" rather as "them." His entry into respectability, initially problematized by a violent past as a monstrous child soldier, is now leveled by a therapeutic process that has transformed and purified him. As a result, the African child soldier has become an adolescent inhabitant of the globalized West, in particular of the United States. Yet the passage quoted above (20), as it divides the narrator's life into three distinct "worlds," displays a sense of uneasiness related to the inability to escape entirely the traumas of the past. Ishmael's traumas, then, are more than personal. Although downplayed in a narrative emphasizing an individual's story of survival and success, they are shared by a whole generation and nation, maybe even by a continent, traumatized by loss of families, communities, and familiar places.

Works Cited

Appadurai, Arjun. *Modernity at Large: Cultural Dimensions of Globalization.* Minneapolis: University of Minnesota Press, 1996.

Beah, Ismael. *A Long Way Gone: Memoirs of a Boy Soldier.* London: Fourth Estate, 2007.

Boyd, William. "Babes in Arms." Rev. of *A Long Way Gone: Memoirs of a Boy Soldier*, by Ishmael Beah. *The New York Times*, Feb. 25, 2007, online. Accessed 8 Apr. 2009.

http://www.nytimes.com/2007/02/25/books/review/Boyd.t.html?_r=1&scp
=2&sq=ishmael%20beah&st=cse

Caruth, Cathy. "Introduction." *Trauma: Explorations in Memory*. Ed. Cathy Caruth. Baltimore: Johns Hopkins University Press, 1994. 3-12.

Crothers, Lane. *Globalization and American Popular Culture*. Lanham: Rowman and Littlefield, 2007.

Gare, Shelley. "Africa's War Child." *The Australian*, Jan. 19, 2008, online. Accessed 8 Apr. 2009.
http://www.theaustralian.news.com.au/story/0,25197,23074110-32682,00.html

Glazer, Ilsa. Rev. of *Armies of the Young: Child Soldiers in War and Terrorism*, by David M. Rosen. *Anthropological Quarterly* 79.2 (2006): 373-94.

Hobson, Janell and R. Diane Bartlow. "Introduction: Representin': Women, Hip-Hop, and Popular Music." *Meridians: Feminism, Race, Transnationalism* 8.1 (2008): 1-14.

Kilby, Jane. "The Writing of Trauma: Trauma Theory and the Liberty of Reading." *New Formations* 47 (2002): 217-30.

Lipsitz, George. "Diasporic Noise: History, Hip Hop, and the Post-Colonial Politics of Sound." *Popular Culture: A Reader*. Ed. Raiford Guins and Omayra Zaragoza Cruz. London: Sage, 2005. 504-19.

Smith, Sidonie. "Narrated Lives and the Contemporary Regime of Human Rights: Mobilizing Stories, Campaigns, Ethnicities." In *Transcultural Localisms: Responding to Ethnicity in a Globalized World*. Ed. Yiorgos Kalogeras, Eleftheria Arapoglou and Linda Manney. Heidelberg: C. Winter, 2007. 143-64.

Toremans, Tom. ""Trauma: Theory – Reading (and) Literary Theory in the Wake of Trauma." *European Journal of English Studies* 7.3 (2003): 333-51.

West, Harry G. "Girls with Guns: Narrating the Experience of War of FRELIMO's 'Female Detachment.'" *Anthropological Quarterly* 73.4 (2000):180-94.

CHAPTER TWELVE

Fronteras Americanas and the Latino Canadian Diaspora: Guillermo Verdecchia's Border Texts

Astrid M. Fellner

In *Fronteras Americanas/American Borders* (1993), a play by Canadian Latino writer Guillermo Verdecchia, a slide projected onto the stage features a statement by Mexican thinker Carlos Fuentes: "Every North American, before this century is over, will find that he or she has a personal frontier with Latin America" (*FA* 54).[1] When Fuentes said "North America," he most likely referred to the citizens of the United States.[2] The incorporation of Fuentes's statement in Verdecchia's play implies that it is equally true that no Canadian is unaffected by Canada's relationship with Latin America. Canada not only shares with Latin American nations concerns about free trade, but is equally impacted by the forces of globalization and the cultural proximity to the United States. Verdecchia's inclusion of Fuentes's quote in his play also implies that American borders can no longer be understood to refer exclusively to the U.S.-Mexican border. In fact, all of Verdecchia's works strongly make the case for a critical position that views the entire continent as a border zone where the United States, Canada and Latin America meet, intermingle, and collide. Verdecchia's persona in the play draws the attention to the American hemisphere as a border

---

[1] In parenthetical citations, Guillermo Verdecchia's play *Fronteras Americanas* will be abbreviated to *FA*. *Citizen Súarez* will be referred to as *CS*.

[2] In a lecture entitled *Latin America: At War with the Past*, which he presented in Toronto in 1984, Fuentes talks the border which divides North and South America, exploring the ramifications of this border in geographic, political, economic, and psychological ways: "Latin America begins at the Mexican border. [...] It is the only frontier between the industrialized and the developing worlds. [...] It is the frontier between two cultures: the Protestant, capitalist, Nordic culture, and the southern, Indo-Mediterranean, Catholic culture of syncretism and the baroque" (7-8). Ironically, in this Massey Lecture Fuentes conflates Canada with the United States as the northern side of the border zone, assuming cultural similarity between the U.S. and Canada.

when he states: "when I say AMERICA I don't mean the country, I mean the continent. Somos todos Americanos. We are all Americans" (*FA* 20). Evoking José Martí's concept of *nuestra America* (our America), Verdecchia cites a long tradition of Latin American thinkers who have endorsed a Pan-American project based on the premise that there is a collective identity in the Americas. Verdecchia's project, however, differentiates itself from the Latin American hemispheric tradition. As Rachel Adams has pointed out, what distinguishes Verdecchia's vision of the American hemisphere from the Latin American tradition is "that Verdecchia speaks as a Latin American in Canada; his reference to the continent positions Canadian themes and settings within a broader American framework" (321-22). Verdecchia's concern to include Canada in a hemispheric view of America is underscored in his play when his persona presents his own version of the history of America. In the section entitled "An Idiosyncratic History of America," he offers a broad historical and cultural overview of the history of the Americas, from the first settlements in the highlands of Mexico and the Andes mountains, the arrival of Christopher Columbus, the War of 1812, to the establishment of the Dominion of Canada in 1867. Juxtaposing crucial historical dates with global cultural events, Verdecchia playfully draws the attention to the interconnectedness of diverse incidents in Europe and the Americas. The inclusion of Canada's winning of the 1969 Stanley Cup ironically concludes Verdecchia's summary of foundational historical events.[3] Crucially, this list of events, as Adams has stressed, "carves out a role for Canada in historical narratives that have traditionally focused on other parts of the Americas" (322).

In the following chapter, I want to take a look at the border texts by Canadian Latino writer Guillermo Verdecchia. Investigating the focus on the North/South border zone in his works, I intend to show how Verdecchia performs the border in his texts and opens up questions of national identity and Canadian *latinidad* to a wider hemispheric lens. In particular, I will analyze Verdecchia's politics of transnational identity in his collection of short stories *Citizen Súarez* (1998). Pointing out the strategies that the author employs in inverting the narratives of nation in North America, I will show that Verdecchia's narratives engage in the critical practice of border-crossing that constantly seeks out the rifts in borders. In so doing, Verdecchia draws the attention to the constructed nature of national binaries, such as the division between Canada and the United States or Canada and Argentina, making a strong case for the inclusion of Canadian literature in an Inter-American paradigm of the literatures of the Americas.

---

[3] Cf. *FA* 29-32.

Canada and the Americas

Since the late 1990s, the awareness of intertwined geographies, movements, and cross-filiations among peoples, regions, diasporas, and nations of the American hemisphere has translated into the reimagination of North American literatures along hemispheric and transhemispheric lines. The (trans-) hemispheric paradigm has become an attractive framework for Americanists because it has allowed critics to approach American Studies from a transnational perspective and to counteract the association of the field of American Studies with the nation state (Fellner 252-58). It raises new and important questions that might have the capacity to "reinvent categories of identity, citizenship, and belonging" (Adams and Casteel 12) within and beyond the borders of the nation-states that constitute the Americas. Consequently, the "hemispheric turn" that has swept across the various sub-disciplines of American literary scholarship attempts to recognize the dynamic, ever-changing elements and contingent nature of the idea of nation.[4] Whereas the transatlantic approach to North American literatures has looked at the relations between Canada and Britain and France, "the hemispheric approach has generally emphasized the relations among and the similarities between the literatures and cultures of the New World, focusing on what distinguishes the cultures and literatures of the New World at large from that of the Old—the colonial past and neocolonial present, for example, racial and cultural diversity, processes of transculturation and creolization, and so on" (Bauer 2010, 251). Paying attention to the multiple crossroads of cultures in the Americas, the (trans-) hemispheric approach has been particularly fruitful for the analysis of colonial American literatures and the study of U.S.-Mexican border narratives.[5]

---

[4] The founding of the journal *Comparative American Studies* in 2002 signaled the institutional recognition of the hemispheric approach to the literature of the Americas. As Ralph Bauer has stated, the phrase "hemispheric turn" was coined by Lisa Voigt and Eric Slauter in the title of a conference they co-hosted at the University of Chicago in 2004 ("Early American Literature" 262 note 3). For an excellent collection of hemispheric scholarship, see Caroline F. Levander and Robert S. Levine, *Hemispheric American Studies*.

[5] Examples of hemispheric scholarship on early American literatures include Ralph Bauer, *The Cultural Geography of Colonial American Literatures: Empire, Travel, Modernity*, Susan Castillo, *Colonial Encounters in New World Writing 1500-1786: Performing America*, and Anna Brickhouse, "Hemispheric Jamestown." Some of the most important examples of recent hemispheric contributions to border studies are Kirsten Silva Gruesz, *Ambassadors of Culture: The Transamerican Origins of Latino Writing*, José David Saldívar, *The Dialectics of Our America: Genealogy, Cultural Critique, and Literary History*, and Jeffrey Belnap and Raúl Fernández, eds. *José Martí's "Our America": From National to Hemispheric Cultural Studies*.

While recent hemispheric scholarship has primarily focused on the relationships between the U.S. and Latin America, Canada is rarely taken into consideration.[6] There are, however, a series of critics who have been at the forefront of expanding the hemispheric paradigm to include texts by Canadian writers as well. In particular, Claudia Sadowski-Smith, Sarah Phillips Casteel, Rachel Adams, Jennifer Andrews and Priscilla L. Walton have analyzed Canada-U.S. border narratives, offering comparative readings from a transnational or even postnational perspective.[7] In "Trans-Scan: Globalization, Literary Hemispheric Studies, Citizenship as Project," Winfried Siemerling has expressed the need for comparative research that moves beyond Canada to include transborder questions in the contexts of wider North American and hemispheric studies. As he states, "[i]n the interest of democratic citizenship that actively participates in global contexts, it seems crucial *both* to maintain and reinforce nationally designated fields of cultural and literary inquiry in Canada *and* to engage in relational and comparative perspectives that also highlight local specificity" (140, emphasis in the original). Siemerling calls for a specific "(TransCanadian) hemispheric studies" (139) that allows Canadian Studies scholars to move across the different literatures and cultures of Canada, metaphorically following the principle of the Trans-Canada Highway. Here I want to take up Siemerling's call and show in what ways the Canadian Latino writer and scholar Guillermo Verdecchia positions his performative construction of Canadian *latinidad* within a transhemisperic framework.

The inclusion of Canadian literature within the hemispheric paradigm is, however, not without problems. "One obvious pitfall of hemispheric studies," as Paul Giles has pointed out, "is the prospect of simply replacing nationalist essentialism predicated upon state autonomy with a geographical essentialism predicated on physical contiguity" (649). For the field of Canadian Studies, which still is an institutionally marginalized field, the treatment of Canadian literature as part of the literature of the Americas furthermore runs the risk of

---

[6] A notable exception is the 2005-issue of *Comparative American Studies*, which has located Canada within the history and culture of the Americas. Offering a compelling rationale for the inclusion of Canada in current varieties of Hemispheric American Studies, the articles in this issue also redirect the discipline of Canadian Studies from its national focus towards a larger, hemispheric perspective.

[7] In particular, see Claudia Sadowski-Smith, *Border Fictions: Globalization, Empire, and Writing at the Boundaries of the United States*, Rachel Adams and Sarah Phillips Casteel, "Introduction: Canada and the Americas," Rachel Adams, "The Northern Borderlands and Latino Canadian Diaspora," Jennifer Andrews and Priscilla L. Walton, "Rethinking Canadian and American Nationality: Indigeneity and the 49th Parallel in Thomas King."

re-marginalizing this budding literature. Levander and Levine have summarized the problem as follows:

> The all too familiar exceptionalist critique of this 'new' American studies scholarship targets scholarship that takes neighboring nations, regions, and communities as its subject because such scholarship too often assumes the U.S. nation as the default unit of intellectual engagement governing 'comparativist' approaches. (2004, 400)

Given the fact that Hemispheric Studies has for the most part originated at U.S. American academic institutions, fear among many Canadian scholars persists that the hemispheric paradigm will reiterate U.S.-centric gestures. As my analysis of the short fiction by the Latino Canadian writer Guillermo Verdecchia will show, despite these pitfalls, a hemispheric approach has also advantages for the study of Canadian literature, especially for Canadian texts that can be subsumed under the category of Canadian border literature.

Verdecchia's cultural productions are not the only Canadian texts that feature the influence of a hemispheric awareness. In fact, images of transnational economy and global influences have started to appear frequently in Canadian literature. In Carol Shield's novel *Larry's Party* (1997), for instance, a Canadian florist muses about the bunches of alstroemeria that have arrived by jet at his florist shop: "This flower, an herb really, started out as a seed way down in South America, in Columbia" (76). From Columbia, he imagines the flowers being "transported across international frontiers, sorted, sold, inspected, sold again" (76). As Rachel Adams and Sarah Phillips Casteel have pointed out, the florist's fantasy "substitutes a vision of Canada's connection with South America for the more predictable Canadian preoccupation with the USA" (6). Clearly, Shield's novel points to an understanding of a Canada whose culture goes beyond the concept of the nation and is part of a larger global and hemispheric economy. Most notably, however, the works of Thomas King have positioned Canadian indigenous writings within a postnational, hemispheric context. In his short story "Borders," King, for instance, depicts the Canadian-U.S. border as a place of different, shifting national and tribal contact zones that are subject to constant change.[8] The border, in indigenous writings is a constant reminder of colonial history, an enduring scar that is the result of the violent appropriations of Native territories over the past four-hundred years. Thomas King, a Canadian citizen who was born in California to a Cherokee father and a German-Greek mother, cannot be claimed exclusively as a "Cana-

---

[8] For excellent analyses of the border narratives of Thomas King, see Arnold E. Davidson, Priscilla L. Walton ad Jennifer Andrews, *Border Crossings: Thomas King's Cultural Inversions*.

dian," "American," or "First Nations" writer. King's life, just like his works, is inexorably shaped by a condition of "in-betweenness"—racially, culturally, and nationally. The question of borders is also central to Verdecchia's work, which explores the repercussions of displacement and the possibility of creating a new awareness that crosses racial and national borders.

Latino Canadian Border Writings

Canadian indigenous writings and Canadian writings by immigrants, one could say, have introduced a new awareness of hemispheric contexts into Canadian literature. In particular, the study of texts that explore border territories and their diverse populations have provided ample opportunity to expand one paradigm to Canadian literature which has become crucial in hemispheric studies: the border paradigm. U.S.-American border theory emerged from the historical specificity of the boundary region of *la frontera* and is usually associated with the field of U.S. Latino/a, and in particular Chicano/a Studies. One of the key texts in Border Studies, Gloria Anzaldúa's *Borderlands/La Frontera: The New Mestiza* (1987), emphasized the concept of borders as boundaries of nation-states that served mainly as the mechanisms that create difference and exclusion. While geographical borderlands in Anzaldúa's text refer to the U.S.-Mexican borderlands, the ideological dimension of the term is not associated with any particular cartographic space but can refer to any border. As Anzaldúa explains,

> [t]he actual physical borderland that I'm dealing with in this book is the Texas-U.S. Southwest/Mexican border. The psychological borderlands, the sexual borderlands and the spiritual borderlands are not particular to the Southwest. In fact, the Borderlands are physically present wherever two or more cultures edge each other, where people of different races occupy the same territory, where under, lower, middle and upper classes touch, where the space between two individuals shrinks with intimacy. (19)

Borderlands, in Anzaldúa's view, also refer to sites that can enable those dwelling in these spaces to negotiate the contradictions and tensions found in diverse cultural, class, and other settings. The notion of borderlands "has also come to denote how the academic study of the United States has recently moved beyond U.S. borders" (Sadowski-Smith 2008, 2). Many critics have noted that contemporary debates about border and Inter-American research are reminiscent of the position held by historian Herbert Eugene Bolton at the beginning of the twentieth century. Before he was Professor of History at the

University of California at Berkeley from 1910 to 1944, Bolton had spent his early career at the University of Texas at Austin where he conducted archival study of the colonial Spanish borderlands. As Claire F. Fox has stated, "The borderlands work eventually led him to develop a hemispheric perspective toward the study of American history" (639). Using the term borderlands, Bolton stressed the common histories of nations in the Western hemisphere. While Bolton's borderlands idea did not catch on in the 1930s and only became important in the 1980s with Anzaldúa's work, it still has not taken hold in Canadian Studies.

Claudia Sadowski-Smith's *Border Fictions: Globalization Empire, and Writing at the Boundaries of the United States* (2008) is the first book-length study to include Canadian border texts within the border paradigm. It is a comparative analysis of transnational cultural representations of the borders that the U.S. shares with Mexico and Canada. As her analysis evinces, a hemispheric approach to Canadian border texts can remap cultural space, encouraging critics to look at Canadian Latino/a writings as part of a transamerican phenomenon that developed out of complex hemispheric politics and histories. The border texts by writers such as Guillermo Verdecchia are clearly influenced by U.S. American border theory but they translate the notion of borderlands into a Canadian context, expanding it "from encounters between Mexican and Anglo cultures to a comparative view of contact zones across the Americas" (Adams and Casteel 10). Verdecchia's works not only make clear that he is conversant in U.S.-Mexican border studies but his works—especially his plays—actively engage the border art of Chicano performance artist Guillermo Gómez-Peña.[9] While his cultural productions dramatize the fraught conditions of the border zone and make use of similar strategies as U.S. Latino/a writers, they also draw the attention to the fact that Canada's border with the U.S. is culturally and politically distinctive from the U.S. Southwest.

Unlike the notion of the border in the U.S., the concept of the border has traditionally assumed a different connotation in Canada, as Canada itself has often been characterized as a border society. As Roger Gibbins explains the

---

[9] Verdecchia, for instance, cites the performative practices of Chicano artist Guillermo Gómez-Peña when one of Peña's stage characters, *el brujo*, appears in *Fronteras Americanas* to diagnose Verdecchia's identity problem as that of a "very bad border wound" (71). Also, since the play does not really have a plot and instead consists of a series of voices, quotations, video, film clips, and images it can reference different traditions. This collage of different voices are held together by the monologues delivered by the character of Verdecchia and the Chicano character of Wideload. By bringing together on the stage a Canadian Latino from Argentina and a Chicano who moved to Canada, the play constructs *latinidad* as part of a larger Latino diaspora that spans national borders.

Canadian border region, "the most important impact comes not from proximity of the international boundary itself, but more from the more general proximity of the United States" (157). The borderlands north of the 5000-mile Canadian-U.S. frontier, sometimes termed the "world's longest undefended border" (Sadowski-Smith 2005, 63) contains important urban and industrialized centers of power and is the home to sixty percent of the Canadian population. As Claudia Sadowski-Smith has stated,

> In the metaphorical approach common in Canada, the border often symbolizes Canadian efforts to resist U.S. cultural, economic, and political intrusions. The border thus functions as a bulwark for definitions of Canadian particularities, which are almost always conceptualized as differences from its southern neighbor (2008, 12).[10]

Verdecchia's play *Fronteras Americanas/American borders* and his short story collection *Citizen Súarez*, for instance, contain many references to Canadian history, settings and cultural referents that crucially draw the awareness of the reader to the fact that these texts are *not* about the United States. Verdecchia's texts remind the reader that the United States is not the only country that has Latino/a communities. Just like the United States, Canada too is the home of a large number of immigrants from Latin and South America. As Hugh Hazelton has shown in *Latinocanadá: A Critical Study of Ten Latin American Writers of Canada* (2007), a body of Latino-Canadian literature is emerging containing works that "share many characteristics of Canadian letters, such as colonialization, the implantation of European culture in an indigenous environment, the gradual freeing from Eurocentric literary modes, and the search for autonomous means of expression" (3). Furthermore, a series of Latino-Canadian playwrights have become important. Chilean-born director and playwright Carmen Aguirre, for instance, has started Vancouver's Latino Theater Group and her play *¿Que Pasa con la Raza, eh?* (What's up with the people?) has received critical attention by scholars like Michelle Habell-Pallán. *Amigo's Blue Guitar* by Joan MacLeod is another border play which focuses on the experience of a political refugee from El Salvador. Like Verdecchia, MacLeod examines the cultural construction of the North-South border zone as a way of expressing positive self-images of Latin Americans in Canada.

---

[10] The border is also an important theoretical and conceptual concept in Quebec Studies where it often refers to the linguistic and cultural problems of the Canadian-American border. See Hugh MacLennan's *Two Solitudes* (1945) for an emblematic literary representation of Anglophone–Francophone tensions in mid-century Canada. For my purposes here, though, I will only focus on the importance of the border in the works of Guillermo Verdecchia.

Verdecchia's texts engage the hemispheric paradigm in order to enact the border and produce a notion of "Canada" as a transnational entity that is deeply entangled in multiple hemispheric connections. Collapsing the North-South distinction into a line that he calls the "Latin-North American border" (*FA* 21), Verdecchia's persona constantly questions the notion of the border:

> Where and what exactly is the border? Is it this line in the dirt, stretching for 3000 kilometres? Is the border more accurately described as a zone which includes the towns of El Paso and Ciudad Juárez? Or is the border – is the border the whole continent? Where does the US end and Canada begin? (*FA* 21)

Suggesting that there are ways of inhabiting a "border zone" which is neither exclusive nor inclusive, Verdecchia carves out a space for the cultural specificity of Latinos/as in Canada, but, as Fuentes suggests in his Massey Lecture, through a bridging of differences "without denying them" (9).

Verdecchia's works represent the Latino/a Canadian diaspora, who unlike other minority communities such as East Asian communities, South Asian and Caribbean immigrants, have not received much critical attention. In fact, the presence of Latino/a writers in Canada is hardly acknowledged in Canadian literary studies. Compared to the 35 million Latinos/as in the U.S, the approximately 800,000 Latinos in all of Canada constitute a rather small number (cf. Adams 315). While the largest number of Spanish-speaking immigrants live in Quebec, there are, however, also sizable Latino communities in Vancouver, Edmonton, Winnipeg, and Toronto. Crucially though, unlike in the U.S. Latinos/as in Canada are usually associated with notions of exile.[11] Because major immigration during the 1970s and 1980s has been composed of Latin Americans who were granted political asylum, critics speak of a Latino/a Canadian diaspora. Recently, however, there has also been an influx of undocumented immigrants from Central America, which has made this community more heterogenous (cf. Habell-Pallán 175).

In *Citizen Súarez*, Verdecchia largely refers to middle-class political immigrants. Conspicuously, and unlike much of Chicano literature produced in the U.S., Verdecchia's texts do not represent the experiences of the working-class and/or undocumented workers. Verdecchia, as my analysis of his short stories will show, is principally concerned with borders in order to investigate how the liminality and the plurality evoked by these borders confound secure conceptions of national, cultural, and personal identity.

---

[11] Cf. Michelle Habell-Pallán 175. For more information on the notion of exile as a theme in Latino-Canadian literature, see Lake Sagaris, "Countries Like Drawbridges: Chilean-Canadian Writing Today."

Performing Latinidad in *Citizen Súarez*

Verdecchia was born in Argentina and came to Canada when he was still a young child. He grew up in Kitchener, Ontario, studied theatre at Ryerson Polytechnic in Toronto, and received an M.A. in English and Theatre Studies from the University of Guelph. Currently, he is a Ph.D. candidate at the Graduate Centre for Theatre Studies at the University of Toronto where he teaches at University College.

Citizen Súarez engages in a performance of a cultural space that becomes the means to negotiate Canada and establish it as a realm of cultural translation, relentless ambiguity, and fertile ambivalence. As I want to suggest, Verdecchia's texts, in fact, produce "Canada" as hemispheric performance.[12] Rather than a stable and fixed place or a coherent nation, "Canada" emerges in Verdecchia's texts as a practice that creates itself through performative acts. Conspicuously, Verdecchia is engaged in constructing Canadian *latinidad*, Latino/a identity in Canada. The term Latino/a is fraught with difficulties, referring to a wide array of cultures and ethnicities. Instead of constituting an essential identity, *latinidad*, as Verdecchia explains in his MA thesis, is "constituted by the various political, cultural, spectacular, legal, activist, and other performances and practices that Latin Americans and their descendants in the diaspora undertake" (6).

Canadian *latinidad* and the concept of the border zone dominate his short story collection *Citizen Súarez*. In a key scene in the story "Letter from Tucuman," the unnamed protagonist states:

> The bus stops. In the middle of nothing. We are all asked to get out and proceed to the little shack on the side of the road. Have we crossed a border? Not that I know of. (Perhaps I'm on the wrong bus. "Excuse me, is this the bus to Pebble Beach?") But here are a bunch of soldiers looking very bored in rumpled uniforms checking our passports and chain smoking cigarettes. No explanation is offered. Nothing exciting happens; no questions are asked. We all troop back onto the bus. (*CS* 78)

This scene, as Adams has pointed out, "might serve as an allegory for a collection that understands American borders as far more dispersed and inchoate than

---

[12] Canada can be said to be performative in the sense that it constitutes the identity it is purported to be. In Verdecchia's texts, Canada can also be seen as a performance, in the sense that it can be analyzed as one. Although not quite the same, I use the concepts of performativity and performance interchangeably here, referring both to the actual performative practices that Verdecchia uses as well as to the performative character of the texts themselves.

the literal boundary lines between neighboring nations" (318). The individual stories of *Citizen Súarez* evoke multiple borders that cross Canada, the United States and Latin America. While some stories deal with the literal crossing of national borders, other stories primarily focus on internal borders.

The story "Meteorite," for instance, recounts the troubles of a Latino Canadian traveling to California upon hearing the news of his father's death and his subsequent search for his father's birthplace in Mexico. On his way from Canada to the U.S., the protagonist meets another man whom he tells that he is Canadian. "You don't look like a Canadian" (*CS* 97), the man responds reminding the protagonist of his Mexican origin. Alienated from his homeland and his family in California, the protagonist decides to go to Mexico, hoping to find a place where he can rest.

In many of the stories, Latin America constitutes a source of nostalgia and serves as a travel destination, but it is also described as being torn by political crises and economic instability. Canada, in turn, provides a refuge from political oppression. Constantly referred to as a cold and white place, which hints both at the weather and describes racial intolerance, Canada is, however, depicted as a sterile place. The protagonist of "Winter Comes to the Edge of the World," for instance, feels estranged in Winnipeg. A political refugee, she feels safe but also "exiled to the edge of the world" (*CS* 123-24) in an "empty white and grey place" (*CS* 123).

In the story "Money in the Bank," a Latino actor struggles with racial stereotypes that North Americans have of Latinos. A light-skinned Latino, he takes on a part in a TV movie-of-the-week and the makeup artist paints his face brown. The actor complains and relates his conversation with the make-up artist: "I have nothing against brown but if they wanted brown they could have hired a brown actor, no? I ask Make-up why she's going so dark with the face and she says 'You're the Cook aren't you? The Latino Cook?'" (*CS* 87). The make-up artist's questions equate *latinidad* with dark skin and manual labor, underlining the racial biases that persist despite Canada's official rhetoric of cultural pluralism.

In "The Several Lives of Citizen Súarez," we learn of the story of the difficult adjustments of the Súarez family after moving to Canada. This story addresses the crisis of citizenship, illuminating the particular conflicts and tensions that shape the life of young Fernando Súarez, the "anti-citizen" of the title story, who refuses to become a Canadian citizen. "Accepting Canadian citizenship, he believed," states the narrator, "would mean relinquishing forever the possibility of travelling freely between those contingent worlds whose existence he sensed and enwrapped" (*CS* 60). While the parents of this young boy are determined to obtain citizenship, he wants to remain between two worlds because he fears that he will lose "his position as a foreigner and his knowledge of the double or perhaps multiple lives he has lived [which] was for him a recondite and marvelous wound" (*CS* 46). As Rachel Adams states,

> Fernando is representative of many characters in Verdecchia's fiction who affirm the perspective that comes through being 'a hyphenated person' who does not fit easily into any one place. At the same time, his story underscores the fact that such ambivalence can only be appreciated from the relative safety and comfort of Canada, where one does not have to worry about being beaten, shot, imprisoned for failing to fit in. (*CS* 319)

Preferring the term "landed immigrant," Fernando understands his connection to Canada in a much larger context than a national one. Thinking of the history of colonialization and slavery, the young boy believes that having arrived in Canada is more in tune with hemispheric American reality than the stable concept of citizenship that he feels would lock him firmly to one nation:

> Landed: arrived safely on terra firma after a perilous ocean journey, like his grandfather who had left Europe and gone to South America, crossing the dark and cold waters of the Atlantic in a rustbucked boat named after the princess no one remembered. Landed: like Colon, like Balboa, like Cabot, like Armstrong, like Cartier, like the Pilgrims, like the Africans, except they weren't immigrants. They were slaves. (*CS* 38)

This story, therefore, offers a counter-narrative to predominant notions of nation and race/ethnicity, performatively constructing Canadian *latinidad* as a position of emotional choice and group solidarity. "Fernando," says another Latino character in the story, "[t]hat's a cool name: Listen, Fernando, you and I are like neighbours, right? We are from the same part of the world, you understand. We share a past, a patrimony. Well, not exactly, but we share a difference right?" (70).

In the diverse portraits of encounters between Anglo America and Latin America, Verdecchia's collection of short stories "compellingly illustrates the portability of the borderlands, showing why this concept has become an organizing paradigm for recent comparative work in American, Canadian, and Mexican Studies" (Adams 319-20). These stories focus on a generation that struggles with citizenship because of political turmoil, travels and the global weakening of the concept of the nation-state. The stories are about people who at times feel lost between countries and languages and who express a desire to belong to a place. Evoking the Spanish and Latin American tradition of fiction writing, Verdecchia, as the book cover states, "speaks in these stories with the fatalistic lyricism of Lorca, the philosophical ambiguity of Paz, and the emotional scalpel of Márquez." His collection of stories thus is firmly rooted in the hemispheric tradition of border texts, constructing a larger consciousness about North American Latinos/as in the Americas.

Conclusion

The continuing critical interest in hemispheric studies testifies to the need for a view of the multiple interdependencies between nations and communities throughout the American hemisphere. Inscribing a north-south rather than an east-west axis that is enmeshed in diverse global movements and crossings, the hemispheric paradigm allows critics to redirect the discipline of Canadian Studies from its national focus towards a larger, hemispheric perspective. In this article, I have shown how Canadian *latinidad* creates itself in Verdecchia's texts through hemispheric performances. The short story collection *Citizen Suárez* offers an expansive view of American borders that treats borders not as geographically specific locations but rather as pervasive cultural phenomena that connect Canada and Latin America in multiple ways while also offering a model for thinking more broadly about the hemisphere from the perspective of Canada (cf. Adams 315). As it turns out, "[h]emisphere and nation are [...] salient categories for understanding his [Verdecchia's] work and, because the nation that most concerns him is Canada, his writing, in turn provides an opportunity to think further about what it would mean to incorporate Canada into prevailing understandings of the American hemisphere" (Adams 315). Verdecchia's hemispheric performances complicate U.S.-centric views that border literature encompasses only texts that deal with the U.S.-Mexican border. Engaging in a dialogue with U.S. American border texts, Verdecchia's work "unmoors the borderlands from their particular location to show how the hemisphere itself has become a crucible for the complex intermixture of Anglo- and Latin Americas" (Adams 325). By de/constructing border zones, those contested spaces where, as Anzaldúa puts it, "two or more cultures edge each other where people of different races occupy the same territory, in which one culture assumes dominance, and may gradually subsume the others" (Preface), Verdecchia's texts enact the border and imagine it as a positive space that enables hybridization. As Verdecchia proclaims at the end of his play *Fronteras Americanas*: "I am a hyphenated person but I am not falling part, I am putting together. I am building a house on the border" (77).

Works Cited

Adams, Rachel. "The Northern Borderlands and Latino Canadian Diaspora." *Hemispheric American Studies*. Ed. Caroline F. Levander and Robert S. Levine. New Brunswick: Rutgers University Press, 2008. 313-27.
-----, and Sarah Phillips Casteel. "Introduction: Canada and the Americas." *Comparative American Studies* 3.1 (2005): 5-13.
Aguirre, Carmen. "¿Que Pasa con la Raza, eh?" *Along Human Lines: Dramas from Refugee Lives*. Winnipeg: Blizzard, 2000.
Andrews, Jennifer and Priscilla L. Walton. "Rethinking Canadian and American Nationality: Indigeneity and the 49th Parallel in Thomas King." *American Literary History* 18.3 (Fall 2006): 600-17.
Anzaldúa, Gloria. *Borderlands/La Frontera: The New Mestiza*. 1987. 2nd ed. San Francisco: Aunt Lute, 1999.
Bauer, Ralph. *The Cultural Geography of Colonial American Literature: Empire, Travel, Modernity*. Cambridge: Cambridge University Press, 2003.
-----. "Early American Literature and American Literary History at the 'Hemispheric Turn.'" *American Literary History* 22.2 (2010): 250-65.
Belnap, Jeffrey, and Raúl Fernández, eds. *José Martí's "Our America": From National to Hemispheric Cultural Studies*. Durham: Duke University Press, 1998.
Brickhouse, Anna. "Hemispheric Jamestown." *Hemispheric American Studies*. Ed. Caroline F. Levander and Robert S. Levine. New Brunswick: Rutgers University Press, 2008. 18-35.
Castillo, Susan. *Colonial Encounters in New World Writing 1500-1786: Performing America*. London: Routledge, 2006.
Davidson, Arnold E., Priscilla L. Walton and Jennifer Andrews. *Border Crossings: Thomas King's Cultural Inversions*. Toronto: University of Toronto Press, 2003.
Fellner, Astrid M. "'América Aqui': Transhemispheric Visions, Border Studies and the Literatures of the Americas." *Exploring Spaces: Practices and Perspectives. American Studies in Austria 8*. Ed. Dorothea Steiner and Sabine Danner. Wien: LIT Verlag, 2009. 251–77.
Fox, Claire F. "Commentary: The Transnational Turn and the Hemispheric Return." *American Literary History* 18.3 (Fall 2006): 638-47.
Fuentes, Carlos. *Latin America: At War with the Past*. CBC Massey Lectures. Toronto: CBC Enterprises, 1985.
Gibbins, Roger. "Meaning and Significance of the Canadian-American Border." *Borders and Border Politics in a Globalizing World*. Ed. Paul Ganster and David E. Lorey. Oxford: SR Books, 2005. 315-31.

Giles, Paul. "Commentary: Hemispheric Partiality." *American Literary History* 18.3 (2006): 648-55.

Gruesz, Kirsten Silva. *Ambassadors of Culture: The Transamerican Origins of Latino Writing*. Princeton: Princeton University Press, 2002.

Habell-Pallán, Michelle. "'Don't Call Us Hispanic': Popular Latino Theater in Vancouver." *Latino/a Popular Culture*. Ed. Michelle Habell-Pallán and Mary Romero. New York: New York University Press, 2002. 174-89.

Hazelton, Hugh. *Latinocanadá: A Critical Study of Ten Latin American Writers of Canada*. Montreal: McGill-Queen's University Press, 2007.

King, Thomas. "Borders." *One Good Story, That One*. Toronto: HarperCollins, 1993. 129–46.

Levander, Caroline F. and Robert S. Levine, eds. "Hemispheric American Literary History." Special Issue *American Literary History* 18.3 (2006).

-----. *Hemispheric American Studies*. New Brunswick: Rutgers University Press, 2008.

MacLennan, Hugh. *Two Solitudes*. Toronto: Collins, 1945.

MacLeod, Joan. *Amigo's Blue Guitar*. Winnipeg: Blizzard, 1992.

Sadowski-Smith, Claudia. *Border Fictions: Globalization, Empire, and Writing at the Boundaries of the United States*. Charlottesville: University of Virginia Press, 2008.

-----. "Canada-US Border Narratives and US Hemispheric Studies." *Comparative American Studies* 3.1 (2005): 63-77.

Sagaris, Lake. "Countries Like Drawbridges: Chilean-Canadian Writing Today." *Canadian Literature* 142-43 (1994): 12-22.

Saldívar, José David. *The Dialectics of Our America: Genealogy, Cultural Critique, and Literary History*. Durham: Duke University Press, 1991.

Shields, Carol. *Larry's Party*. London: Harper Collins: 1998.

Siemerling, Winfried. "Trans-Scan: Globalization, Literary Hemispheric Studies, Citizenship as Project." *Trans.Can.Lit: Resituating the Study of Canadian Literature*. Ed. Smaro Kamboureli and Roy Miki. Waterloo: Wilfrid Laurier University Press, 2007. 129-40.

Verdecchia, Guillermo. *Citizen Suárez*. Vancouver: Talonbooks, 1998.

-----. *Fronteras Americanas/American Borders*. Vancouver: Talonbooks, 1997.

-----. "Staging Memory, Constructing Canadian Latinidad." M.A. Thesis. University of Guelph, 2006.

ABOUT THE CONTRIBUTORS

About the Authors

Astrid M. Fellner is Professor and Chair of North American Studies at Saarland University in Saarbücken, Germany. From 2008-09 she was "Distinguished Visiting Austrian Chair" at Stanford University. Her publications include *Articulating Selves: Contemporary Chicana Self-Representation* (2002) and several articles in the fields of U.S. Latino/a literature, Colonial American Literatures, Canadian literature, Gender Studies, and Cultural Studies. She has also finished a study entitled *Bodily Sensations: The Female Body in Late-Eighteenth-Century American Culture*. She is the co-editor of *(Anti-) Americanisms* (2005) and *Making National Bodies: Cultural Identity and the Politics of the Body in (Post-) Revolutionary America* (2010), and the editor of the forthcoming collection *Body Signs: The Body in Latino/a Cultural Production*.

E. M. Ester Gendusa studied Foreign Languages and Literatures at the University of Palermo, Italy, before completing her M.A. in "Gender, Culture and Politics" at Birkbeck College (London) under the supervision of Professor Lynne Segal. She has recently taught English language at the University of Palermo where she is currently a Ph.D. student. Her main research interests lie in the interrelation between Gender, (Post-)Colonial and Cultural studies. She has published articles on Doris Lessing, Bernardine Evaristo, Arundhati Roy and Erna Brodber. She has translated into Italian essays by Peter Hulme and Chantal Zabus as well as Alastair Niven's interview with Bernardine Evaristo. She is currently working on a volume on Doris Lessing's *The Grass is Singing*.

Joel Kuortti is Professor of English at the University of Turku and Adjunct Professor of Contemporary Culture at the University of Jyväskylä, Finland. His research fields are post-colonial theory, Indian literature in English, transnational identity, hybridity, and cultural studies. His publications include *The Salman Rushdie Bibliography* (1997), *Place of the Sacred: The Rhetoric of the Satanic Verses Affair* (1997), *Fictions to Live In: Narration as an Argument for Fiction in Salman Rushdie's Novels* (1998), *Indian Women's Writing in English: A Bibliography* (2002), *Tense Past, Tense Present: Women Writing in English* (2003), *Writing Imagined Diasporas: South Asian Women Reshaping*

North American Identity (2007), *Reconstructing Hybridity: Post-colonial Studies in Transition* (ed. with Jopi Nyman, 2007).

Delphine Munos is a doctoral student in the Department of English and American literatures at the University of Liège, Belgium. Her research interests include South Asian literature, Indian women writers of the diaspora, transnationalism, race and gender in literary representations of migrant identity formation, and issues pertaining to whiteness and globalization. Her Ph.D. dissertation examines the notion of a "diasporic hereafter" in the literature of the North American Indian diaspora and focuses on works by Mohsin Hamid, Jhumpa Lahiri, Bharati Mukherjee, Shauna Singh Baldwin and Ginu Kamani.

Jopi Nyman is Chair and Professor of English at the Department of Foreign Languages and Translation Studies at the University of Eastern Finland in Joensuu, Finland. He is the author of several monographs and essay collections in the fields of literary and cultural studies. Professor Nyman's most recent books include the monograph *Home, Identity, and Mobility in Contemporary Diasporic Fiction* (2009) and the edited collections *Post-National Enquiries: Essays on Ethnic and Racial Border Crossings* (2009) and *Reconstructing Hybridity: Post-Colonial Studies in Transition* (co-edited with Joel Kuortti; 2007). His research interests include British, American and post-colonial literatures and popular culture.

Jonathan P. A. Sell is a senior lecturer in the Department of Modern Philology of the University of Alcalá, Spain. By training a specialist in early modern literature, his interest in rhetoric has led to a number of articles on the relationship between allusion, metaphor, and the construction and negotiation of identity in contemporary writers such as Seamus Heaney, Salman Rushdie, Caryl Phillips and Zadie Smith. This is also the topic of the monograph he is currently completing. As for his main field of research, recent publications include *Rhetoric and Wonder in English Travel Writing, 1560-1613* (2006) and *Conocer a Shakespeare* (forthcoming), a commissioned work inviting Spanish readers to "get to know Shakespeare."

Josiane Ranguin is completing a dissertation on the work of Caryl Phillips at Paris IV- Sorbonne, in Paris, France. Her article "'Foreign Home'" in Caryl Phillips's *The Final Passage*" was recently published in the anthology *(Re-) Mapping London: Visions of the Metropolis in the Contemporary Novel in English* (2008). Her areas of interest include French and English-language Caribbean literature, post-colonial writing and film studies.

Silvia Schultermandl is assistant professor of American studies at the University of Graz, Austria, where she teaches courses in American literature and culture studies. Her research interests lie in multi-ethnic American literatures and transnational feminism. She is the author of *Transnational Matrilineage: Mother–Daughter Relationships in Asian American Literature* (2009) and has published widely on contemporary American literature including ethnic American literature, canonicity, and 9/11. She recently put together a special issue for *Interactions* on Asian American and British Asian culture. Her collection of essays, *Growing Up Transnational: Identity and Kinship in a Global Era* (co-edited with May Friedman) is forthcoming from University of Toronto Press in the spring of 2011.

Kathy-Ann Tan works in the American Studies department at the University of Tübingen, Germany, where she teaches courses on contemporary American and Canadian writing, Language poetry, and Cultural Studies. Her first book was titled *The Nonconformist's Poem: Radical "Poetics of Autobiography" in the Works of Lyn Hejinian, Susan Howe and Leslie Scalapino* (2008). She is currently working on her second book project (Habilitation) on globalization and citizenship in contemporary North American fiction.

Şebnem Toplu is an associate professor at Ege University in Izmir, Turkey. She is the author of *Cultural Materialism: Text and Context Relation in Jane Austen's Works* (2001) and *Diverse Aspects of Italy and Italians in Contemporary British Literature* (2001), both published by Università degli Studi di Modena e Reggio Emilia, Italy where she lectured as visiting professor for three years. She wrote various articles on eighteenth century British literature, contemporary British fiction, postcolonialism, autobiography, multiculturalism, transnationalism and ecocriticism. She is the department head of English Translation Studies and editor of *Interactions* journal since 2002. Her ongoing book project is entitled *Fiction Unbound: Bernardine Evaristo*.

Jessica Weintraub received her M.A. in poetry from the University of California, Davis and her Ph.D. from the University of Tennessee, Knoxville. She currently teaches at St John Fisher College in Rochster, NY. Her dissertation, a novel called *A Unified Theory of Love*, is a fraught love letter to the East Tennessee landscape in the 1940s and during the 2004 American Presidential Election. Her poems have appeared in *Terrain, Poetry Scotland, in*tense, Spark, New Millenium Writings*, and her story, "Fluency" was published in the anthology *Outscapes*. Her scholalry article "From AOK to Oz: The Historic Dictionary of American Slang" was reprinted in *Discovering Popular Culture: A Longman Topics Reader*. Her current novel, *A Holding Place*, follows three girls as they negotiate the shifting terrain of friendship, love, and identity against the backdrop of 1980's multiculturalism.

INDEX

9

9/11 80, 130

A

A Bend in the River 54
A House for Mr. Biswas 45, 52, 53
A New World Order 206
A Passage to India 187
A Way in the World 46, 55
absence 28, 31, 64, 74, 141, 142, 144, 146, 149, 151, 153, 155, 156, 164, 167, 202, 207
acculturation 43
affectual economy 217
Aguirre, Carmen 238
allegory 103, 199, 207, 241
America 9, 16, 20, 28, 31, 36, 38, 54, 67, 105, 121, 139, 144, 150, 215, 217, 228, 231, 232, 234, 235, 238, 239, 241 - 243
American Dream 139
American mainstream 31, 143
Anderson, Benedict 10, 25, 27, 198, 204, 206, 212
Anne Frank's Diary 216
Anzaldúa, Gloria 29, 236, 237, 243
Appadurai, Arjun 13, 29, 220, 221
Appiah, Kwame Anthony 51, 159, 183
Arab Americans 28
Arendt, Hannah 26, 59
Arnold, Matthew 82
Ashcroft, Bill 49, 93, 107
Ashley, Bernard 215
asylum 197, 198, 200, 201, 212, 239
authenticity 33, 35, 44, 52, 82, 185, 216

B

Balsari, Saumya 10, 19, 79, 82, 90
Bammer, Angelika 43
Banerjee, Mita 83
Barnouw, Dagmar 45
Bartlow, R. Dianne 222
Bauer 233
Belsey, Catherine 179, 180, 183
Bengaliness 144
Between Woman and Nation 27, 37, 108
Bhabha, Homi 45, 79, 83, 90, 114, 139, 187
Bildungsroman 116
body 31, 36, 54, 121, 125, 133, 151, 160, 173, 180 - 182, 199, 200, 203, 205, 209 - 211, 238
Boehmer, Elleke 105
Bolton, Herbert Eugene 237
Border Crossings 199, 235
border studies 130, 131, 233, 237
Border Theory 131
borders 9, 11, 12, 15, 18, 21, 39, 50, 113, 127, 128, 131, 132, 172, 192, 199, 212, 221, 231 - 233, 236 - 241, 243
boundaries 9, 10, 25, 27, 31, 35, 36, 38, 39, 44, 46, 48, 79, 101, 128, 132, 142, 145, 152, 165, 172, 176, 192, 200, 203, 205, 207, 209 - 212, 236
Bourdieu, Pierre 113, 114, 117, 131
Brah, Avtar 89, 90, 97, 106, 160, 161, 166, 173
Brahmin 88
Braidotti, Rosi 107
Bramen, Carmen Tirado 13, 35
Brazil 19, 96, 104, 105
Brickhouse, Anna 233
British 9, 13, 15 - 18, 20, 21, 46, 88, 89, 93 - 100, 104, 107, 108, 112, 113, 160 - 168, 176, 184, 187, 192, 197, 198, 201, 204, 206 - 208
Britishness 95, 97, 106, 164, 198, 208
Broeck, Sabine 184
Bulgaria 66
Butler, Judith 25 - 27, 30, 62, 68, 73, 118

C

Canadian Studies 234, 237, 243
canon 10, 32, 36, 95, 102

capitalism 139, 183, 221
Carby, Hazel 98
cartography 105, 111, 128, 199
Caruth, Cathy 152, 224 - 226
Castillo, Susan 233
Castro 156
Chakrebarty, Dipesh 184
childhood 29, 32, 39, 44, 49, 81, 117, 119, 129, 141, 143, 160, 164, 168, 169, 216, 218, 219, 226
Childs, Elaine 72
Childs, Peter 139
Chuh, Kandice 34, 35
class 11, 27, 53, 83, 84, 88, 94, 112, 114, 119, 131, 148, 155, 159, 161, 169, 176, 184, 187, 190, 191, 199, 203, 206, 207, 209, 236, 239
Clifford, James 139
Clingman, Stephen 197, 201, 204, 211
Coetzee, J.M. 55, 56
Colin 64
colonialism 44, 94, 96, 97, 183, 187
community 18, 25, 29, 31, 45, 46, 80, 98, 99, 102, 114, 143, 147 - 150, 161, 164, 167, 170, 172, 173, 184, 202, 206, 209, 221, 222, 239
contact zones 44, 235, 237
Corley, Martin 83
Coste, Didier 175
Craft 162, 166
Crèvecoeur, Hector St. John de 26
Cromwell, Oliver 80
Crothers, Lane 222
Culler, Jonathan 156

D

Das Gupta, Monisha 148
Davis, Angela Y 35, 98
Dayal, Samir 46
Derrida, Jacques 181
Desai, Anita 16
detective story 19, 118, 132
diaspora 17, 79 - 81, 84, 87, 89, 106, 139, 141, 152, 159, 162, 168, 221, 237, 239, 240

displacement 43, 46, 79, 80, 90, 128, 159, 199, 201, 207, 208, 216, 221, 236
Divakaruni, Chitra Banerjee 140
Dooley, Gillian 43, 52, 55, 56
Dr Jekyll and Mr Hyde 64
du Gay 162
Dustin, Moira 171
Dutta, Abhijit 81

E

Empson, William 73, 74
Engles, Tim 119
Ermath 95
Eros 175, 180
Espinoza, Alex 16
essentialism 10, 12, 27, 33, 60, 62, 234
Ethnic Life Writing and Histories 35
Eurocentric 14, 114, 238
European Union 113

F

Fekete, John 59
fiction 18, 20, 30, 35, 39, 44, 46, 54 - 56, 66, 72 - 74, 83, 130, 144, 161, 171, 192, 215, 235, 242, 243
Figlio, Karl 145
Filipovici, Zlata 216
Finding the Center 44, 45
fluidity 12, 19, 139, 159, 173, 199
Forster, E.M. 71, 72, 74, 175, 186, 187
Foucault, Michel 175, 176
Fox, Claire F. 10, 237
Fraser, Antonia 80
Freud 70, 181
Friedman, Susan Stanford 16, 46, 113
Fuentes, Carlos 231, 239
fundamentalism 179
Fuss, Diana 12

G

Gaonkar 65
Garcia, Cristina 16
gender 11, 25, 27, 29 - 31, 33, 35, 38, 39, 79, 86, 90, 93 - 96, 98, 99, 102, 103,

105 - 108, 112, 119, 125, 131, 159 - 161, 169, 170, 199
Gibbins, Roger 238
Gibson, Andrew 64
Giddens, Anthony 131
Giles, Paul 234
Gilman, Sander L. 177
Gilroy, Paul 16, 17, 67
Glixman 127
global youth 223
globalization 10, 14, 17, 43, 48, 114, 159, 215, 221, 231
glocal 114
Going Global 36, 37
Gombrich, E.H. 72
Gomez☐Pena, Guillermo 127, 131
Gómez-Peña, Guillermo 237
González, María Martínez 159
Greenblatt, Stephen 16, 69
Grewal, Inderpal 9, 10, 36, 79
Griffin, Connie D. 167
Griffiths, Paul 52, 53
Gruesz, Kirsten Silva 233
Guerrillas 45, 54
Gussow, Mel 55

H

Habell-Pallán, Michelle 238, 239
habitus 113, 117
Half a Life 44, 46, 51, 52, 55, 56
Hall, Edward T. 119
Hall, Stuart 12, 19, 115, 168, 199
Handke, Peter 68
Hanks 64
Hazelton, Hugh 238
Head, Dominic 60
Hemispheric American Studies 233, 234
hemispheric turn 233
hip-hop 220 - 223
Hirsch, Marianne 152
History of English Language Teaching 80
Hobbes, Thomas 63, 70
Hobson, Janell 222
Hollinger, David 12
Holocaust 152, 224

home 10, 20, 31, 37 - 39, 51, 53, 54, 55, 80, 84, 87 - 89, 114, 115, 120, 122, 124, 125, 130, 145, 146, 148, 154, 159, 161, 162, 164, 165, 169, 172, 173, 198 - 200, 202 - 204, 206, 207, 209 - 212, 224, 225, 238
homeland 18, 19, 38, 139, 140, 203, 241
Homo Sacer 127
homophobia 33
hooks, bell 98
Howie, Gillian 12
Hume, David 63
hybridity 13, 17, 46, 67, 72, 79, 87, 89, 90, 155, 159, 168, 176 - 178, 186
hyphenation 13, 29, 67

I

identity politics 10 - 12, 18, 19, 20, 26, 29, 30, 33 - 36, 107, 111 - 115, 126, 127, 132, 199, 221
In a Free State 47, 53, 55
India 19, 43, 49 - 54, 81, 84, 85, 87, 139, 140, 142, 144, 147, 149, 151, 160, 180, 181, 185, 188, 193, 205
Indian-American 139, 146, 150, 155
Indianness 146 - 149, 153 - 155
integrity 44, 117, 205, 209

J

Jamaica 66, 97, 181, 185, 194
Jewish 18, 60 - 62, 67, 69, 177, 202, 211
jouissance 178, 194
Joyce, James 64, 188, 190, 192

K

Kaddish 61, 68, 69, 72, 74
Keating, AnaLouise 34
Keitetsi, China 215
Kilby 224
Kim, Sur-yon 116
King, Thomas 234 - 236
Kristeva, Julia 59, 70

L

labor 127, 180, 241
Lahiri, Jhumpa 11, 20, 82, 140 -142, 144, 145, 147, 148, 150, 154, 155, 156
Lasdun 64
latinidad 232, 234, 237, 240 - 243
Lausberg 75
Lawrence, D.H. 64
Lazreg, Marnia 37
Ledent, Benedicte 207
Lee, Chang-Rae 11, 19, 115, 116, 129, 130, 132
Li, Florence Hsiao-ching 18, 72, 115, 128
Lie, John 161
life writing 26, 35, 215
Lim, Shirley Geok-lin 10, 14, 15, 18, 27, 30 - 33, 35 - 39
Lima, Maria Helena 95
Lipsitz, George 221
London 19, 45, 50, 51, 53, 61, 65, 71, 81, 86, 87, 95, 96, 98 - 100, 103 - 107, 161 - 163, 165, 167 - 169, 171, 172, 173, 176, 182, 184, 185, 188
Los Angeles 127 - 130
Lowe, Lisa 9, 190
Luckhurst 210, 211
Luckmann, Thomas 131
Lyall 179, 185

M

Machado Saez 211
MacLennan, Hugh 238
MacLeod, Joan 238, 239
Magic Seeds 44, 46, 51 - 53, 55, 56
Malaysia 30, 31
marginality 12, 28, 31, 43, 172
Martí, José 232, 234
Martin, Denis-Constant 59
Marx, Karl 26
Mauss, Marcel 113
McLeod, John 100, 103, 107
Mead, George Herbert 62, 63
media 68, 69, 132, 139, 171, 221
mediascapes 220
Mediterranean 96, 231

melancholia 152
memory 32, 35, 88, 104, 125, 126, 129, 140 - 142, 145, 151 - 155, 162, 164, 178, 182, 187, 194, 210
mesearch 33
metropolises 130
Midnight's Children 64
migration 15, 16, 18, 19, 29, 38, 43, 47, 79, 81, 112, 115, 127, 129, 141, 144, 151, 152, 159, 162, 172, 176, 199, 200, 201, 203, 204, 208
Miguel Street 44, 54
Milstein, Brian 192
mimicry 19, 44, 79, 83, 87, 89, 90, 166
Mimicry 45
Minor Transnationalism 14
Mirza, Heidi Safia 94, 108
Mishra, Pankaj 149
Mishra, Vijay 139, 140, 141, 151 - 153, 155
mobility 9 - 11, 14, 18, 111, 112, 114, 115, 223
modernity 9, 11
Mohanty, Chandra Talpade 21, 33 - 35, 38, 98, 183, 193
Moore, G.E. 71, 81
Morris 184
Morrison, Toni 16, 200, 203, 210, 212
Moss, Laura 72, 176, 179, 181, 185 - 187
Motherland 18, 140, 141, 149, 151, 153, 155
Mukherkjee, Bharati 140
multiculturalism 11, 13, 34, 36, 59, 66, 111, 112, 120, 127, 130 - 132, 159, 161, 171, 177
Murray, Patricia 106

N

NAFTA 131
Naipaul, V.S. 10, 16, 18, 43, 44 - 56
Nasta, Susheila 99, 102, 159
nationalism 100, 205
nation-state 9, 11, 13, 16, 18, 27, 38, 108, 112, 113, 132, 243
New York City 116, 121, 122, 217, 227
Nigeria 19, 96, 97, 104

Nixon, Rob 45
Nostalgia 129, 149
novel-in-verse 95
nunchi 119

O

Ohmae, Kenichi 113, 132
Olson 63
other 10, 11, 14, 15, 28, 31, 34, 43, 53, 54, 59, 69 -72, 108, 133, 152, 153, 194, 208, 225
Other 21, 35, 37, 80, 82, 90, 97, 102, 126, 142, 143, 156, 183, 190
otherness 12, 156, 223

P

Pan-American 232
Paul de Man 224
performance 11, 12, 20, 26, 30, 35, 36, 61, 62, 67 - 69, 72, 73, 124, 131, 165, 211, 221, 223, 237, 240
personal experience 27, 28, 33, 43, 100, 106
Phillips, Caryl 11, 66, 197 - 199, 200, 201, 203 - 207, 209, 211, 212
postmemories 152, 153
Powell, Enoch 161
Pratt 44
presence 32, 71, 94, 95, 117, 142, 144, 146, 149, 153, 155, 167, 197, 220, 225, 239
Punday, Dan 193

R

race 11, 30, 33, 34, 38, 79, 83, 93 - 98, 103, 105, 107, 108, 112, 125, 159, 177, 185, 193, 199, 202, 203, 206, 242
racism 12, 27, 33, 100, 112, 203, 205
Radhakrishnan 178, 184, 185, 193
Reading and Writing 44, 53, 54, 56
religion 131, 160, 161, 170, 171, 182, 188, 191, 199
Revolutionary United Front 215
rhizome identity 111

Ricoeur, Paul 59, 70
Robbins, Bruce 159
Roman Empire 209
Rosen, David 219
Rushdie, Salman 10, 16, 55, 64, 88, 204
Russell, Bertrand 71, 74

S

Sagaris, Lake 239
Saldívar, José David 234
Scattered Hegemonies 36
Schuurman, Frans 113
Segal, Lynne 94
Segura, Denise A. 172
Self 37, 73, 142, 143, 167
selfhood 9, 11, 18, 19, 27, 30, 32, 39, 44, 45, 108
sexism 33, 222
Shield, Carol 235
Shohat, Ella 184
Sidney, Philip 69, 70
Siemerling, Winfried 234
Sierra Leone 215, 217, 220, 227
slavery 104, 203, 220, 224, 242
Smith, Sidonie 11, 63, 72, 216, 218
Sollors, Werner 12
Sommer, Doris 166, 191, 192
Sommer, Roy 184, 185
Sources of the Self 47
space 14, 16, 18 - 20, 29, 34, 37, 38, 47, 48, 60, 65, 69, 89, 90, 97, 99, 100, 103, 104, 106 - 108, 113, 114, 128, 129, 133, 139, 140, 141, 146, 147, 152, 159, 161, 162, 164, 173, 178, 182 - 184, 187, 189, 192, 194, 197, 201, 203, 204, 206, 210, 212, 227, 236, 237, 239, 240, 243
Spivak, Gayatri Chakravorty 12, 25 - 27, 30, 62, 79, 85, 86
Stanley, Sandra Kumamoto 11
Stein, Mark 104
Sterne, Lawrence 64
Stoler, Ann Laura 176
Stone-Mediatore, Shari 34, 35, 193
subaltern 79, 85 - 87, 96, 98
Suleri, Sara 34

survival 80, 87, 90, 201, 215, 217, 223, 228

T

Tan, Amy 19, 32
Taylor, Charles 47, 59, 62, 69, 192
telos 61
The Enigma of Arrival 50, 51, 55
The European Tribe 203, 205
The Little Mermaid 179
The Middle Passage 54
The Mimic Men 45, 54
The Mystic Masseur 43, 53
The Namesake 82, 150
The Nature of Blood 201, 203
The Suffrage of Elvira 53
Thompson, Molly 60
Toplu, Sebnem 20, 105
topography 176, 183, 207
Toremans, Tom 225
traditionalism 87 - 89
transculturation 166, 233
translation 15, 20, 79, 182, 240
Transnational Asian American Literatures 36
trauma 20, 65, 140, 152, 201, 215, 223 - 226
Trinidad 43, 44, 47 - 49, 53
Truth, Sojourner 26
Turner 184, 199
Ty, Eleanor 17, 29

U

U.S. Census 28
U.S. exceptionalism 140
Unaccustomed Earth 140, 141
Unheimliche 143
United States 9, 12, 13, 27, 29 - 32, 34, 36, 38, 46, 49, 50, 66, 80, 93, 98, 114, 120, 131, 140, 146, 147, 149, 151, 160, 199, 215, 217, 223, 227, 228, 231, 232, 234, 236 - 238, 241

V

Verdecchia, Guillermo 11, 20, 231 - 243
Vietnam War 224
violence 20, 96, 99, 101, 116, 175, 178, 185, 187, 209, 215 - 219, 222
Viswanathan, Gauri 15

W

Walkowitz, Rebecca L. 15, 16, 199, 200
West, Harry G. 219
Western civilization 44, 52, 56
Western Europe 49
Western modernity 215
Where Angels Fear to Tread 187, 190
Who Sings the Nation-State? 25, 26
Williams, Patrick 139
Wood, James 61, 64
Woolf, Virginia 64, 69, 70, 71, 190, 191
World War II 45, 66, 176, 189
writing diaspora 140

X

xenophobia 12, 33, 122

Y

Yamashita, Karen Tei 11, 19, 115, 127, 130 - 132
Yeats, W.B. 175, 194
Yoshino, Kenji 33
Young, Lola 108

Z

Zavella, Patricia 172
Žižek, Slavoj 152